William H. P. Greswell

The Growth and Administration of the British Colonies, 1837-1897

William H. P. Greswell

The Growth and Administration of the British Colonies, 1837-1897

ISBN/EAN: 9783337151744

Printed in Europe, USA, Canada, Australia, Japan

Cover: Foto ©ninafisch / pixelio.de

More available books at **www.hansebooks.com**

The Growth and Administration of the British Colonies

1837—1897

By

REV. WILLIAM PARR GRESWELL, M.A.

Late Scholar of Brasenose College, Oxford
Author of "Africa South of the Zambesi", "History of the Dominion of Canada", &c.

LONDON
BLACKIE & SON, LIMITED, 50 OLD BAILEY, E.C.
GLASGOW AND DUBLIN
1898

Contents

CHAPTER I
Our Colonial System - - - - - - - - 7

CHAPTER II
Pioneers of Colonial Progress and Reform (1837–1897) 36

CHAPTER III
The Growth of the British-American Colonies (1837–1897) - - - - - - - - - - 54

CHAPTER IV
The Growth of the British-Australasian Colonies (1837–1897) - - - - - - - - 77

CHAPTER V
The Growth of our African Colonies (1837–1897) - 106

CHAPTER VI
The Growth of Colonial Constitutions—Canada - - 129

CHAPTER VII
The Growth of Colonial Constitutions—Canada - - 161

CHAPTER VIII
The Growth of Colonial Constitutions—Australasia - 192

CHAPTER IX
The Growth of Colonial Constitutions—South Africa - 218

Appendix—Details of the Canadian Constitution - - 243

INDEX - - - - - - - - - 249

The British Colonies.

Chapter I.

Our Colonial System.

A remarkable feature of the British Empire in the nineteenth century is the secret, sudden, and almost unofficial nature of its growth. At home, there has been scarcely any visible sign of extended Colonial greatness or any symbolism of increased authority outside the well-known mercantile circles or the more exclusive *entourage* of departments of state. A Territorial District has been proclaimed, a Province created, and a Protectorate added to the area of our Empire without exciting at home more than a temporary and passing interest in the minds of the British public. The fierce search-light of modern Europe had not yet been turned upon our distant territorial expansions in the early days of the Victorian era, and even to Britons themselves it might have seemed a small matter at the time that British Kaffraria, for example, had achieved a separate administrative status in South Africa, or that Queensland had been divided from New South Wales in Australia, or that the Province of Manitoba had been carved out of the lordly domain of the Great North-West, or, indeed, that a new centre of Colonial activity had been created anywhere. The private diaries of such heroes of exploration as Livingstone and Franklin, and the stirring exploits of our sportsmen and travellers have had great attractions for the youth of England, always ready to take up a life of adventure and risk. The more tangible and material facts of political and statistical interest, which contribute to form the very groundwork and structure of our Colonial Empire, have been generally ignored as matters scarcely deserving public notice, still less the attention of those who direct the course of school or university instruction. The system of International Exhibitions, inaugurated in 1851, and especially the exhibition in London of the products of our Colonies and India, in 1886, came, therefore, to most Britons living at home, as a remarkable revelation of hitherto unappreciated facts. Following close upon the Exhibition came the Colonial Conference of 1887, termed in the *National Review* "our first Amphictyonic Council", and extracting the hope from Lord Salisbury that it would be "the parent of a long progeniture".

The way in which we have "pegged out claims for posterity" is now the commonplace of our public life. But, for a long time, the builders of our Colonial Empire have lacked "a sacred poet" if not an apologist. Even now we seem half inclined to apologize for our greatness. Venice was more self-conscious when every year the stately Bucentaur, gilded from stem to stern and filled with the noblest of the city, went seawards from the classic Canal, and the great Doge himself dropped a ring into the Adriatic and claimed in mystical fashion the sovereignty over the sea. Great Rome, also, knew how her world-wide empire was increasing when, time after time, the triumphal cars, with captives and the spoils of war, ascended the Capitol, and thanksgivings, *coram populo*, were returned, and the *porrecta majestas imperi* was kept before the eyes of the citizens. More sober is the British fashion, and doubtless more solid. There has been little fuss and no official programme. In a certain sense the very remoteness of our Colonial Empire, its unknown condition, the apathy of the State, the indifferentism of the Cobden School on the subject, the rebuffs of officialdom frequently administered to too forward colonists, have, one and all, worked an unexpected good. Europe thought that if we cared so little, officially, for our Colonies, and did not give them a separate Department of State till 1854, there could not be much in them. It has so happened that, until quite lately, the affairs of Africa, and of Australasia, were considered to be beyond the pale of European diplomacy. If a Colonial question becomes nowadays an European question it was not always so. This is the marked feature of the latter years of the Victorian era. Our Colonies were suffered to go on just as they pleased, and it was difficult to find out much about them.

The protracted indifference of Continental powers to our colonization may be accepted as a partial explanation of our success as a colonizing nation. But it would be idle to ignore individual temperament, and that tenacity of purpose that has run through the thread of our enterprises. The Anglo-Saxon race is noted for its individualism, and in our Colonial Empire, with its wide horizons, and free spirit, fostered by the freest institutions in the world, there has existed an unrivalled field for the play of individualism. Sir John Seeley has remarked in his *Expansion of England* (p. 8), that we "seemed to have conquered and peopled half the world in a fit of absence of mind". If there has been any want of alertness it must have surely been with the official world and the gentlemen who had charge of "The Plantations" and Colonies. British sailors and British traders have gone wherever ship could carry them, without State bounties or State bribes, from the days of Raleigh and Gilbert, Dampier, and scores of others, to the present day, until it seems as if the great

Epic the nation wants now is an "Epic of Commerce", and a patriotic Camoens to write it. To this spirit Edmund Burke paid an eloquent tribute when, in his speech on "Conciliation with America" he said (March 22, 1775): "Whilst we follow them" (the whaling crews of New England) "among the tumbling mountains of ice, and behold them penetrating into the deepest frozen recesses of Hudson's Bay and Davis's Streights . . . we hear that they have pierced into the opposite region of polar cold, that they are at the antipodes, and engaged under the frozen Serpent of the South". At the same time Burke noticed that in following their interests "the Colonists in general owe little or nothing to any care of ours". If Burke meant that colonial enterprise outran official despatches and official encouragement, we shall have constant illustrations in all the continents and islands of the world of this trait in the national character. Indeed the spirit of colonization has run in the teeth of accredited policies and departmental warnings.

Roosevelt, in his *Winning of the West* (vol. i. p. 37), remarks that from the date of the triumphant peace secured by Wolfe's victory the British Government became the most active foe of the spread of the English race in America. For many years there was an attempt to bar the colonists from the Ohio Valley. It was the position taken up by England at Ghent in 1814, when her Commissioners tried to check natural progress by the erection of a great neutral belt of Indian territory guaranteed by the king. It was the rôle which her statesmen endeavoured to play when, at a later date, she strove to keep Oregon a waste, rather than see it peopled by Americans; and it was the same motive which kept the North-West so long a wilderness and a home of the trapper rather than of the agriculturist. The new lands across the Atlantic were regarded as being won and settled for the merchants and traders at home rather than for the colonists themselves. This was a continuation of the old policy of the French Government in Canada.

Lord Selkirk, who was on the side of *bonâ-fide* colonization in the North-West, laying, as we shall see, the beginnings of Manitoba and the Red River Settlements with the aid of hardy Scotch colonists, observed that, when Canada was a Province of France, the fur-trade was carried on under a system of exclusive privileges. The governor granted licences to trade with the Indians to certain favoured individuals, generally officers of the army, within certain prescribed limits. These licences could be revoked if the Government thought fit to revoke them. This was not a policy of true Colonial expansion. It was part and parcel of the old trade policy of monopolies and of keeping colonies in leading-strings simply as trade depots and trade centres, or convenient halting-places. The idea was never formulated that the "Hinterland"—to use an expression much in vogue just now—was ever likely to be useful as the abode of "homing-off" colonists. There was only one hive to which the honey could be brought, and this was the Mother-country, and this rudimentary conception of Colonies explains much.

In the old days British Colonial policy was not very different from that of her continental neighbours. The Dutch, as long as they kept the Cape, discouraged the exploration of the interior, magnifying to travellers and botanists, like Sparrman and Thunberg, its perils and difficulties, never being willing that their colonists should "trek" away into the interior, and thus losing all kind of control over them. From the departmental point of view everything should be concentrated at the company's offices and the Government Castle at Cape Town. In the same way the French, having formed their fishing, fur, and lumbering stations in North America, were by no means anxious that the French Creoles, or native-born French colonists, should get out of official control and become "coureurs de bois", adding nothing to the value of the trade with the mother-country. This "trekking away" was a dangerous policy also, as it brought the government into collision with native tribes.

The growth, therefore, of the British Colonies is all the more wonderful because British colonists have received so little encouragement. The colonizing virtues have asserted themselves in spite of difficulties, like the Roman military virtue, eulogized by Horace, of which he said, epigrammatically, *Merses profundo, pulchrior evenit*. Not only have British colonists had to deal in the Victorian era, as we shall see, (1) with departmental neglect, but (2) with parliamentary misrepresentations, (3) with private misconceptions, (4) with literary contempt and general indifference. Yet the hardy plant has grown and thriven, trusting to its own vitality, in complete and utter contrast to other Colonial methods and systems. What greater difference could there be between the inception of a modern German colonizing project, with its blare of official trumpets, and the infantile struggles of some of our colonies! More than once the infant Hercules seemed as if he would be strangled, but he has emerged victorious.

In following the history of our Colonies all over the world, we are following, chapter by chapter, the unfolding of our own national spirit, bold in adventure, patient in toil, and ready in resources of mind and body. South Africa has been much *en évidence* lately, and it is in this country, perhaps, that we may best find recent illustrations of the progressive spirit of the British colonists on the one hand, and the reluctance of the home government on the other, to undertake new responsibilities. How often in past times have we not heard that the best policy was for Great Britain to confine her direct rule and influence to the narrow Cape Peninsula and the naval station at Simons Bay, and leave the rest of the South African continent alone! That there was no continuous policy in South Africa was proved abundantly in recent times by the debates in parliament arising out of our wars there. Further back, in Earl Grey's time, the main, if not the sole, reason which induced Great Britain to take an official interest in South Africa was the necessity of protecting those bands of settlers whom, under the hard stress of the times following upon the Napoleonic wars, she had planted as a kind of advance guard on the Kaffrarian borders in 1820. A forward policy never commended itself to him, and even in 1852 he discusses the old heresy of abandoning all South Africa, except the Cape Peninsula. Further, it was Earl Grey's friends who carried out, by letters patent, the abandonment of the Orange River sovereignty, that most fatal error of Colonial administration. There has always been a Penelope's web in South Africa, and reversals of policy follow one another quickly. Students of South African history remember how Lord Glenelg undid the work of Sir Benjamin D'Urban, and gave back the province of Queen Adelaide, as it was called, to barbarism and the Kaffirs, with the inevitable result that barbarism had again to be met. This was in 1835-1836. Lord Glenelg, as Charles Grant, was Colonial Secretary to Lord Melbourne, and a Whig. His feelings were in unison with those of Wilberforce, Clarkson, and Buxton, but it may well be doubted whether he had any sympathy with Colonial expansion. Later on, in the case of Basutoland, Lord Cardwell wrote in 1866 to the Cape governor, Sir Philip Wodehouse, that any step involving an extension of rule at the Cape was far too serious in its bearings to be entertained by Her Majesty's government.

The question of our Colonial administration, responsible for so much that is wayward and vacillating, deserves a careful study, as it is seldom explained; and we cannot approach the subject of Colonial expansion in the Victorian era without knowing the form and character, and to some extent the inner working, of that department which has governed everything. In his celebrated report on the affairs of Canada (1838), to which it will often be necessary to allude, Lord Durham noticed that one reason to account for Canadian maladministration, so conspicuous when Queen Victoria ascended the throne, was to be found in the frequent changes in the office of the Secretary of State to whom Colonial affairs were entrusted. Since Lord Bathurst had retired from that charge in 1827, he observed that there had been no fewer than eight Colonial Secretaries; and the policy of each one had been marked, more or less, by a difference in method from that of his predecessor. This is exactly what Sir C. Adderley (Lord Norton) has noticed in his work on Colonial Policy (p. 2). Two evils naturally resulted—*Firstly*, the imperfect knowledge of the chief secretary himself and the necessity of appealing, therefore, so often to subordinates; and, *secondly*, the want of stability in the general policy of the government. These evils were pointed out and emphasized by a Select Committee of the Colonial House of Assembly in Upper Canada, at the time of the Canadian troubles of 1837–1838. Another evil, and this a most serious one, was also indicated by Lord Durham, viz., that the course of Canadian politics so often had reference to the state of political parties in England instead of to the actual wants and necessities of the colonists.[1] Nobody knew "how soon some hidden spring might be put in motion at the Colonial Office which would defeat the best-laid plans".

The plain fact seems to be that the growth of our

[1] *Report*, p. 137.

Colonies has been a very different matter from their administration. Indeed, their growth has not followed upon or been the natural consequence of their administration. The history of the Colonial Office has been the history of an office that has never quite known or controlled its own sphere of work in times gone by, however excellent its work is now. From 1670, speaking roughly, Colonial affairs were attached to the Board of Trade. This may be explained by the fact that originally the plantations were regarded only in the light of trade centres, bound hand and foot to the mother-country by every conceivable restriction, and by all kinds of navigation laws. The principal business of these plantations or colonies would naturally, therefore, be concerned with trade.

In 1802 Colonial affairs were attached to the War Office, and Lord Hobart was the first Secretary of State for War and the Colonies, which union of office lasted until 1855. This confusion of departmental work will explain much, as we shall find, that needs explanation. Had British colonization been more distinctly and avowedly an affair of state, or had an Emigration and Colonization Bureau furnished a separate portfolio for a cabinet minister, a greater importance would have been attached to Colonial affairs. As the empire grew steadily there was a terrible pressure of work, and Colonial affairs were constantly in a muddle. Sydney Smith remarked in 1819, that "one and no small excuse for the misconduct of Colonial Secretaries is the enormous amount of business by which they are distracted. There should be two or three Colonial Secretaries instead of one. The office is terribly overweighted."[1]

For more than fifty years of this century the Colonial Office was attached to the War Office, and the inconveniences of the system, coming to a climax, were

[1] *Edinburgh Review.*

exposed in a debate raised by Sir John Pakington in 1855.[1] At this date the management of our Colonial affairs revealed "a state of public business hardly decorous", to use Sir John Pakington's words. The Colonial Secretary was at Vienna conducting negotiations at the close of the Crimean War, whilst not a day passed in London without the arrival of some important Colonial despatches. The Australian Constitution Bills were hung up; the state of affairs in South Africa, when Moshesh was moving and the Basutos were restless, required attention; there was a convict question in Van Diemen's Land, and a critical state of affairs in Victoria. All these matters were urgent, yet the machinery of administration was unequal to the task. Sir C. Adderley (Lord Norton), in backing up Sir John Pakington, gave a somewhat cynical view of the situation. The period in Colonial affairs, he said, was most critical, and the time for a combination of two public offices, War and the Colonies, most unfortunate. At the close of last century, when Mr. Dundas (Lord Melville) was offered the War Office, it was observed that he had all work and no patronage. The Colonial Office was therefore thrown in, where at that time there was little or no work, but where there existed a considerable amount of patronage. The consequence of the junction of the War and the Colonial Departments was a state of such confusion in the office that it was wittily described by Lord Derby as "The Office at War with all the Colonies".

The kind of confusion, financial and otherwise, which followed upon the amalgamation of these two offices was indicated in Sir Henry Parnell's (Lord Congleton) work on *Financial Reform.* Sir Henry, who was chairman of a Parliamentary Committee appointed in 1828 under Canning's brief administration, was the means of intro-

[1] Hansard, March 12, 1855.

ducing a new system of "audit" in our public departments, and exposed many abuses and irregularities. Amongst other things, he pointed out that under the heading of "Army Extraordinaries" a great deal of wasteful and illegal expenditure was concealed from Parliament and the public. For instance, there were sums paid at home to Colonial agents, there were sums drawn from abroad for Colonial expenses, although they were wholly for civil Colonial purposes and not for military expenditure. The evidence of Mr. Sargent before the Committee of Finance showed that besides being Paymaster of the Forces to a very large amount, he was also a Paymaster for Civil Contingencies, for the repairs of Windsor Castle, for emigration to Canada, for the ecclesiastical establishments in the West Indies. These facts are instructive, because they show why our Colonial administration was so often at fault, and why, from the point of view of the Colonial reformers, it was so hard to attack. There is nothing more stubborn in defence than a vested interest, and when it came to the point it was difficult for Whig or Tory to tear away from the War Office the good things that had appertained to it so long. The union of the two offices might be an anomaly, and the public inconveniences might be great, but nothing would be done until the state of the case came to be, as expressed by Sir John Pakington in 1855, under the Palmerston régime, "barely decorous". Then the separation took place.

Colonial history has moved very quickly since then, and so great and important has the work of the Colonial Office become that, in some cases, it appears still to require further definitions. Our responsibilities in the Continent of Africa have become so great in every quarter that they may, at no distant date, monopolize the care and attention of a separate department. Even now there is in certain portions of our African territories a confusion of jurisdiction and administration. On the west coast of Africa the boundary questions, in themselves a puzzling affair, between France and Britain, and Germany and Britain, involve a constant bandying to and fro of evidence between various authorities, each paramount in its sphere. The presence of a Trading Company in Nigeria complicates the question still more, and when a case of exercising sovereign rights occurs there is more than one shoulder upon which the responsibility may fall. A certain unity of administration is necessary here as in Central Africa.

The exact legal and international status of a Protectorate is uncertain. A Protectorate has been a decent mantle of jurisdiction adopted of late to throw over large spheres of administration, but what are the precise limitations of rights? It has often happened that a Protectorate has involved the jurisdiction of the Foreign Office, not the Colonial Office. In West Africa the Colonial Office, however, administers the Protectorates that come under the Hinterland of our Crown Colonies, whilst the Protectorates of East Africa are under the Foreign Office. In South and Central Africa the Colonial Office administers territories south of the Zambesi, but north of that line the Foreign Office exercises control, so that this extraordinary complication of jurisdiction exists, viz., that part of the territories of the British South Africa Company is under the Foreign Office and part under the Colonial Office. No empire has ever shown more varied forms of administration than the British Empire. Leaving the Indian Empire out altogether, there exist in our Colonial Empire no fewer than 43 distinct governments.

When Lord Derby said that the War Office was at war with all the Colonies, he might have made this the text of a more elaborate essay than appears on the surface. For, from one point of view, the War Office has been antagonistic to our Colonies so far as the military spirit has been opposed to the spirit of Colonial freedom. It has so happened that military governors have been almost a necessity in what are now our Responsible Colonies. In South Africa, New Zealand, and even Tasmania the opposition of the natives has been a factor to be reckoned with, and therefore such military governors as Sir George Arthur in Tasmania, Sir Henry Pottinger, Sir George Cathcart, and Sir Harry Smith in South Africa, were regarded as an absolute necessity. In addition to native embroilments in South Africa there have been differences with the "Trek" Boers; and Sir Harry Smith figures as the hero of Boomplatz in South Africa, where he defeated the Boers, and also of Aliwal in India. In Australia the convict element has required the iron hand of the military governor and prison warders rather than the persuasive eloquence of the civil administrator. Such a governor as Bligh in New South Wales (1806) was autocratic and stern, and the colonists then said that the British Government, when they appointed him to rule in Australia, had spoiled an excellent seaman to make a very inefficient governor; but what could they expect? No doubt the position of a governor in the midst of a mixed free and convict population was hard. Then such occasions as the Ballarat riots required the soldier's arm, when, in 1854, there was open insurrection, and "diggers'" law prevailed, with a cry for a "Republic in Victoria". In Canada regiments were constantly needed, both in the war with the United States in 1812–1814, and at the time of the Papineau Rebellion of 1837. Such governors as Sir George Arthur and Sir John Colborne and Sir Francis Head seemed to be better representatives of the Imperial Government than a plain civilian in broad-cloth. Even after the Canadian rebellion there were Fenian scares, frontier disputes, and difficulties with the United States, of a chronic kind, which needed the coarser methods of autocratic government rather than the more wary and compromising rôle of a constitutional governor.

But, once established, it was hard to exorcise the spirit of militarism from the Colonial Office and from Colonial administration. Moreover, the spirit of militarism was necessarily in opposition always to the spirit of constitutional freedom. It was difficult to change the quarter-deck and the parade-ground for the somewhat embarrassing precincts of the chamber of a Colonial Legislative Assembly, where the governor had to walk warily and circumspectly. It was a mistake, so recently as in the seventies of this century, when the Transvaal was taken over, to appoint a military officer like Sir Owen Lanyon as administrator of affairs in the Transvaal acting under Lord Wolseley. No appointment could possibly have been made more unsuited to the occasion, as the people, the Boers, a homely folk in themselves, preferred always a plain official in broad-cloth, like their own President Brand and President Kruger, rather than an officer of the "rooibaatjes" or redcoats.

If the British Colonies suffered from departmental neglect and confusion at the beginning of the Victorian era, they were hardly better off from the point of view of parliamentary representation. The case for Canada in 1837-38[1] almost went by default, although Arthur Roebuck, member for Bath, spoke as Canada's paid agent, and Mr. Leader held a brief also on behalf of the Colonists. But there was a strong objection, as we shall see, within the walls of Parliament itself, against Roebuck's speaking in the capacity he did. There were no opportunities of parliamentary questionings as now, there were no Colonial agents, few interested pecuniarily in the Colonies as capitalists and lenders of loans. We

[1] See Chapter VI.

shall see how the Canadian crisis called into being a distinct class of "Colonial Reformers" in the House of Commons; but these reformers were not always a tower of strength to their cause. They were comparatively unknown men, and had begun to form a kind of "Adullamite Cave", agreeable neither to Whig nor Tory, splitting away from Lord John Russell and the official champions of English parliamentary reform. Colonial politics formed only one plank of their platform, only one item of a tolerably large programme, and parliamentary programmes often suffer from being too large. They were allied, again, with what was known then as the new school of "Philosophical Radicalism", with whom were associated the names of Grote, Mill, Hume, Molesworth, John Tooke, Austin, and the Benthamite school. Their *personnel* was not particularly attractive, and they were the victims of fads, carrying with them, even as a political sub-section, the seeds of disintegration. Charles Buller, member for Liskeard, and one of the set, observed to Grote in 1836, speaking of the impossibility of arriving at any unanimous opinion amongst themselves, that their duties would soon be confined to "telling" Molesworth. The tie that bound them all together was of the slenderest description. Molesworth himself, member for Pencarrow, was of a somewhat impracticable and morose disposition. The programme of the Philosophical Radicals formed a certain political manifesto, and, doubtless, had much to commend it; but it seems clear that the cause of the Colonies did not gain much from being incorporated in it. In the *London and Westminster Review* of 1837–1838 John Stuart Mill thought that the time had come for a political declaration with the watchwords of "The Ballot", "Justice to Ireland", and "Justice to Canada", and called upon the somewhat uncertain Lord Brougham to take the lead of "a Moderate Radical Party". But was Brougham the right man to lead? or could he have led?

The parliamentary arrangement here suggested was a tactical mistake, and could be popular to no great party in the state. Why complicate the Canadian situation in 1837 by introducing the old and extremely controversial question of Irish reform? What had the ballot, no doubt a most desirable public measure, to do with the especial grievances of the French Canadians in the valley of the S. Lawrence?[1] Apparently, no party could or would consider Colonial questions on their own merit, the very fault indicated by Lord Durham. It is an old-standing grievance lasting well up to our own times. Seldom in our annals have Colonial subjects been handled in the spirit of pure criticism and with an accurate knowledge of facts. It is a matter of comparatively recent history that South African affairs have been discussed in a most violent and partisan spirit in the House, and that the "South Africa Act" of 1877, providing for the confederation of the various South African Colonies and States, was treated as a kind of Irish question in the House, and made a peg for parliamentary obstruction. Only just lately all parties seem to have breathed a serener atmosphere, and to have realized, once and for all, that Colonial affairs are matters of too great and too imperial a bearing to be bandied to and fro with the shibboleths of parliamentary sub-sections.

It may be questioned whether Mill was himself altogether sound in his general attitude towards colonization. Perhaps the subject of England's Colonial Empire, with its tangled web of sentiment and adventure, private idealism and public effort, its passionate patriotism and pride of race, its conflicts with barbarism, its Christian missions, evangelizing zeal, and its self-righting spirit of justice and philanthropy, overriding at

[1] See Chapter VI.

times, as on the slave question, all canons of political economy, constituted in reality a bad, if not altogether unsuitable subject for the philosopher of exact logical thought. British colonization represents a dynamical force and the play of an infinite variety of human motives, rather than the operation of mechanical laws, falling into their place with exactitude and precision. We may try to compare and correlate causes, argue correctly, and deduce with accuracy; but, suddenly, a wave of feeling, a gust of sentiment, overthrows the carefully-built edifice. The story we have to deal with is as varied as a troubadour's tale, and its episodes like those of the Arabian Nights, its "moving incidents" resembling those of Othello's life, with a superabundant display of many personalities.

In his work on *Representative Government* (p. 325), Mill expressed himself to the effect that over and above the commerce which she might equally enjoy after separation, England derived little benefit, except in prestige, from her dependencies, and the little she did derive from them was quite outweighed by the expense they entailed and the dispersion they necessitated of her naval and military forces. Here is the bald commercial fact stated plainly and without reserve. It is the view that, upon closer inspection, we shall see had much to recommend it to a large number of the Whig and Radical politicians, an economic rather than an enthusiastic view, with too much of the dry light of reason about it. It is the kind of doctrine we insensibly imbibe by a perusal of the *Government of Dependencies* (1841), by Sir George Cornwall Lewis. The subject-matter is discussed in the correct academic spirit, and with due reference to ancient precedent. But here, on the growth of the British Empire, was a subject out of keeping with all precedence, contradictory and anomalous. Walter Bagehot has said of Lewis that "he was puzzled about the passions of mankind; he had so little passion himself. . . . There was a want of enthusiasm about him both in appearance and in reality. . . . His memory was a dry memory just as his mind was a dry light. . . . Somebody called him a sagacious dictionary, and, apart from his massive simplicity of understanding and his immense accumulation of exact knowledge, there was nothing very remarkable about him." Although Lewis was in the front rank of the Liberal party, entering parliament five years after Cardwell, and filling many important posts officially, his influence as a teacher and guide on Colonial affairs cannot be said to have been strong and illuminating. He was out of sympathy in reality with his subject, and ought to have left it alone altogether.

It is possible to find fault with the Whigs as Colonial administrators at the beginning of the Victorian era; but was there *ever* a school of Parliamentary Colonial reformers with a party name and an official position who could supplant them and make up for their want of imagination and sympathy? In 1830 Sir Henry Parnell, the chairman of Mr. Canning's Parliamentary Finance Committee, expressed himself thus in a work on financial reform: "It is clear that the public desires no commercial advantage from the Colonies which it might not have without them. . . . The history of the Colonies for many years is that of a series of losses, and of the destruction of capital, and if to the many millions of private capital, which have been thus wasted, were added some hundred millions that have been raised by British taxes, and spent on account of the Colonies, the total loss to the British public of wealth, which the Colonies have occasioned, would appear to be enormous. . . . The discovery of the real sources of wealth has shown the folly of wasting lives and treasure on Colonial possessions." In a word, Sir Henry Parnell proposed to get rid of Ceylon, the Cape, Mauritius, and our North

American provinces at once. "With respect to Canada," he wrote, "including our other possessions on the Continent of North America, no case can be made out to show that we should not have every commercial advantage we are supposed now to have, if it were made an independent State. Neither our manufactures, foreign commerce, nor shipping would be injured by such a measure. On the other hand, what has the nation lost by Canada? Fifty or sixty millions have already been expended; the annual charge on the British Treasury is full £600,000 a year; and we learn from the Second Report of the Committee of Finance, that a plan of fortifying Canada has been for two or three years in progress, which is to cost £3,000,000."[1] These passages are particularly instructive, as they prove the apathy of some of our public men on the subject of a Colonial Empire, and they were written *before* the days of Free-trade. The Tory party, to judge from such an organ as the *Quarterly*, was not, however, always averse from an extension of territory, especially as an asylum for our emigrants, but it was distinctly hostile to the extension of Colonial liberty and Colonial freedom. It was an extension of empire under the leading-strings principle; and in the Canadian crisis of 1837 the Tories voted, of course, against a policy of what appeared to them a surrender of prerogative.

Colonial life in the beginning of this century had lost much of its pristine idealism, and lay under such deep shadows of slavery and convictism that even a Bishop Berkeley would have found it more than a Herculean task to cleanse it. Earl Grey, during the Russell administration, is theoretically in favour of Colonial emancipation and Colonial responsibility, and he is constantly writing down most correct sentiments. Still there is little enthusiasm, and certainly not much real faith.

[1] Parnell's *Financial Reform*, 1830.

When a test case arises, he shows an impatience and an anger hardly in keeping with his theories. For instance, when the Cape colonists boycotted the convict-ship *The Neptune*, in 1849, which threatened to deluge the Colony with the Bermuda convicts, he lost his temper entirely. Nevertheless, he was wrong, and his action was inconsistent with his statements, for he had said that no colony, which was not in the commencement a penal settlement, should be forced to receive convicts. He gives with one hand and takes away with the other. Earl Grey meant well when he wished to give representative government, but he desired to reserve all official posts for English nominees, and could not believe that the colonists were really able to govern themselves even in the minor public departments. Upon the larger question he seemed still at sea, and did not grasp the exact conditions under which representative government might be conceded, and was prepared to give to the West India Islands what he would give to the Australian colonies. John Noble, a Cape colonist and the author of *South Africa, Past and Present*, has said of Earl Grey, that while no Secretary of State held a higher character for ability, the turn of his mind was unfortunately influenced very strongly by the old opinions and associations respecting the course to be pursued towards the dependencies of the Empire. Theoretically he acknowledged that colonists were entitled to the self-government they were perpetually asking for; but in reality he was continually asserting the autocratic control of Downing Street in every action and every function. The consequence was that he proved to be the "blister" of the Colonies. Upon the whole question of Colonial enfranchisement it was clear that the Whigs were really feeling about for a policy, and had not made up their minds as to "how", "when", and "where" self-government—a question always facing them in Colonial administration—should and ought to be conceded. In this sense they were "Opportunists" and not thorough-going believers in a Colonial form of government, broadly-based and yet loyal. It was a question, again, that unfortunately cut into their ranks and divided their party occasionally. Sir Charles Adderley, a Liberal, criticised severely at times Earl Grey's Colonial administration. Perhaps, also, it was the predominant West Indian influences and West Indian associations, with their trade questions and class difficulties, that were always colouring the conceptions of our Colonial life; for West Indian life was a peculiarly composite colonial life, full of anomalies.

The West Indian heiress was then the conventional character in the pages of our novelists, sugar-growing by far the greatest of our Colonial industries, for the days of the Australian squatter or South African diamond merchant were not come yet. The province of Colonial administration was not properly defined, and it was the good old times of personal government and absolutism. "Good-bye, my good fellow, and let us hear as little of you as possible", were reported to be Earl Bathurst's parting words to a Colonial governor; and these instructions were fairly well carried out. What the true conditions of Colonial life were in each particular case few cared to know. There was little geographical knowledge, few statistics, and little appreciation of real facts. That the infant Hercules was growing very fast out of swaddling-clothes and parental control few even in the official world imagined, until a crisis came. The surprise was, that the infant had grown at all.

Lord John Russell was probably the most imperialistic of the old Whigs, and his manifesto of Colonial policy, put forward in 1850,[1] is a remarkable declaration. He

[1] Hansard, Feb. 8, 1850.

sketched the growth of our Colonies from 1600 to 1815, and discerned in their history from the first certain general principles. It was a notable fact, he said, that Colonists had carried with them the freedom and institutions of the mother-country; there was no room to doubt that the same laws under which men lived in England should be established in a country composed of Englishmen, and he quoted from the Stuart Patent granted to the Earl of Carlisle, "Know ye that all and every subject should be as free in Barbados as they that were born in England". But did Lord Russell really believe in his heart of hearts that political enfranchisement and political freedom in the old country (such as he himself had helped forward so much) should have its exact counterpart and precise imitation in the Colonies? It would seem that Lord Russell kept to himself important reservations on this point. The ideas of our old Colonial policy were hard to alter, and we feel that almost all statesmen regarded the offshoots of our race as "dependencies" in the strict interpretation of the term. Lord Russell is not over-sanguine that similarity of institutions and an identical training in the privileges and freedom of citizenship will keep the Colonies in close political connection with Great Britain. "I anticipate," he said in 1850, "with others, that some of our Colonies may so grow in population and wealth that they may say, our strength is sufficient to enable us to be independent of England, the link is now become onerous to us; the time is come when we can, in amity and alliance with England, maintain our independence. I do not think that time is yet approaching. But let us make them as far as possible fit to govern themselves; let us give them, as far as we can, the capacity of ruling their own affairs, let them increase in wealth and population; and whatever may happen, we of this great Empire shall have the consolation of saying that we have contributed to the happiness of the world." This language is cautious and statesmanlike, but it lacks faith and enthusiasm. Lord Russell makes a more important announcement on the subject of the Empire in general. "Having shown the increase," he said, "I come now to a question which has been much agitated, and which has found supporters of very considerable ability, namely, that we should no longer think it worth our while to maintain our Colonial Empire. I say in the first place, with regard to this proposal, that I think it our bounden duty to maintain those Colonies which have been placed under our charge; . . . they form part of the strength of the Empire, . . . and give harbours and security to trade. . . . I think that the persons who talk about giving up our Colonies do not consider the probable result. These Colonies would apply to other countries, *e.g.*, the Cape to Holland, Mauritius to France; and who can doubt that they would take them?" This is explicit enough, and it seems to mark a certain definite change in our Colonial policy.

John Bright bears testimony to these opinions of Lord Russell in a speech delivered by himself on Dec. 4, 1861. "I recollect", he said, "Lord John Russell, some years ago, in the House of Commons, on an occasion when I made some observation as to the unreasonable expenditure of our Colonies, and said that the people of England should not be taxed to defray expenses which the colonists themselves were well able to bear, turned to me with a sharpness which was not necessary and said, 'the honourable member has no objection to make a great empire into a little one, but I have'."[1]

It must be remembered that John Bright himself, speaking on the subject of Canadian Confederation (Feb. 28, 1867), said that for his part he wanted the population of these Provinces to do that which they believed to be

[1] *John Bright's Speeches*, edited by Thorold Rogers, vol. i. p. 179.

best for their own interest—to remain with this country, if they liked it, in the most friendly manner, or to become independent states if they wished it. If they preferred to unite themselves with the United States, he would not complain even of that.[1]

A change in the official view of our Colonies was destined to come sooner or later. In 1847 Herman Merivale had succeeded Sir James Stephen as permanent Under-secretary of State for the Colonies, an office he held until 1859. This fact may possibly be some explanation of the change in the official front. It has been stated by Mr. E. G. Wakefield, the son of Edward Gibbon Wakefield, that Archbishop Whately, who had a good deal of correspondence with the Colonial Office on the subject of emigration in 1845, always considered Sir James Stephen "a decided enemy to, and indeed sceptic in, Colonization", and gave it as his opinion, further, "that he had small hope for the Colonies while the principal rule over them was exercised by a man who held an obstinate opinion that they could not and ought not to succeed".[2] The power and influence of permanent secretaries is great especially when the heads of their departments are constantly changing.

Herman Merivale (1806–1874) was more sympathetic. In 1837, as Professor of Political Economy at Oxford, he delivered a course of lectures on British Colonization which made a great impression, and led to his appointment in the Colonial Office. Amongst other matters his essays contained an able criticism of Wakefield's methods of colonization, to which we shall frequently have occasion to refer. Herman Merivale was open to suggestions, and must have smoothed the path officially for Colonial reform, for, in 1856, Mills dedicated his work on the "Colonial Constitutions" to Mr. Merivale as "the early

[1] *John Bright's Speeches*, edited by Thorold Rogers, vol. i. p. 163.
[2] *The Founders of Canterbury*, vol. i. p. 6.

and consistent advocate of that enlightened and progressive system of Colonial policy now happily adopted by Great Britain". It was fortunate that, in spite of all the difficulties and impediments in the path of British colonists, a proper *modus vivendi* was formed between the Colonizing world and the Departmental world. This era of greater harmony and more complete knowledge was continued with conspicuous success by Sir Robert Herbert, who succeeded Lord Blachford in 1871.

As has been already remarked, the administration of our Colonies during the greater portion of the Victorian era has been singularly free from interruption on the part of our Continental neighbours. This is fortunate, otherwise we might have paid more heavily for some of our mistakes. Had Europe been so eager in the forties and fifties of this century to acquire colonial possessions as she is now, the school of Goldwin Smith and of Colonial Disruptionists, so conspicuous in the "sixties", would have had ample opportunities of being satisfied. Just at present Colonial administration trenches very closely upon the work of the Foreign Office. Instead of the Colonies being a mere appendage to other departments of State, these departments of State, one and all, seem to hang upon the Colonial Office. The rod of the Colonial Office, like Aaron's rod, has almost swallowed up the rest, and if there is any ground of friction between ourselves and other European States, it generally resolves itself into a Colonial question. This fact is partly shown in the confusion of Colonial Administration in the Colonial and Foreign Offices, to which allusion has already been made, as existing in South and Central Africa.

There has been a continuous rivalry with France, and a great deal of diplomatic snarling on Colonial questions during the Victorian era, but hardly enough to make an occasion for a fight. The French are extremely sensitive on the subject of their Colonial Empire, and hug with perhaps a pardonable pride the remnants of their former Transatlantic empire. In the spirit of resigned regret Chateaubriand wrote: "We are excluded from the New World when the human race is recommencing—the English and Spanish languages serve to express the thoughts of many millions of men in Africa, in Asia, in the South Sea Islands, and the continent of the two Americas: and we, disinherited of the conquests of our courage and genius, hear the language of Racine, of Colbert, and of Louis XIV. spoken merely in a few hamlets of Louisiana and Canada under a foreign sway". In Canada the actual territory left to France are the Islands of S. Pierre and Miquelon, together with the right of fishing and curing fish round a certain portion of the coast of Newfoundland, known as "The French Shore" right. Thither the French fishing-fleet sail every year from the ports of Normandy in a somewhat picturesque procession, and a spirit of maritime adventure is thus fostered amongst the hardy sailors of their coasts. Indeed, the Newfoundland fishing-fleet is considered to be the nursery of the French navy. To encourage it the French Government give bounties.

The French Colonial system is entirely different from our own, and encourages bounties and State subsidies of all descriptions. Protection and not Free-trade is the watchword of their system. In the scramble for the continent of Africa, France has gained more actual territory than any other Power. If she has lost elsewhere she has won 2,000,000 square miles of territory here. She has visions of a West African Empire, and a Trans-Saharan Railway, and a through communication from the Mediterranean to the Gulf of Guinea, and she has amassed territory between the Middle Congo and the Ocean, covering an area of 257,000 square miles, according to Mr. Stanley, the African explorer. These are all still "undeveloped estates", and await the hand of the trader and the practical organizer. Still, in the nineteenth century we miss some of the old vigour of French colonization which was so evident in the sixteenth and seventeenth centuries. No one has trod worthily in the footsteps of the great Coligny and taken his model of a scheme of colonization, which was to be prompted by patriotism and religious fervour alike; there is no class of statesmen, like Richelieu and Colbert, with magnificent ideals; there are no such men in the nineteenth century as the Jesuit explorers of Canada, as Biart, Gabriel Lallemand, Isaac Jogues, Jean de Brebeuf; there are no such men, *œkists* in every sense of the term, as Jacques Cartier, Champlain, la Salle, and Frontenac.

Not that there have been no French explorers or missionaries in the nineteenth century. Far from it, for there have been many, especially on the Continent of Africa, but in their aims and projects there has been little coherence. The French people themselves blow hot and cold upon Colonial ventures, and if such a policy as that of Jules Ferry is approved one day it is execrated the next. The want of political stability has interfered greatly with schemes of colonization, and after such expeditions as those of Tonquin and Madagascar there is always an angry and discontented feeling as to whether the game is worth the candle after all. Judging of French colonization by Algeria, it would seem, like Hindustan, never likely to be a country adapted for *bonâ-fide* colonization. There is a curious admixture of East and West, a *congeries* of all types in the towns; but a Frenchman cannot become an Algerine as British immigrants, when they reach our Colonies, become Canadians or Australians. Militarism flourishes in

Algeria, and if we trace French colonization elsewhere we find the bad theories of convictism, which we have long since exploded by means of better prison discipline, still hanging around such outposts as New Caledonia and Cayenne. When it was suggested in the last century that we should convert a tropical and West African station into a penal settlement, the idea was denounced by Burke as a most unjustifiable alternative to death.

Perhaps the most remarkable event of modern times in its bearing upon our Colonial Empire has been the entry of Germany upon a career of official colonization. It has long been noted, as an aphorism, that France had colonies but no colonists, and Germany colonists but no colonies. It has been part of the official programme of the German Government to supply colonizing or trading areas. Too long had the thrifty German peasants and artisans, flying oftentimes from the "conscription", drifted across to the United States in thousands, and it was deemed a patriotic task to arrest the flow. In 1884 Prince Bismarck, speaking before a Reichstag Committee on the subject of the subvention of mail steamships to Asia and Australia, laid down the lines of a German Colonial policy which was not to establish colonies on the French or English pattern, but to protect German subjects and traders wherever they had established themselves. An era of Colonial annexation set in, and Germany took Damaraland in South Africa, a portion of New Guinea, New Britain, and parts of the hitherto unappropriated regions of the Continent of Africa on the east and west coasts. Under the special patronage of the Emperor William the movement has grown, although there is considerable opposition to large naval expenditure in Germany itself. Individually, the Germans are good colonists and keen business men, and have learned a great deal from ourselves, becoming, in the commercial world, Great Britain's most formidable rivals. But it is more than doubtful whether there is room for a "Greater Germany" which can compete with "Greater Britain", the number of German civilian colonists numbering only 32,000 at the present time.[1] Germany is pervaded with the spirit of militarism, and is, therefore, a bad nursery for Colonial administrators. As we know from our own Colonial history, the spirit of militarism and bureaucracy is always at variance with the spirit of free and tolerant colonization. Germany's agents in the Cameroons have not been successful; Dr. Peters' career in East Africa was disgraceful; Germany's action in Hayti, quite recently, has been obnoxious; her high-handed proceedings in China breathe a spirit of *hauteur* and bureaucratic impulsiveness which will inevitably recoil upon her. Germany is torn also with Socialistic doctrines, distinctly adverse to the present monarchical system, and if a Greater Germany, resting upon trade extensions, ever arose, it would probably strengthen the backbone of resistance to the autocratic rule of the Crown, and bring about social and political changes in the framework of German society. Enough has already been done to show how completely different German Colonial administration is from our own. When the Germans were intriguing to get into the Transvaal, the late Sir Bartle Frere warned the Boers that the little finger of German bureaucracy in the Transvaal would be far thicker and heavier than the loins of the British administration. In spite of all its mistakes and blunders, British Colonization is the pioneer of peace and industrial progress everywhere, and has thrown open to the whole world vast areas of the world's surface for Free-trade and Free colonization. Far different is the exclusive and Protectionist spirit of France and Germany,

[1] *Times*, December 25, 1896.

who close their colonies to the outside world, and build round them a Chinese wall of tariffs.

Chapter II.

Pioneers of Colonial Progress and Reform (1837–1897).

The real pioneers of colonial reform and progress in the Victorian era would appear to be individual men who, outside the ranks of office and of party, have pleaded the cause of the colonists. Abroad or in the Colonies themselves, and on the ever-widening frontiers of our Empire, there has been one class of pioneers; at home, another. The one worked with axe and spade, the other with pen and paper. For lack of regular machinery special pleaders have been required to represent Colonial interests and advocate right methods of emigration and colonization. It must not be forgotten that in the ranks of the Colonial reformers of 1830–1840, to whom allusion has already been made, there were a certain number distinguished above their fellows for their especial knowledge of Colonial affairs, and also for the personal enthusiasm with which they wrote and spoke about them. These men were more useful out of parliament than in it. Although nominally it chanced that they were of the party of Grote, Hume, Mill, and the rest, they must be distinguished from them, and appear to have exercised a peculiar influence of their own in many channels, an influence which was not exactly that of perpetual opposition, from the mere narrow party point of view at home, to Lord John Russell and the Whigs of that day, who had carried the Reform Bill in England, but did not extend another class of reforms to the Colonies.

Pioneers of Colonial Progress.

These men were social reformers and philanthropists, first of all, in the great interest they took in national emigration as the best form of charity, and political extremists in the last resort. In all great movements there is an esoteric side, an inner set of doctrines and principles moulded by a few great thinkers, generally abreast of the times.

In the colonial politics of 1830–1840 the ideas of that strange and brilliant enthusiast, Edward Gibbon Wakefield, were plainly discernible. He was the prophet of a new movement, and gathered round him sympathizers from every quarter. It is remarkable how often our colonial history has been shaped and moulded by sentiment and enthusiasm, and how seldom by the absolutely dry reasonings of political economists. A kind of Colonial Mahdism has often given colour to our annals of colonization. It was a time of dire distress and poverty in many parts of England, and to Gibbon Wakefield the necessity of a broad and national system of emigration from England to fill up the wide spaces of our Colonial Empire, and to create strong limbs of one great united body, appeared in the light of a plain political duty. Ideas no less magnificent, and perhaps more practicable, than the shadowy viceroyalties of Colbert and Richelieu, moved through his ever-fertile brain when he designed in New Zealand the outlines of the Otago settlement with Captain Cargill and Dr. Aldcorn of Oban, and the Canterbury settlement with Godley, Bishop Hinds, and Lord Lyttelton, and others. In the one case the Free Kirk of Scotland, and in the other the Church of England was to be represented, and the settlements thus assumed from the beginning a religious character. It was Wakefield's notion also to direct Irish colonization to Canada on a colossal scale, and the suggestion was made by him to Daniel O'Connell and William Smith O'Brien.

Mr. Wakefield was the author of a system of colonization by which public land in the Colonies was sold and not given recklessly as hitherto, the proceeds being applied to emigration surveys, roads, churches, and schools. In 1836 South Australia was founded on these principles, Wakefield taking the chief share of the founder's work. His first "trumpet-sound in the arena of colonization", as Rusden, the historian of Australia, describes it, was an anonymous letter published in London (1829), purporting to be "A Letter from Sydney". We shall have occasion to point out how Canada and New Zealand, as well as Australia, engrossed by turn the attention of this remarkable man. He was the first really to introduce some kind of order and method into our whole system of colonization. Men, women, and children were flocking promiscuously, under the stress of circumstances, from Great Britain to the colonies, forming that notable exodus which has been such a feature of the nineteenth century and of the Victorian era. They wanted guidance, and Wakefield tried to supply it. The accommodation on board ship for the ordinary emigrants, and for the government batches of convicts, was execrable. Latter-day legislation has rendered all this impossible, and "Plimsoll's mark" is an outward sign of proper solicitude for our seamen; but it is incredible to think how, sixty or seventy years ago, human beings were huddled together in ships which were simply death-traps. The dangers of a storm were as nothing to the pestilence that, from lack of sanitary precaution and bad water, brooded in the cabins. It was the "horrors of the middle passage" over again to reach England's colonies. If so many people were to leave the shores of England in order to seek new fortunes, argued Wakefield, let them be sent in the right way and at the right time, and, when they land, let them find provision made for them; let them see the form of a civil government, churches, schools, and all the institutions they have been accustomed to see at home. Surely this was the least the State could do. Indeed mere humanity could ask no less. No one understood the problems of colonization better than Wakefield, both from actual experience of Colonial life and also from special knowledge of his subject. He was alive, also, to the pressing constitutional reforms needed in Canada in order to put the machinery of government there upon a sounder basis than that of 1837, and, together with Charles Buller, as a wise and trusted assessor in the task, helped materially to colour Lord Durham's Report on Canada, to which we shall have occasion often to allude as a charter of colonial liberties. To him, as well as to Roebuck, John Stuart Mill has assigned a meed of praise in his work on *Representative Government*. Lord Norton acknowledges his debt to him in the draft of the New Zealand Constitution Act, "which he drew up under his guidance",[1] and Herman Merivale, in his *Lectures on Colonisation*, says, that "the success of the Australian Colonies was in a great measure to be attributed to the lessons taught by Gibbon Wakefield and his disciples".

It is worth noticing, *en passant*, that the activity of Wakefield was not always pleasing to the Whigs and to Lord John Russell. In the *Edinburgh Review* of 1840, in an article on the "New Theory of Colonization", the writer observes, "Whenever Lord John Russell shall undertake the task of answering the weekly attacks upon him and his office in the *Spectator* and the *Colonial Gazette*, we shall be in a position to estimate the real worth of what might be called the Wakefield theory of the Colonial Office". These remarks are instructive, as they point to a cleavage and disagreement, possibly natural in its way, between the official world and the free-lances of our Colonial policy, such as Wakefield and his comrades.

[1] *Colonial Policy*, p. 137.

Roebuck as a writer on Colonial policy figures better than as a speaker in Parliament on this subject, his personality as an orator being somewhat aggressive, and earning him the title of "Tear 'em". On the pages of a little book, written by him in 1849, on *A Plan for the Government of Some Portion of our Colonial Possessions*, he discourses in a more amiable and certainly more attractive vein upon the condition and prospects of the British Empire. He combats the popular theory that "a colonist in the mind of the official is a man ever on the verge of rebellion". He looks forward in a very remarkable way, and tries to prepare the ground by a wide anticipatory system of Colonial legislation. There were, he noticed, three great Colonial systems growing up— (1) in British North America, (2) Australasia, (3) South Africa. Each would, in his judgment, become a centre of administrative activity, upon which the hand of the statesman would mould the features of a state. The outlying regions, such as those in Canada, would be incorporated as "settlements", others as "provinces". These "provinces" in their turn would be grouped together for federal purposes, and the hand of the surveyor would be busy in marking definite boundaries, counties, townships, and parishes, each parish being divided into lots and sold by authority. Referring especially to Canada, he wrote (p. 224): "By care and fairness the affections of these people (the French-Canadians) may, I hope, be regained: they would form a great item in the Federal Union I have prepared, and that Federal Union would effectually check the tendency of Upper English Canada to Americanise—would knit Nova Scotia, New Brunswick, Prince Edward Island, and Newfoundland into one powerful Confederation, which would be for centuries a bulwark for England, and at all times a check and counterpoise to the advancing power of the United States. I contemplate an extension of our dominion across the Continent, the formation of new States north of Lake Superior." He bade Canadian statesmen be the rivals of those of Washington, able to meet them on equal terms, and thus resist the encroaching power of the United States, which had just annexed Mexico. He always considered the extension of the power of the United States to the North Pole as an event likely to prove "fatal to the maritime superiority of England". At the same time he thought that Canada would soon be independent, and did not realize that a Confederation of Canada could exist and still be in political partnership with the mother-country. Nevertheless, he strikes a distinctly imperial note, and has a thought for England's navy. His Canadian patriotism may be partially explained by the fact that he was educated in Canada and spent many years of his early life there. Roebuck is very different from Goldwin Smith, to whom we shall have occasion to refer, who, a generation afterwards, contemplated with equanimity, if not with approbation, the possibility of the absorption of Canada by the United States. Charles Buller (1806-1848), the friend of Wakefield, and secretary to Lord Durham in Canada, and, according to Thomas Carlyle, "the genialest Radical he ever knew", and "quite a bit of sunshine in my dreary Edinburgh element", had, in all probability, a greater personal influence within the esoteric circle of Colonial reformers even than Roebuck. Everyone, we are told, who came within Buller's presence was amused by the keenness of his wit, which never wounded, and was impressed by the sincerity of his purpose for good.[1] Standing 6 feet 3 inches in height, and a yard in breadth, a striking contrast to the smaller frame of Roebuck, he was of great bodily strength, thought not of a robust constitution. Harriet Martineau and John Stuart Mill

[1] *Dictionary of National Biography.*

were both indebted to him for information on Canadian affairs; and although it is said that Buller was always open to Mill's suggestions, it may well be questioned whether his was not the larger and more sympathetic mind on the practical subject of colonization and emigration as a matter of State politics. It is worth while to quote here in outline some ideas on Colonial policy as given by Charles Buller on a notable occasion in the House of Commons (April 6, 1843); for, although spoken under different circumstances than those of the great Burke, his words deserve to be ranked with them. Assuredly the occasion was an epoch-making one; and the dignity of Colonial life never had a better vindication. Waxing eloquent on the subject of the convict question, he observed that "neither Phœnician, nor Greek, nor Roman, nor Spaniard—no, nor our own great forefathers—when they laid the foundations of an European Colony on the Continent, and in the islands of the western world, ever dreamed of colonizing with one class of society by itself, and that the most helpless in shifting for itself. The foremost men of the ancient Republics led forth their colonies: each expedition was in itself an epitome of the society which it left. The solemn rites of religion blessed its departure from its home; and it bore with it the images of its country's gods, to link it for ever by a common worship to its ancient home. The Government of Spain sent its dignified clergy out with some of its first colonists. The noblest families in Spain sent their younger sons to settle in Hispaniola and Mexico and Peru. Raleigh quitted a brilliant Court and the highest spheres of political ambition in order to lay the foundation of the Colony of Virginia. Lord Baltimore and the best Catholic families founded Maryland; Penn was a courtier before he was a colonist; a set of noble proprietors established Carolina, and entrusted the framing of it to

John Locke; the highest hereditary rank in this country below the peerage was established in connection with the settlement of Nova Scotia; and such gentlemen as Sir Harry Vane, Hampden, and Cromwell did not disdain the prospect of a Colonial career. In all these cases emigration was of every class, . . . and thus was colonization always conducted, until all our ideas on the subject were perverted by the foundation of our convict colonies; and emigration, being associated in men's minds with transportation, was looked upon as the hardest punishment of guilt or the necessity of poverty." This vindication was needed if Australian political life was destined to be fully emancipated and to be fully responsible.

It was well that this timely reminder of the dignity of Colonial life should have been made. Literary men of the correct and orthodox stamp had not done their best for the honour and heroism of Colonial life. The slave-traffic, convictism, and buccaneering had worked their worst influences upon the minds and judgments of men. The shadow of the "hulks" was upon chivalric adventure as well as the lowest trade venture of the Oil Rivers. Men of the nineteenth century still thought with Samuel Johnson and Oliver Goldsmith that Colonial life was far-off, unreal, unallied with our ideals, stained with disloyalty or crime. "Sir," said Johnson to the faithful Boswell in 1769, "the Americans are a race of convicts, and ought to be thankful for anything we give them short of hanging." There was a great ignorance of all Transatlantic conditions, and at the same time Johnson confessed that "he had read little and thought little on the subject of America". In the seventeenth century there had been a race of optimists and of idealists in the work of British colonization, such as Bacon of Verulam, Baltimore, Raleigh, and in the sceptical and indifferent eighteenth century itself, at the beginning of it, the great

Berkeley, the most enthusiastic perhaps of all, but they seemed as prophets in the wilderness. Their day had gone by, their chivalry had evaporated, and enthusiasm, such as that which fired Elizabethan men, was at a discount. Canada remained at the beginning of the Victorian era just as Oliver Goldsmith had described it in his *Letter of a Chinese Philosopher* (speculating on the causes of war between England and France), a country "cold, desolate, and hideous", much as the French king himself is said to have described this fair heritage when General Wolfe succeeded in winning Quebec, as "only a few acres of snow". Sydney Smith, writing to the *Edinburgh Review* on Australia, in 1803, is not much better informed. Criticising the schemes of Australian convict colonies, he asked, "Why are we to erect penitentiary houses and prisons at the distance of half the globe. If we really wanted barren islands we could find them nearer home, or, supposing these deficient, we might discover in Canada, or the West Indies, or on the coast of Africa, a climate malignant enough, or a soil sufficiently sterile to revenge all the injuries that have been inflicted on society by pickpockets, larcenists, and petty felons." All this is well-nigh incredible to us, and proves that even the most rudimentary knowledge of geography was wanting in the leaders of thought of a country busily engaged in building up a great empire. It must be noted that, in contrast to the dearth of interest shown generally with regard to all Colonial topics which concerned the vast masses of our people most nearly, it is only just to mention the late Robert Stephen Rintoul, the editor of the London *Spectator*, who assisted Gibbon Wakefield by propagating his views. Colonial topics occupy such a prominent and important place in the public press now that it is simply right to recall those who gave them their due importance in the days of neglect. There is no feature more marked in our daily life now than the desire to know and to be informed concerning our Colonies. This is as it should be, and, so far, the non-official and Press world is influencing the official world.

If there was apathy before, there were reasons for it. The scene was far off, and before the days of quick communication news came slowly. There might be a fight for the liberty of the Press, as at the Cape, when Pringle and Fairbairn dared to upraise their voices against Lord Charles Somerset, the despotic governor of the Cape, but it was too Lilliputian to notice, hardly an echo reached the reading public in England. Members of Parliament did not, as now, engross the attention of the House with questions relating to Colonial affairs. As the items of Colonial administration and expenditure were concealed and covered by the vote for Army expenditure and army extraordinaries, it was almost impossible to raise any questions in the voting of the estimates. Sir Henry Parnell, the Chairman of the Finance Committee (1830), recommended that "accounts should be laid before the Treasury at least quarterly of the revenue and expenditure of our foreign possessions, and that a Colonial budget should be stated to the House of Commons every session by the Chancellor of the Exchequer, and all Colonial expenses should be voted on a distinct estimate".

Things have changed now if we look at the list of questions asked in parliament now of the Colonial Secretary. Our newspapers, which, a decade or so ago, scarcely gave a paragraph to Colonial news, now place it in the forefront. At one time it was "India and the Colonies", now it is the "Colonies and India", as if the two sets of interest to all Britons had changed places. Telegraphic summaries, not only of government proceedings and business, but also of the pleasures and pastimes of our cousins at the Antipodes, reach us every morning and are discussed at the breakfast-table. How great and wonderful the contrast! By a sudden revulsion of feeling, as it were, in the latter years of the Victorian era, beneath the quickening fire of a new and stimulating power, poets-laureate discern the greatness of the British Empire. Lord Tennyson, in his *Ode to the Queen* (1887), spoke of Canada and of Canadian loyalty at last in the true and worthy strain; and a Canadian poetess, Agnes Maude Machar, answers back:

> "We thank thee, Laureate, for thy kindly words
> Spoken for us to her to whom we look
> With loyal love, across the misty sea.
> . . . .
> For we have British hearts, and British blood
> Shall leap up, eager, when the danger calls!
> Once and again our sons have sprung to arms
> To fight in Britain's quarrel—not our own—
> . . . .
> Canadian blood has dyed Canadian soil,
> For Britain's honour, that we deemed our own."

There is no danger now of Rudyard Kipling's *Lady of the Snows* being forgotten in our national literature, but, not long ago, the high-priests of English literature uttered few Tyrtean strains in the days of struggle and adversity. In the "thirties" and "forties" of this century there was still the cold sneer of "Botany Bay" over some of our honest enterprises, as we learn from the writings of Sydney Smith on the subject of Australia and Convictism.

There were other educating and pioneering agencies at work, working on non-official lines, which helped on, directly and indirectly, the cause of colonization. Such was the Royal Geographical Society of London, which, under the auspices of the "Raleigh Travellers' Club", united, in 1830–1831, with the African Association (already famous for having sent out Hornimann, Houghton, and Mungo Park to West Africa), and gave a lasting impulse to British colonization and British exploration everywhere. Such also was the Royal Agricultural Society of England, founded in 1837-1838, which held its first annual encampment at Oxford in 1839. The Colonies of Great Britain, whose wealth is mainly pastoral and agricultural, have been the first to feel the good results of its enlightened enterprise. There is no country in the world better adapted than Great Britain for improving and maintaining the best breeds of cattle and sheep and oxen. The mother-country has been able to give to her colonists the very best stock and the very best machinery in the world, and there has always been a most profitable exchange between the two.

Somewhat later in date, the Royal Colonial Institute, now a most important body in London, with a membership of nearly 4000 members and an influential council, came into existence, and assumed in relation to the Colonies a position similar to that filled by the Royal Society as regards Science, and the Royal Geographical Society as regards Geography. It is impossible to overrate the valuable services done to the Colonies in London by the Royal Colonial Institute. It was on June 26, 1868, that a few gentlemen, amongst them being Viscount Bury (Earl of Albemarle), Mr. A. R. Rocke, Sir James Youl, and other representatives of Colonial interests, met together with the object of forming a society. As long ago as 1837 a society had been formed, under the title of the Colonial Society, for the purpose of affording a meeting for all those interested in the various dependencies of the Empire, and that had been succeeded by the "General Association for the Australian Colonies", inaugurated in 1855 for the purpose of furthering the welfare of the Australian Colonies, and more especially of promoting the several Constitution Bills of these Colonies then before the Government. Of this Association the Right Hon. Hugh Childers and Sir Arthur

Hodgson and Sir Charles Nicholson were prominent members. The Royal Colonial Institute was the lineal successor of the Colonial Society and of the Australian Association. The key-note struck at the inaugural meeting in 1868 is important, as attention was drawn to the paramount necessity of diffusing a knowledge about our Colonies, which was lacking, and at the same time the necessity of a closer union between Great Britain and the Colonies was affirmed. In the presence of 200 noblemen and gentlemen Lord Bury said that at the outset the one great object of this Society would be to disseminate accurate information upon all Colonial subjects. This was all the more necessary because there had sprung up a school of politicians whose leading idea appeared to be that Colonies were an excrescence of our Empire rather than an important element, an encumbrance rather than a material element of strength. He then openly alluded to the teaching of Professor Goldwin Smith. At this crisis the cause of our Colonies needed all the advocacy it could get.

It may be asked what could have been the arguments of those political philosophers who had discovered that Colonies did not pay. Briefly speaking, these very Colonies were losing their interest as trading centres by the break-up of the old system of commercial monopolies, according to which the Colonies were close preserves, and were jealously guarded by all kinds of legislation from foreign intruders. Since the recognition of the principles of Free-trade by the leaders of the great parties in the State, the Colonies were "superfluous for the supply of what we consume, and equally superfluous for the consumption of what we produce". We had done for ever with bounties and discriminating duties. We bought such products as lumber, corn, and fish not in the close or privileged markets of Canada, Nova Scotia, and Newfoundland, but in the open markets of the world. The West Indies no longer were the only sugar market we possessed, but we could buy this wherever we chose. The manufactures of Liverpool, Leeds, and Manchester went with no less profit to foreign countries than to our Colonies, and it was discovered that, compared with the amount of trade in those days which we carried on with foreigners, that of our Colonies was comparatively small. Wealth, trade, and the enjoyment of a high commercial position in the world came to us quite independently of our Colonies. There was the sentiment of possession and the glory of colonization, but what were these? Great Britain could be quite as powerful in the family of nations without Canada, Australia, Ceylon, and the West Indies. Then there were the questions of cost and defence. The Kaffir, Maori, and countless other small wars on the frontier of an ever-extending empire were a burden to the taxpayers at home. The bills were enormous in South Africa, and Sir William Molesworth stated in Parliament (July 31, 1855) that our regular military expenditure then amounted to £400,000 and £500,000 a year besides the series of Kaffir wars, which, on the average, had cost this country £1,000,000 a year.[1] A Parliamentary Committee sitting in 1865 to investigate the affairs of West Africa had recommended that we should withdraw from all our West African possessions except Sierra Leone. It was mainly the item of expense that appealed to the Committee, the West Coast Squadron costing the government £1,000,000 a year. Moreover, the malarious character of the coast was particularly detrimental to British officers and sailors, the loss in life from this cause alone equalling that of many a small campaign. True it was that England was doing a service to humanity in coast-guarding West Africa and preventing the slave-trade, but we were not backed up well

[1] Adderley, *Colonial Policy*, p. 174.

by other nations in our laudable efforts, especially with the demand for Cuban slaves, and Sir Charles Adderley remarked that "a wall of English corpses round the African shores could not stop the egress of slaves".

There was a time when these arguments were hard to meet. All the more credit to those who did stand by the Empire and its integrity, and to England's merchants and traders who would not be driven from their vantage-ground. Great Britain is treating with France now in a careful, if not a jealous humour for those fragments of Hinterland in West Africa which twenty or thirty years ago seemed to be so valueless to her. Behind all the worry, cost, and infinite trouble of our settlements in Africa, no matter whether in the west or south, or indeed elsewhere, there was a vision of better times and of a more prosperous era. As the Continental world failed to be drawn into our Free-trade principles, and raised their tariffs higher and higher against our manufactures, it was wise to retain every spot on earth where England could have, commercially, free ingress and egress. The Protectionist policy of the world's nations has driven "Free-trade England" along the path of Empire with accelerated speed. The wisest amongst us in the commercial world saw this, and we held to our heritage. This very heritage is useful for the growth of raw material on the one hand, and for the sale of manufactured goods on the other.

There has been no more powerful pioneer of true Colonial progress than the late Right Honourable W. E. Forster, who, when called upon to give an address to the Philosophical Institution, raised his voice in 1875 on a notable occasion in Edinburgh against the school of "Little Englanders". This speech may be regarded in certain respects as a landmark amidst the utterances of our public men. He spoke with warmth and enthusiasm upon our Colonial Empire, and prophesied that the union between Great Britain and her Colonies would last, because, no longer striving to rule them as dependencies when they were strong enough to be independent, we should welcome them as our partners in a common and mighty Empire. Mr. Forster alluded to Professor Goldwin Smith, and reminded his hearers that twelve years ago a voice from Oxford had declared our Colonial Empire to be an illusion for the future and a danger to the present, but that now fortunately this voice was no longer heard in England. Professor Goldwin Smith had gone to Canada, where his eloquent arguments for disruption convinced the Canadians no better than ourselves. There was an enthusiasm and manliness in the character of Mr. Forster which charmed and fascinated his followers. There were two sides to his character, the philanthropic and the imperialistic, as his biographer, Mr. Wemyss Reid, points out. Mr. Forster felt keenly and conscientiously the responsibilities which we owed to the subject races of our Empire, and this accounts for his South African policy, which has been productive of much good to his country. He also felt himself to be a "citizen of no mean city", and this led him, as a detached politician, when he left his arduous duties in Ireland, to take up the cause of Imperial Federation. It was wittily remarked of Mr. Forster by his friends, that when he identified himself with the Federation League "he was going about dry places seeking rest, and that he found the League". From that date forward to the day of his death the question of the Unity of the Empire was his engrossing thought.

Nor must it be forgotten how, in 1872, Lord Beaconsfield saw the value of "reconstructing as much as possible our Colonial Empire, and of responding to those distant sympathies which may become the source of incalculable strength and happiness to this land".

Sir John Seeley (1834-1895), who held the Chair of

Modern History at Cambridge in 1869, and published in 1883 his *Lectures on the Expansion of England*, gave the intellectual stimulus that was required to a movement already in the air. His work was immediately recognized, becoming the standard book of reference on Colonial policy. Colonial politics, by their very greatness, are now raised above all party considerations. Lord Rosebery, on more than one notable occasion, has responded to the note of a true Imperialism; the Right Hon. J. Chamberlain is a prominent champion of Greater Britain, and an enthusiastic leader of the new movement. With regard to Lord Salisbury, it has been fortunate that when Europe woke up from her sleep of indifference to Colonies, his unrivalled diplomacy was at the service of his country to maintain boundaries and to define England's rights.

But apart from personal influences, there were others of a still more powerful character. Science was destined to play an important part in the growth and consolidation of the British Empire, and as a pioneering agency science has worked many silent revolutions. In 1853 a United States naval expedition had surveyed the bed of the Atlantic, and Commander Berryman reported that from Newfoundland to Ireland, a distance of 1640 miles, there was a plateau at the bottom of the sea which seemed designed by nature to hold the wires of a submarine cable, and keep them out of harm's way. In 1858 Ireland and Newfoundland were connected by wire, and Queen Victoria and the President of the United States exchanged messages of congratulation. After the first trembling words this wire failed; but the beginning was made and the way was shown, and soon a "girdle was put round the world". Further, science stepped in to aid us in the building of ocean steamers, and in giving ease and comfort to passengers, and shortening the length of voyages everywhere. On the frontiers of our growing Empire she placed repeating-rifles in the hands of our soldiers and Colonists, before which the native tribesmen withered away like leaves before the storm; she gave the traveller new drugs and medicines, and taught him to combat disease—a medicine-chest as well as a useful box of ammunition; she gave him concentrated food, better rules of health, better clothing, and increased comforts; she gave him more exact instruments wherewith to find his latitude and longitude, whether on the wide ocean spaces or on the trackless continents; she gave wings to commerce, spurs to discovery, and the power, through machinery, of "a hundred-handed giant" to the individual man. People spoke to one another from the ends of the earth, and smoothly glided along the railway from one portion of the Colonies to another. If there were disintegrating forces at work science helped to reverse them, thus consolidating, metaphorically and actually, the outlying regions of our Empire.

One extraordinary result brought about by the workings of mechanical science has been the cheapening of freight by water all over the world. The shipbuilders and merchants of Great Britain, working from the basis of a country admirably qualified to help them with its stores of coal and iron, and a skilful class of mechanics, such as those of the Clyde, have succeeded in securing the greater part of the carrying trade of the world. The ocean, especially in connection with an inland water-system as that of Canada, furnishes the best highway possible. Ocean is no longer *dissociabilis*. It has been possible to land corn and beef at Liverpool at extraordinarily low rates. This, together with the Free-trade principle, has reacted on our agriculture in Great Britain; but the very despair of agriculture, unnatural as it seems to be, forces Great Britain to look abroad and to adhere more closely to her Colonial Empire as part of her life-blood.

Chapter III.

The Growth of the British-American Colonies (1837-1897).

The growth of our Colonial Empire during the Victorian era reveals a principle of spontaneous life very different from that of all other European countries. There have been no bounties to encourage our sailors and merchants, no subsidies to aid our Colonial department, no bureau to direct our colonists. As above hinted, British colonization has forced itself into every imaginable corner of the world by sheer persistence and perseverance, often in spite of official protests and the cry of Departmentalists, so that the various chapters of British colonization strike the eye, again and again, as triumphs of individualism. There were certain portions of the world where, in 1837, the British Empire could grow, and others where it was compelled to remain stationary, simply from geographical considerations. In the West Indies, a group which first naturally invites attention, it was impossible to overflow beyond the shores of the islands, and it was only possible to advance in such continental possessions as British Guiana and British Honduras, which have been always associated, historically and geographically, with the West Indian Islands. The tropical regions of Central and North America have, however, never presented themselves to the British colonists as *bonâ-fide* colonizing homes. Campéché Bay and its neighbourhood had been a favourite resort of the logwood cutters and buccaneers in the seventeenth century, and there had been an attempt to plant a colony of Scotchmen on the Isthmus of Darien after the Treaty of Ryswick (1697). But this latter project had failed, and the survivors were transferred

Growth of British-American Colonies. 55

to Jamaica. The "Mosquito Shore" is a tract of country stretching from Cape Gracios à Dios southerly to Punta Gorda on S. Juan's River, and in 1847 Lord Palmerston declared that the king of the Mosquito Indians was under the protection of the British Crown. In British Guiana and the Orinoco Valley there have been no great additions in the Victorian era, and its area is much the same now as it was when it was ceded to Great Britain by the Netherlands in 1814. There has been a disputed boundary question recently between Great Britain and Venezuela which called forth an assertion of the Monroe doctrine from the United States, and embroiled for a time the diplomatic relations between Great Britain and the United States. The dispute has come under arbitration, but it is evident that there is no scope, even if there were any desire, on the part of Great Britain for territorial aggrandizement in Central America. We simply desire to stand upon whatever legal rights we inherited from the cession of Berbice, Demerara, and Essequibo to us by the Netherlands, as far as maps and documents can substantiate our case.

The West Indian Islands alone, amongst our Colonial possessions, present a picture of comparative retrogression in the Victorian era. Undeservedly, perhaps, they have fallen from their high estate. Figures prove how important they were amongst our other Colonies in population and wealth in 1838.

Colonies.	Population.	Value of Imports.	Proportion per head.
North American Colonies, ...	1,400,000	£1,992,457	£1 7 0
West Indies, ...	1,000,000	3,393,441	3 8 0
Cape Colony, ...	150,000	623,323	4 3 6
Australia, ...	130,000	1,336,662	10 5 0
Mauritius, ...	90,000	467,342	5 3 6

These are the figures given by Herman Merivale in

his *Lectures on Colonization* (p. 248); and if his further statement that the value of the West Indian exports sometimes reached, and even passed, in 1833, the value of £8,000,000, be accepted, it is clear that the West Indian trade interests overshadowed all others. In 1891 the value of West Indian imports was £8,360,253, and that of their exports £8,618,858; but if we contrast them with those of the colony of New South Wales alone in 1891, leaving out of sight the six other Australasian colonies, we shall find that they fall behind them, the value of the imports from the United Kingdom to the Pacific colony being £10,580,230, that of the exports £8,855,405.[1] Figures are more eloquent than words sometimes, and, although it would not be correct to say that the West Indian colonies have absolutely decayed during the Victorian epoch, it is clear that they have lagged far behind our Pacific colonies. Nor, indeed, can they approach the prosperity of the North American and South African groups. There have been several reasons to account for the present state of the West Indian group. The abolition of the Slave-trade in 1807, and the Slave Emancipation Act of 1834, undermined the prosperity of the sugar planters. The Emancipation Act belongs to a category of reforms by itself. It was a self-sacrificing measure, because Great Britain lost heavily in cash, owing to the heavy sums paid in compensation to the planters, amounting nearly to £20,000,000, and, moreover, the measure brought paralysis into the sugar industry, which had been long established, and had furnished Great Britain with an immense amount of trade in times past. When thousands of negroes were given their freedom, it was idle to expect from them, in the midst of their first sensation of freedom, an orderly and rational restraint. The islands were fertile, and celebrated for their bananas and other fruits. The negro

[1] Coghlan's *Seven Australasian Colonies*.

was satisfied with little, and loved to bask in the sun in a climate just suited to him.

There was nothing more impulsive in the whole course of our history of colonization than the impatience of Sir Eardley Wilmot and the band of philanthropists with him, who pressed on with irrational speed the emancipation of the West African negroes. Lord Derby, Secretary for the Colonies at the time, had wisely prepared a seven years' apprenticeship before the era of complete freedom began, but before four years of the probationary period had elapsed, the new system came into full play. It is calculated that no less than 800,000 black semi-barbarians, without sufficient training, were admitted to the full right of British citizenship. The *Civitas Britannica* is a great and noble heritage, but it could hardly stand the test, in this case, of being squandered. That free labour would be the instant sequel of an unparalleled act of state generosity was a sanguine estimate of the situation. It was destined to be falsified by the fact that the labour market had almost immediately to be supplied by coolies imported by the planters from Asia, under indentures. On the question of a market for West Indian sugar, it might have been thought that British legislators, guided as they were so completely by the emancipation theories, would have made a distinction between sugar grown by means of slave labour (for the emancipation theory was not endorsed at once by other nations) and that grown by free labour, and would have given a preference to the latter. For some time they did, but presently the doctrine of Free-trade intervened, and in 1846–1848 it was decided to give no preference to any product of our colonies, whatever the circumstances of its growth and production. This decision came during the administration of Lord Grey. Involving, as it did, the "equalization of the duties" on free-grown and slave-grown sugar, this measure put the Colonial productions at a great disadvantage in European markets. Mr. Washington Eves observes in his work on the West Indies that sugar production fell to a point then from which it has never recovered. Estates had to go into Chancery because the proprietors were unable to manage them, large districts of the colony of Jamaica returning to the condition of bush. Two of the leading principles of English statesmanship at the beginning of the Victorian era, viz. Slave Emancipation and Free-trade, reacted with most disastrous results upon our West Indian Colonies. Home legislation, although it gave compensation, almost strangled the sugar industry.

There was another grievance. In past times the Crown had drawn large sums from the islands in the shape of a 4½ per cent "upon all dead commodities of the growth or produce of the islands of Barbadoes, Antigua, St. Kitts, Nevis, Montserrat, and the Virgin Islands, by means of which court functionaries in the days of the Stuarts and the Georges were paid. This tax was first levied in 1663, being the price paid for getting rid of proprietary claims, and lasted till 1838. The colonists pointed out that a sum of more than six millions, being three times the fee-simple value of the islands, had been raised altogether by their imports, which, upon the introduction of Slave Emancipation, became absolutely unbearable to them.

In Jamaica the shrinkage of capital and the general depression of the sugar industry led to a disturbed state of politics. Times being bad, there was constant friction between the Legislative Assemblies and the Imperial Parliament on the question of revenue bills. The assemblies, invested from the beginning with representative institutions, were constantly standing up for their constitutional privileges, whilst the Crown was equally determined to maintain its prerogative. It must always be remembered that West Indian political representation meant naturally the representation of a class, viz. the planters, for no one was ever bold enough to assume that the West Indian negroes could be entrusted with the franchise, parliamentary representation, and responsible government. The Black Republic of Hayti, an outcome of the doctrine of the French Revolution, lying close to the doors of Jamaica, thundered a lesson into her ears she never forgot. There was always a fear that a leader more powerful and less wise than Toussaint L'Ouverture might arise in our Colonies, and although poets, like William Wordsworth in his "Odes to National Independence", might idealize this particular man and the mission, so far as he was a victim of Napoleon, no one but the scattered planters living in isolation amidst a teeming population could realize the actual danger of black revolutionists. There had been numerous Maroon wars and servile revolts in Jamaica, no less than twenty-seven of them in 150 years of the island's history. The expense of putting down one of these, that of 1760, was £100,000, the rising of 1832 cost £161,596, exclusive of the value of property destroyed, estimated at £1,154,583; besides a loan of £500,000 granted by the Imperial Government to assist the planters.[1]

The climax in Jamaican history was reached in 1865, during the governorship of Mr. Eyre, when a number of rioters at Morant Bay openly raised the cry of rebellion. They were dispersed, chiefly owing to the prompt action of Governor Eyre, who, however, was recalled and charged with unnecessary violence. But the direct effect of it all was the surrender of the Jamaican Constitution and the substitution of direct Crown control. The whole case was beset with difficulties, and opinion at home, largely influenced by John Stuart Mill, was led, in many instances, to sympathize

[1] *Quarterly Review*, No. 277.

with the negroes, but the planters, being on the spot, welcomed a strong assertion of law and order. There was no doubt that this outbreak, in addition to other causes, hindered the progress of the Colony, and had a bad effect generally throughout the West Indies.

The latest difficulty the West Indian planter has had to contend with is the competition of Europe by means of beet-grown sugar in Germany and elsewhere. The beet-growers themselves receive considerable bounties from their respective states, and thus the West Indian sugar-grower has been placed at a serious disadvantage in the open markets of Great Britain. One remedy that has been suggested is to levy a countervailing duty at the British ports upon continental sugar to the exact amount of the continental bounty in each case, thus placing our own West Indian planter upon fair and equal terms with the beet-grower. But this appears to some to be a departure from the principles of Free-trade, although from the abstract point of view nothing appears to be more reasonable. The case of the West Indies has, however, been deemed worthy of more than one Parliamentary Commission, and the planters themselves, in their struggle to keep abreast with the general progress of the Empire, have not lacked advisers. They have been told long ago that, with sugar in its uncertain state, and the labour market precarious, it is not advisable to have all their eggs in one basket, and that they ought to devote attention to other products. Sugar has been a blessing and a curse to the West Indies. For a long time it was a blessing, so it seemed to the planters. It built up vast fortunes. The stately homes of England rose in their grandeur upon the labour of slaves in the West Indies. It is difficult to realize, now that our perspective is altered, how great an assault was made by the Emancipation Act and Free-trade upon class interests, and these some of the most important in the land. There was this much to be said for the West Indies as a source, in past times, of national strength. Under the old navigation laws, and under the old monopolist *régime*, their trade helped to call and keep in existence our mercantile marine, and thus to create a nursery for our seamen. In those long and bitter struggles of the eighteenth century it was the wealth of the West Indies that helped England materially to stand the strain and cost of incessant wars, and these wars, carried on vigorously and with success, were the beginning of a wider empire than that of the West Indies themselves.

Thus, for historical and sentimental reasons, the West Indian Islands and Possessions are particularly deserving of Great Britain's care.

Indeed, there is no portion of our Colonial Empire so intimately bound up with the inner life, literature, and history of Great Britain as the West Indies. But at present, it would seem, they cannot grow—not indeed in the way we should wish. White labour cannot help the islands, although Cromwell thought it could, and sent to Jamaica more than 2000 labourers. The climate makes it a black man's country, the paradise of the West African negro, who never wishes to return to West Africa after having tasted the joys of the West Indies. New products may arise, like the sisal-hemp industry in the Bahamas, and fruit-growing in all the islands for the United States may partly take the place of the sugar-cane. For the British official and British capitalist there may be an opening, but not for the British colonist seeking a new home in a new country in the sense he seeks it in North America, South Africa, and Australasia.

In Canada there was a far wider field than in the West Indies, and here the growth of wealth and population has been remarkable. In 1838 Merivale calculated that the whole population of our North American Colonies was 1,400,000, and in the census of 1891 it reached 4,829,411. In 1838 the value of all North American imports was stated by the same writer to be £1,992,457: in 1891 the value of Canadian imports was £24,650,884, of which £8,639,903 came from the United Kingdom. Judging from Lord Durham's official report in 1838, the population of Canada was very scattered, being separated by long and difficult distances, especially where water-carriage was absent. Along the banks of the S. Lawrence the French seigniories had been planned in a peculiar way, and the tenure was not freehold, but regulated according to an antiquated feudal system, to which we shall have to call attention. This tenure prevented a free flow of capital, and checked expansion in every quarter. The seigniories were clustered along the S. Lawrence for a distance of 90 miles below Quebec and 30 miles above Montreal, each seigniory containing from 100 to 500 square miles, parcelled out by the proprietors in small lots to each inhabitant. This portion was generally 3 arpents or acres in breadth, and 70 to 80 in depth, commencing from the banks of the S. Lawrence and extending back into the woods. In the United States there was a better system altogether, and a more active demand for property, which could be bought outright without any servitude or incumbrance. Land sales yielded a large revenue to this Government, no less than £20,000,000 in 40 years, according to an estimate given by Lord Durham in his well-known Report.

The expansion of Canada has been westwards. The advice to immigrants has been "Go out west and grow up with the country", and before them has stretched the virgin forest or prairie, with its lakes and rivers and boundless prospects. The whole of the region to the North-West had been granted, in 1670, to Prince Rupert and a company of proprietors by Charles II., and converted into a company called "The Hudson Bay Company". Practically, the reign of this proprietary company lasted, with certain changes, till 1870, a period of 200 years. Never in the world was such a hunting preserve known. There were factories and forts, such as Fort York and Moose Factory on the Hudson Bay Shore, Fort Resolution on the Slave Lake, Fort Edmonton in the Saskatchewan Valley, and scores of other small trading centres, but no great towns. Solitary trappers roamed through the desolate forests; and by the lakes the Indians traversed the country along the well-known "trails" or tracks; or, when occasion demanded it, they constructed their frail birch canoes and with inimitable skill and courage found their way by stream and torrent to the very ends of the continent. Far to the north the continent sloped down along a strange and melancholy space called "The Barrens" to the Arctic Ocean. On the West the range of the Rockies, running up the continent, seemed to cut it in twain, and keep the "Pacific Slope" and the milder regions of Columbia separated from this unknown prairie waste. Its vastness is hard to realize. Granted that a traveller had come to the extreme western towns of the Lake regions of Canada, perhaps 1000 miles inland, there still stretched before him a space of 2000 miles of Hudson Bay Territory to the Pacific Coast. The latest surveys have made the area of Canada 3,470,000 square miles, nearly equivalent to the land surface of Europe, which is 3,986,000 square miles.

The administration of the Hudson Bay Company was of a peculiar kind. From their factories or forts they employed the whole Indian population of 100,000 as keepers, and the strictest possible rules prevailed as to the protection of fur-bearing animals. The territory was divided into four departments, 33 districts, and 152 posts, in which 3000 agents, *voyageurs*, and servants were employed. Money was not known in the country, and business was conducted upon a tariff that had been long in use, the standard of value being the skin of the beaver, two martens being equivalent to a beaver, and twenty musk-rats to a marten, and so on along a scale well-known to the Indians. A report of the Great Exhibition of 1851 showed that 120,000 sable skins were imported into England from the Company's territories, a million musk-rat skins, and that since the beginning of the trade more than £20,000,000 worth of skins had been imported. But this huge monopoly was destined soon to disappear, and some large portions of this preserve to be reclaimed.

From Winnipeg to the Rockies it was discovered that the whole country sloped upwards in three remarkable steppes or elevations, the first rising to 800 feet, the second to 1600 feet, and the third to 3000 or 4000 feet. The total area of prairie ground along these steppes has been estimated to exceed 192,000 square miles, or more than three times the size of England and Wales. Before the time of the Queen's accession explorers had traversed portions of it and made their surveys. Hearne had followed the Coppermine River down to the Arctic Sea, and Mackenzie had seen the mouth of the Mackenzie River, Captain Cook in his voyage in the North Pacific had touched at Nootka Sound, and Franklin's instructions from Lord Bathurst took him past the forts and factories of the Hudson Bay territory to the shores eastward of the Coppermine River.

In 1837, Dease and Simpson, two officers of the Hudson Bay Company, had mapped portions of the polar basin next to the surveys of Franklin.

The first prize won from the North-West was Manitoba. The result of all the journeys and exploration of our travellers was to throw light upon the geographical problems of the Continent. It was discovered that, after all, the country was adapted to agriculture and the purposes of colonization, and one of the earliest pioneers in the region was Thomas Douglas, Earl of Selkirk. This nobleman had been chairman of the Hudson Bay Company, and had been able to acquire from them 116,000 square miles of territory, a goodly principality in itself. Thither he was desirous of leading, in the fashion of an ancient œkist, a band of Highlanders; and the journey of these men from the little fishing village of Helmsdale across the Atlantic, past the drifting icebergs of Davis Straits, through Hudson Bay, and down the Nelson River to their final destination at Winnipeg, is deserving of a conspicuous place in our epics of commerce and colonization. Lord Selkirk took part in the enterprise himself, and encouraged the clansmen to persevere; and they were not slow to respond to his example as their chief and leader. Scotsmen have accomplished wonders in the work of British colonization, especially in Canada, but they have seldom been engaged in a more fruitful project than the Selkirk Settlement, 1811-1816. It is precisely efforts of this sort which differentiate British colonization from that of our European neighbours. The Earl of Selkirk deserves to be ranked with Lord Baltimore, who took a settlement first of all to the peninsula of Avalon in Newfoundland, and afterwards to Maryland in the United States; and also with William Penn, founder of Pennsylvania. His name, as Thomas Douglas, Baron Daer, is preserved in Fort Daer and Fort Douglas.

There is a touch of pathos in the clan feeling that bound these adventurers together. Coming to Prince Edward's Islands with a detachment of 800 emigrants in three ships, Lord Selkirk says, "I arrived at the place late in the evening, and it had a very striking appearance. Each family had kindled a large fire near their wigwams, and around these were assembled groups of figures whose peculiar national dress added to the singularity of the scene. Confused heaps of baggage were everywhere piled together before their wild habitations, and by the number of fires the whole wood was illuminated. At the end of this line of encampments I pitched my own tent, and was surrounded in the morning by a numerous assemblage of people, whose behaviour indicated that they looked to nothing less than the happy days of clanship." The Selkirk Settlement commanded the warm sympathy of Sir Walter Scott, who testified to the "generous and disinterested disposition of the founder, who was carrying out, almost single-handed, such a wise scheme of national emigration. Winnipeg, originally known as Upper Fort Garry under the Hudson Bay Company, was founded at the confluence of the Red River and Assiniboine, and became the doorway leading to the prairies beyond. For many years it was an isolated settlement, separated from the most advanced point of civilization by 400 miles of uninhabited country, the route following a chain of lakes and rivers, presenting obstacles to boat navigation, especially in the river rapids, which necessitated constant "portages". It soon got to be known for certain that a continuous belt of country could be settled and cultivated from the Lake of the Woods to the Rockies.

Beyond the Rockies lay British Columbia, amidst a tumbling sea of mountains right down to the Pacific. Here, too, the Company's officers had their ports, and a monopoly of the fur-trade. In 1842 they sent Sir James Douglas westward, and in 1846 announced formally to the Colonial Office that they had explored and occupied Vancouver's Island, and wished to be formally inducted into possession of it. They had already selected Victoria as their port and capital on the south-east coast, up the Straits of Fuca, which divide the island from the American State of Washington. Long ago, as far back as 1778, some London merchants had made a trading-port here at Nootka Sound, when the Spaniards claimed some rights, which were surrendered, however, to British authorities in 1792. In 1849 the Crown granted the Island of Vancouver and its royalties in free-socage to the Hudson Bay Company with a reserved power of resuming it when necessary. This occasion was destined presently to arise, as Sir James Douglas reported that a large influx of Californian miners and speculators coming to the gold regions rendered the task of administration beyond his powers. Goldfields settle many Colonial problems, and the gold of Columbia led, after a change of the seat and form of government, to the erection of the combined Colonies of British Columbia and Vancouver's Island in 1866. It is somewhat remarkable that the goldfields of Klondike, which are reported to be of such fabulous wealth, promise to lead to further developments through and beyond British Columbia, on the east of the 141st degree of longitude. Hither are rushing, as in the case of British Columbia in the "fifties", hosts of United States adventurers. Readers of our Colonial annals may be reminded of old Martin Frobisher's great expedition in 1576, when he sailed to the north with his imagination fired and his cupidity excited, as Richard Hakluyt tells us, by the prospect of gold-mines lying in the very centre of Arctic snows and the islands of hyperborean seas. When he reached Anne Warwick's Sound he loaded his vessel with a promising ballast of shining sand and mica which he thought to be gold; and, in 1578, so great was the enthusiasm of the age that fifteen vessels sailed from Harwich for Frobisher's Straits in hopes of the golden mountains. There is nothing new under the sun, and if there is a rush to the Klondike goldfields in 1898, far in the regions of the Arctic, it is well to remember that in the annals of our adventurous nation there was a somewhat similar rush 320 years ago. The Elizabethan adventurers were disappointed with their beautiful "glistering stones", which turned out to be pieces of iridescent spar known as Labrador spar; but at Klondike the El Dorado is more substantial and remunerative.

For many years of the Victorian era the boundaries between Canada and the United States were not definitely settled, and led to much friction. There were three disputes, the first relating to the Maine frontier, settled in 1842, the second to the valley of the Columbia River, known as the Oregon dispute, settled in 1846, the third known as the San Juan controversy, settled in 1872, by which the coast boundary between the United States territory of Washington and the island of Vancouver was definitely fixed. It cannot be said that Great Britain emerged from any of these disputes with success. The United States have told France to leave North America, and they have delivered the same message to Spain, although they have technically disguised the roughness of their notices to quit by the Louisiana purchase of 1803, and the Florida purchase of 1819, a disguise hardly covered by their proceedings in Texas and Mexico. But with the increase of their prosperity their ambition has grown, and by the well-known Monroe doctrine the United States have signified the desire of their republic to have a monopoly of the Continent. It has been difficult to negotiate with the States, knowing this to be one of their cardinal points of policy, and rather than incur the risk of war, Great Britain has given in. The Maine dispute was inherited from the Treaty of Paris of 1783, recognizing the independence of the United States, and turned chiefly upon what interpretation ought to be given to "the highlands which divide those rivers which empty themselves into the river S. Lawrence, from those which fall into the Atlantic," also as to what were the sources of the Connecticut River. There was a certain looseness of geographical definition in the original maps and treaties which encouraged litigation. But for a long time nothing was said, until 1814, when certain proceedings, called the Ghent negotiations, were inaugurated. These failed, as did the appeal to the King of the Netherlands in 1827. Matters, however, were brought to a head in 1842, when Lord Ashburton was appointed by Sir Robert Peel to proceed to Washington as plenipotentiary to settle the Maine frontier, and also to come to agreement about the right of search in vessels carrying slaves from the West African coast. The United States gained practically all the territories in dispute; and to this day Canadian patriots indignantly refer to the "Ashburton surrender".

Meanwhile the Oregon question was ripening, and this difficulty soon became more pressing than the Maine question. If we go back to 1783 we find that the United States sought no empire beyond the Rockies; and Great Britain, if she rested upon the discoveries of Sir Francis Drake in 1579, who coasted down the country and gave it the name of New Albion, might have assumed sovereignty then at a very early date, even as far south as San Francisco. There was a difficulty in 1789 between British and Spanish subjects, and by the Nootka Sound Convention Great Britain, not wishing to colonize these regions herself, bargained for free and open colonization and trade for the subjects of both countries. In 1792 George Vancouver went to the North Pacific coast to receive the surrender of Spanish possessions near Nootka Sound, as hinted above.

British merchants and traders, ever to the front, were constantly seen on the Californian coast. Amongst them was Sir Edward Ellice (1781–1863), a managing director of the Hudson Bay Company, who figured in the English political life and Canadian politics of the early portion of the Victorian era. His father had taken the English side in the struggle with the United States, and had removed as a United Empire Loyalist to Montreal. Edward Ellice came home and was educated at Winchester, became the friend of such reformers as Sir Francis Burdett and Sir C. Cam Hobhouse, and married a sister of the second Earl Grey. Lord Norton has said that he knew more on the subject of colonial politics than any of his contemporaries. His interests, however, were bound up with Canada and the fur trade, and towards the Great North-West and the Pacific coast he was one of our earliest pioneers. In 1820 it is said that one of his ship captains brought to him from California a splendid specimen of gold in quartz rock, and if Ellice had taken the trouble to obtain a cession from the Mexican government, which at that time was no doubt possible, as this government was in difficulties, the English might have been the first to pass south of the river Columbia and take possession of San Francisco. There would have been no Oregon dispute, and Ellice would have been the richest man in Europe. But by the break-up of Mexico the United States had their attention directed powerfully to the Pacific coast-lines; and ultimately the Oregon boundary question resolved itself into the adoption by Great Britain of the boundary along the 49th parallel, which at present exists. The growth, therefore, of British North America was arrested on the Pacific coast by circumstances which our statesmen could not well guide. But the opportunity of territorial expansion lay before them, and they might have been beforehand with the United States in securing the reversion of this part of Spain's colonial domain.

The San Juan controversy arose out of the Columbia question, and was really part of the whole Oregon dispute. San Juan is a small island in Rosario Straits, and lies in the channel dividing Vancouver Island from the

Growth of British-American Colonies. 71

continent. In 1855 the legislature of Washington Territory, now separated from Oregon, passed an act including the island in their assessments, and, as the Hudson Bay Company possessed a factory here, there was friction at once. San Juan was not a very important island in itself, but from a strategic point of view it held such a commanding position that it was called the "Cronstadt of the Pacific". In 1859 the situation became acute when one of the American squatters shot a hog belonging to the Hudson Bay Company. Out of this incident a crisis arose, and the island was jointly occupied by American and British troops. The whole question was referred to the German emperor for arbitration, and decided against Great Britain. It has been said that faulty maps and a barely adequate geographical knowledge have been partly the cause of these international misunderstandings. It has been proved over and over again in the course of our colonial history that, considering how wide our Empire is, and upon how many states, civilized and uncivilized, it borders, the best guarantee for peaceful possession and quiet progress is a scientific boundary line, decided by a joint-commission. The law of trespass can then be known with exactness. Neutral zones like that of Oregon in North America, or even those portions of Kaffraria in South Africa, set aside as No Man's Land, between Kaffirs and colonists, have always sown the seeds of dangerous and embarrassing disputes. It is fortunate that before the discovery of the Klondike goldfields an International Boundary Commission surveyed the Canadian and Alaskan line along the 141st degree of longitude. The result has been to show exactly within whose jurisdiction the goldfields lie.

There is no doubt that boundary disputes, trenching as they did so often upon open rupture, hindered the progress and growth of the Dominion of Canada. By 1870 the Great North-West was fairly well known, and it had practically received its exact geographical definitions. In that year the Hudson Bay Company parted with their monopoly of government, and the North-West was transferred to the newly-formed Dominion of Canada, the Company receiving £300,000 compensation, retaining their forts and trade, and a right to a twentieth part of the lands. This was the introductory step to the erection of Manitoba into a separate province. In 1871 this province received two remarkable bodies of immigrants, that of the Russian Mennonites or Quakers, and that of the Icelanders who were settled at the Reserve called Gimli, numbering nearly 10,000 altogether. The extraordinary fertility of the Red River Valley and the adaptibility of its soil, as well as that of neighbouring river valleys, became known to every emigration office or bureau, whether public or private, in Europe.

Into the details of the marvellous growth and progress of Canada it is impossible to enter here. One by one great provinces, judicial districts, and principalities in their area and capabilities, have been incorporated in the Dominion, the *constitutional* growth of which will be subsequently noticed. The vague and ancient geographical expression of "Rupert's Land" resolved itself into such definite areas as Manitoba, Kewatin, Assiniboia, Saskatchewan, Alberta, Athabasca, and beyond the Rockies was British Columbia, equal in promise to any one of these. In 1877 Lord Dufferin said of Manitoba, that from its peculiar characteristics Manitoba could be regarded as the keystone of that mighty arch of sister provinces which span the Continent from the Atlantic to the Pacific. It was at Manitoba that Canada, emerging from her woods and forests, first gazed upon the rolling prairies and unexplored North-West, and it was from here she took a new departure. When we reflect that at the beginning of the Victorian era even the name of Manitoba was unknown to geographers, and that the Red River settlers were regarded as beyond the pale of ordinary Canadian colonization altogether, the fact of Manitoba being a "keystone of an arch" of provinces in 1872 is indeed remarkable.

Probably Manitoba would have remained in isolation much longer than it did had it not been for the Canadian Pacific Railway. We shall have to admire the Confederation of Canada as an act of supreme statesmanship, reflecting the highest credit upon the far-sighted discrimination of all those concerned in it. From another point of view the Transcontinental Railway must elicit our admiration as an engineering feat of extraordinary boldness, carried through with the greatest engineering skill, connecting together the most distant parts of the Dominion. Indeed, it would seem as if the railway were an almost necessary antecedent or concomitant of the political scheme of Confederation. By it intercourse was facilitated between all parts of the vast Dominion: along the line, as through an artery, pulsated the life-blood of the State: commerce flowed easily, local prejudices were diminished, and the unity of Canada demonstrated. Rarely have such moral and political results followed upon the enterprise of the engineers and surveyors of a railway.

As long ago as 1838 Lord Durham had advised railway communication as a cure for political and racial discontents. Isolation seemed to be the brooding curse of the country, intensifying national prejudices, and rendering trade difficult, and concentration of effort impossible. The Canadian Pacific was to have been commenced in 1873, but after some delays, owing to the vastness of the undertaking and the conflict of interests involved, the task was only seriously approached in 1880 under contract to be finished in 1891. It was completed in half the stipulated time, the last spike that finished the two ends, which had been working towards one another both from east and west, being driven in by Sir Donald Smith, in November, 1885, at a place called Craigellackie, 2569 miles west of Montreal. The main difficulties of construction were encountered in the Rockies, and the Selkirk range in British Columbia. In one place the line, twisting in repeated double loops, descends 600 feet in six miles, and accomplishes just two miles of actual progress.

It was soon realized that this magnificent enterprise was not merely an intercolonial railway but an imperial highway. British Columbia and Vancouver, although 6000 miles distant from London, could be reached in a fortnight. In the old days the Pacific coasts of North America could only be reached by San Francisco, Panama, or the stormy Cape Horn. The latter route was used by the old explorers, and meant a voyage of several months for a sailing ship. The hand of the modern engineer has altered all this, and changed the perspective of the world as by a sudden stroke. Beyond the province of British Columbia lay the vast spaces of the Pacific Ocean and New Zealand, Fiji, and Australia, and no sooner had the eye rested upon the Rockies than it was carried westwards and followed the sun in his course. Never had the *oceanic* character of the British Empire, as opposed to the mere *thalassic* view, been more signally proved than by the linking of the two shores of Canada together, and the opening up of Asia through Canada.

At the time of the Confederation of Canada all the canals of the country became the property of the Dominion Government, the total expenditure on this means of communication being valued at £10,000,000. Canadian canals must be classed with Canadian railways in the vast facilities they afford for internal communication. Canada is studded with lakes and threaded by magnificent rivers, most of them for six or eight months of the year becoming natural highways of the utmost value. The land of the birch canoe was destined to be the land of the steamboat, all conditions being most favourable to this means of progression. The adaptability of Canada in this respect had not escaped the notice of one of the pioneers of the North-West, Sir Edward Ellice, who in 1806 had made the first passage in the *Fulton*, the first steam-ship ever launched. But his wildest dreams may possibly be transcended by the events of the near future. When the ice has burst up on the Mackenzie River there is one of the finest water-courses in the world for 1500 miles, and for some years past the Hudson Bay Company have had steamers on this river. Should the Klondike goldfields prove to be the great El Dorado they promise, the best way to approach them will be on the Canadian side along the old fur-traders' "trails", or possibly via Edmonton on the Canadian Pacific Railway. Time, indeed, which achieves marvels with the aid of nineteenth-century science, may bring about a Hudson Bay route for a certain portion of the year, and thus the problem of the shortest " North-West Passage" be solved at last by steamship and railway.

In connection with the Canadian Pacific a system of land-survey and township allotments has been inaugurated. These townships start from the international boundary line and run north in blocks. They are divided by lines called "principal meridians", the first meridian, a kind of Greenwich, starting from a point on the boundary between 97° and 98° W. longitude. The level and uniform character of the country favours these chess-board divisions and blocks, and lends itself easily to a survey. The unit of the township's survey is one square mile, or 640 acres, which is divided into quarter-sections of 160 acres. This quarter-section has been held out to the immigrant as a freehold given to him on condition of three years' residence and cultivation, with payment of an office fee of £2. This is one of the best and simplest land titles in the world, and as, in the North-West, the surveyor has been beforehand with the occupier, the latter knows at once by his number and by a reference to the map where his home and patrimony may be. The surveyed lines are indicated on the ground itself by pillars and stones at the corners of the divisions and subdivisions, all numbered according to their position to the prime meridian. An intelligent settler when travelling in the surveyed districts is able quickly to read off his position by reference to a single pillar, and thus the land-surveyor has left behind him a series of directing posts and signboards, showing the way, as well as fixing enduring monuments of township demarcation. In each township there is so much land reserved for school and public purposes, thus the infant locations lie upon the ground ready for the purposes of emigration and colonization. Moreover, the prairie is boundless, and the soil deep and practically inexhaustible in these surveyed regions of Canada.

It is instructive to contrast this method of settlement with those haphazard conditions which were prevalent at the beginning of the Victorian era, to which Lord Durham, Charles Buller, and Gibbon Wakefield called attention, when the wretched emigrants, after long and terrible voyages on the Atlantic, were flung almost literally like bales upon the wharves of Quebec and Montreal. There was this difference, that the bales of merchandise had a label and a destination, but the human chattel had none. Living on bad food and unwholesome water on board ship, swindled by the pursers, and ignorant of the conditions and climate of the country before them, the emigrants were more fit subjects for the lazaretto when they arrived than for the hardships of colonization. Yet, in 1837 no fewer than 22,000 had found their way to Canada. Very often they drifted over the Canadian boundary into the United States, and Great Britain lost tens of thousands of her colonizing subjects. Lord Durham wrote, after exposing the terrible privations and utter bad management of our methods of emigration: "It is far from my purpose, in laying these facts before Your Majesty, to discourage emigration to your North American Colonies. On the contrary, I am satisfied that the chief value of those Colonies to the mother-country consists in their presenting a field where millions even of those distressed at home might be established in plenty and happiness. All the gentlemen whose evidence I have quoted are warm advocates of systematic emigration. I object, along with them, only to such emigration as now takes place—without forethought, preparation, method, or system of any kind."

Chapter IV.

The Growth of the British-Australasian Colonies (1837-1897).

In 1838 the population of our Australasian Colonies was calculated by Merivale to be 130,000; in 1891 it had reached 3,809,895. In 1838 the value of imports from the mother-country to Australia was valued at £1,336,662, or £10, 5s. 0d. per head; in 1891 the "Seven Colonies of Australasia" imported from the United Kingdom goods to the value of £30,823,474. For the same year the total value of all imports and exports amounted, collectively, to £84,651,488.[1] The growth of population and the increase in trade has been more marked in

[1] Coghlan's *Seven Colonies of Australasia.*

Australasia than in the Canadian Dominion, or, indeed, in South Africa. There have been several reasons to account for this: amongst them, that the serious rivalries of European powers have never been witnessed on their shores. "Notasia", or the Land of the South, was far off, especially in the old sailing days. It is generally accepted that the honours of Australian exploration lie with the Dutch, and that Dirk Hartog (1616), Edel, Peter Nuyts, Carpenter, and Tasman were the chief of its early discoverers. Hence the name New Holland, which adhered to Australia at the beginning of the Victorian era, and Tasmania or Van Diemen's Land. But first the Netherlands and then Spain had to give way before the British fleet, and by the capture of Manilla, towards the end of the eighteenth century, a blow was struck at Spanish commerce from which it never recovered.

More serious was the intervention of France in the South Pacific. Nothing shows more clearly the world-wide rivalry of France and England than the competition of their sailors and colonists in the South Pacific at the end of the eighteenth century and at the beginning of the nineteenth. Nor was the question of sovereignty in those seas settled till the Victorian era had well begun. France has boasted of many intrepid sailors and many far-sighted leaders in the work of exploration and colonization; but she has not always had the wish, even if she had the capacity, to back them up. Montcalm himself was not well supported in his defence of Canada far back in the earliest days of French occupation. When Colbert and Richelieu had once planted their "viceroyalties" they seem to have let them shift for themselves. Bougainville, a daring French commander in the Canadian war of 1763, surely made a bold stroke when, without taking counsel of his country, he conveyed the French Canadians of New Brunswick and Acadia far south to the Falklands, or, as they were called, the

"Iles Malouines" (the resort of the S. Malo sailors), in order to redress the Colonial fortunes of France. The Falklands constituted a great vantage-ground in those early days of Cape Horn traffic, for by this route sailed the world's adventurers and traders to the southern seas. But the jealousy of Spain for her somewhat shadowy Colonial rights was aroused, and the French adventurers received notice to quit, and Bougainville obtained some compensation. But at the expense of his scheme Great Britain profited eventually by this rivalry of France and Spain. Thus Bougainville's project, which might have led to a definite Colonial policy in the southern seas by France, fell through. But it was not till December, 1832, that H. B. M. sloop *Clio* hoisted the British flag and asserted sovereignty over the Falklands. In 1841 the question was raised in the House of Commons whether the Falklands were not adapted for the purposes of a penal settlement.

The vision, however, of a French Pacific colony and an empire in Australasia was not so quickly dispelled. Great Britain had planted the Botany Bay convict settlement in 1788 under Governor Phillip, but she had no title to any part of the continent except its Pacific coastline, which had been declared to be British by Captain Cook in 1770. The enterprise of our sailors, especially of the whaling crews (a factor not to be ignored in the story of colonization), had made the traders of this country familiar with the coasts of Tasmania, New Zealand, and Australia—wherever, indeed, the sperm-whale was to be found in the Pacific. Still, the daring adventures of whaling crews did not constitute a claim, nor was it equivalent to a formal annexation. At the very time of Governor Phillip's arrival in Botany Bay in January, 1788, he saw there two French ships under La Perouse, who had explored many islands of the Pacific, Norfolk Island, and New Zealand. After the fashion of those times the French and English commanders exchanged courtesies with one another, and some of the English convicts, only just arrived at Botany Bay, made overtures to La Perouse, and asked him to carry them away with him. But the French commander dismissed them with threats, and gave them a day's provisions to return with. The subsequent fate of La Perouse in the Pacific, resembling in its mystery and uncertainty that of Sir John Franklin in the Arctic, prompted a number of French expeditions into southern waters, such as that of D'Entrecasteaux. This tale of the sea was finally unravelled by Dillon, an English sea-captain, in 1827, who found fragments of a theodolite, pieces of china, portions of barometer tubes, in the Island of Mallicolo in the possession of the natives, just as Dr. Rae, the Arctic explorer, chanced upon the silver spoons with Sir John Franklin's crest, buttons, and other articles, in the remote settlements of the Eskimo. New South Wales was occupied under the Pitt ministry, and the name of Thomas Townsend, Lord Sydney, connected by marriage with Pitt's family, was associated with the scheme. The question has sometimes been asked: "Was it simply to found a convict station, now that North America was closed to Great Britain, that Governor Phillip was sent out on his well-known commission to Botany Bay; or was it with some wider scheme in view?" Mr. Rusden, the historian of Australia, thinks that there was some other motive in the minds of ministers than the simple transference of convicts; for there were places much nearer which might have been utilized. This motive might be traced to Colonial rivalry with France.

It is curious that it was in June, 1800, a few months before the retirement of Pitt, that the French Government fitted out two armed vessels for an expedition round the world under Captain Baudin. Baudin's instructions were wide, and included an ambitious programme. He was to touch, first of all, at Mauritius, then a French colony. Thence he was to sail to the southern and eastern coasts of Van Diemen's Land, and afterwards survey the south-west coast of New Holland, penetrating behind the islands of S. Peter and S. Francis, and so explore that part of the continent concealed by these islands, where a strait might possibly be found to offer a communication with the great Gulf of Carpentaria. After these explorations they were to direct their course to Cape Leeuwin, and examine the unknown parts of the coast to the northward. The expedition, after wintering at Timor, was then to sail through Endeavour Strait to the eastern point of the great Gulf of Carpentaria, to survey the whole circuit of its coast, finishing their survey at the North-west Cape. A glance at the map will at once show how particular was the attention paid by the French to the Australian continent. Napoleon himself had encouraged the scheme at the very time that he was pushing his reserves across the Simplon Pass on his noted campaign, thus showing the scope of his ambition and his determination to foil, if possible, Great Britain. The very nomenclature given by Peron, the editor of Captain Baudin's narrative, suggests a great deal. There was *Terre Napoléon* assigned to 900 leagues of coast from Cape Wilson to Cape Leeuwin; also Cape Richelieu, Bay Talleyrand, Capes Suffren, Marengo, Josephine's Gulf, and the great Gulf of Buonaparte, and the Archipelago of Jerome. The continent of Australia, however, was never destined to be more than French in name, and this only for a short time. The *Terre Napoléon* exists only in the narratives of the French explorers. No doubt this was to the chagrin of such Frenchmen as Talleyrand, who is reported to have said: "Deprive England of her colonies, and you break down her last wall, you fill up her last ditch".[1] The renewal of war

[1] *Quarterly Review*, vol. lxxviii.

between England and France in 1803, and Nelson's splendid victory of Trafalgar, destroyed these hopes of rebuilding the French Colonial Empire which was lost in 1763, and reduced the French navy to comparative impotence for almost a generation. For a long time the idea of a settlement in Australia haunted Frenchmen—as late, indeed, as 1840. Lord Russell, who was then Colonial Secretary, thus describes an official interview on this subject: "During my tenure of office at the Colonial Office a gentleman attached to the French Government called upon me. He asked how much of Australia was claimed as the dominion of Great Britain. I answered, 'The whole of it', and with that answer he went away".[1]

But French energies were not limited to Australia: they were also directed towards the settlement of New Zealand. In 1837–1838 there was just a chance that the French nation, by means of the intrigues of a certain Baron de Thierry, would hoist their flag in New Zealand and create a French Colony in the South Pacific. There was an inclination on the part of the government of France to give an official sanction to French enterprises in that direction. Count de Mole, the President of the Council of France, had expressed his determination to appoint De Thierry as French consul in New Zealand. Mr. Angas, a watchful guardian of British interests in those waters, wrote to Lord Glenelg, and after alluding to the great increase of French warships in the South Seas, and the danger, generally, of French intervention, observed: "I need not remind your Lordship that the French vessels easily destroyed the English settlements at Sierra Leone, . . . and your Lordship is also aware that New Zealand is at present nominally an independent nation, in which British interests are represented by a consul, and that in its present position and relation

[1] Spencer Walpole's *Life of Lord John Russell*, vol. i. p. 339.

to this country the French may establish a settlement there with as much propriety as the British, provided De Thierry possesses sufficient influence with the leading chiefs to obtain their concurrence". Indeed, M. Guizot, in his *France under Louis Philippe*, alludes to the convenience of securing a place of rest in the South Pacific. In 1839 a company was accordingly formed at Nantes and Bordeaux for the purpose of founding a French Colony in New Zealand. However, these projects were nipped in the bud by Great Britain in 1839-1840, when the first governor was sent to New Zealand, and the Treaty of Waitangi was entered into with the Maoris. The same kind of danger was averted in the South Island also, when Captain Owen Stanley, brother of the late Dean of Westminster, hoisted the British flag at Akaroa. Commenting on this *fait accompli*, M. Guizot confessed that the French could not set up against the anterior possession of the British Government, and Captain Thouars, a French admiral, who had been round the world in the *Venus*, turned his attention elsewhere, and presented to the French Minister of Marine a report on the Marquesas Islands.

It will be convenient to summarize here the remaining efforts of continental states to found Colonies in the South Pacific. In 1841 Thouars occupied these islands, and thence in 1842 he sailed to Tahiti. British interests here were entrusted to Consul Pritchard, who, for his stand against Admiral Thouars, was made a prisoner on the French flag-ship. The British Government entered a strong diplomatic protest against this high-handed step, and the " Pritchard incident" was dangerous for a time. However, it ended in the recall of the too zealous French admiral, the annulling of the annexation, and the payment of a handsome indemnity to Consul Pritchard. In 1853 the French admiral, Fébvrier-Despointes, hoisted the French flag on New Caledonia, an island so called by its discoverer, Captain Cook, and then on the Pine Islands, and then the Loyalty Islands. In 1864 Napoleon III. resolved to convert New Caledonia into a penal settlement, in preference to French Guiana, and up to the fall of the empire convicts were sent thither in large numbers, and were well guarded. After the suppression of the Commune, New Caledonia was selected by M. Thiers as a good place to deposit the scum of revolutionary Paris, and whenever they escaped, as they frequently did, owing to lax supervision, they became the scourge of the Pacific, and especially of the Australian Colonies. In the "eighties" the *Récidiviste* question created a good deal of friction between Australia and the French authorities, but there has never been any real obstacle to the uninterrupted flow of Australian prosperity. The projects of Germany in annexing part of New Guinea and calling it Kaiser Wilhelm's Land, in renaming New Britain as the Bismarck Archipelago, and occupying the Marshall Islands, only prove how late, and therefore how insignificant, European annexations have been in the South Pacific. During the Palmerston ministries (1855–1865) England was strong in Europe and on good terms with France, her only serious rival in the work of colonization. Soon after 1865 France herself was destined to be engaged in her life-and-death struggle with Germany, and the effects of the campaigns of 1870 are still lasting in Europe.

Freed from the competition of Europe, the story of South Pacific colonization is simple as contrasted with the complex narrative of North America, where the United States constituted a political influence always to be reckoned with, and often dangerous to the growth of Canada. Nor has the native terror hung over any part of Australasia with the same persistence as it has haunted South Africa for nearly a hundred years. There have been troubles with the Tasmanian natives, encounters with the Australian "black fellows", generally discreditable to the white men concerned, and formidable wars with the Maoris of New Zealand, the most stalwart savages of the South Pacific. The Tasmanians have disappeared altogether, the Australian aborigines are scattered in insignificant bands, the Maoris are domesticated and incorporated in the body politic of New Zealand, and are far more harmless than the Kaffirs of South Africa. For a long time past native difficulties of an acute character have ceased to exist in the colonies of Australasia.

The story of the early struggles of New South Wales need not be described here. It is gloomy and dispiriting to the last degree. Few realize what a struggle it was, and how hard was the task of the first administrators. The wretched convicts themselves were desperately ignorant, and some of them, when landed in Australia, still thought that by running away overland they could reach their native country.[1] On board ship one of the amusements of the convicts was to choose the most abandoned characters as "captains of the deck", whilst the next in the scale of villainy were the "petty officers", and so on. Starvation stared the settlement in the face more than once, and in great haste on one occasion the *Sirius* was sent to the Cape, and the *Supply* to Batavia, for provisions. Governor Phillip sent 200 convicts with seventy soldiers to Norfolk Island, where there was a chance of their being able to support themselves, and at the beginning of this century Tasmania was added to the original colony of New South Wales.

It is a somewhat remarkable fact how often in the history of British colonization the beginnings of a colony have been not only bad and discouraging, but such as might warrant almost absolute despair. The first colony

[1] Cunningham's *Two Years in New South Wales*, 1827.

taken to Virginia by Sir R. Grenville was a failure, and the second, going out in 1587, underwent great hardships. Indeed our North American colonization was so slow that after thirty years it was stated by Purchas that "there were of bulls, cowes, heifers, calves a hundred and forty-four, horses three, and as many mares, goates and kids, two hundred and sixteen". The beginnings of the Australian settlements, whether in the penal group or in Western Australia and South Australia, were almost as bad. May we not infer that the perseverance and fortitude of the race, never to be daunted by adversity, constitute the great secret of the success of our colonization? The methods have been miserable, the mismanagement great; nevertheless the right instinct has carried the badly-conceived purpose through, and made the policy successful in the end.

The beginning of Queen Victoria's reign is a signal for many of our Pacific colonies to begin a corporate existence also. The first process is that of dividing off from the original centre of administration in New South Wales. Tasmania was separated from New South Wales towards the end of 1825. In 1836 Governor Bourke proclaimed the thriving little settlement at the mouth of the river Yarra to be within the jurisdiction of New South Wales, and appointed a resident police magistrate. In 1837 he visited this Port Phillip district, planning the town of Melbourne and naming it after the Queen's first prime minister. Fifteen years later the whole of the Port Phillip district was declared to be a separate land district of New South Wales, an event which foreshadowed the ultimate separation of 1851. The same process is observable in the case of Queensland. This immense area, comprising an area of 430 millions of square miles, much larger than New South Wales and Victoria combined, with a coast-line extending over 2500 miles, was, in 1842, defined as "The Northern

District of New South Wales", with a view to its ultimate separation. This, however, was delayed until 1859, when the territory to the north of the 29th parallel of latitude was proclaimed a separate colony.

In grouping our Australian Colonies we shall see how from the parent colony of New South Wales the outlying settlements of Norfolk Island, Tasmania, Victoria, and Queensland all had their beginnings. This process of division promises to be continued, at least in one case.

Queensland has long since shown signs of a desire to be divided into two separate colonies of North and South Queensland, the northern portion being distinguished for its more purely tropical character and products. If so, there would be a governing centre not only at Brisbane, lying at the extreme south, but also at some town farther north.

A northward extension of Australian influence was, in 1883, attempted by the Colony of Queensland. The vast island of New Guinea had recently attracted many prospectors for gold; and there was a fear that Germany would annex all the eastern parts of the island. As the British Government persistently declined to take any steps to avert such annexation, Queensland, in 1883, declared those parts of the island to be British territory. This bold and patriotic action was at first annulled by the Home Government; but owing to pressure from the colonists, and the increasing claims of Germany to the north-eastern part of New Guinea, the south-eastern portion was, in 1888, annexed to the British Crown. For judicial purposes British New Guinea is part of Queensland.

One of the social features of this group is its enormous urban population, especially in New South Wales and Victoria. In 1891 Sydney had a population of 383,386, forming 34·11 per cent of the whole population, Melbourne, a population of 490,902, forming 43·09 per cent of the whole population. The beginnings of Melbourne are all the more remarkable because, unlike Sydney, they lie just within the limits of the Victorian era. It is difficult to imagine that it was only in 1835 that John Batman sailed from Tasmania, after tossing about Bass Strait for nineteen days in his adventurous little sloop called the *Rebecca*, made his way to the lonely site of Melbourne, and obtained a grant of land from the wild natives who lived there. After Batman, John Pascoe Fawkner took a party in the *Enterprise* from Launceston and began to form a settlement in the wilderness. There have been many transformation scenes in the histories of our Colonies during the Victorian era, and many marvellous stories of progress, but none surely more striking than that of the change which, within the space of sixty years, has passed over the neighbourhood of Port Phillip. Until the recent check caused by bank failures, that progress was well sustained. The visitor to Melbourne to-day can scarcely realize from what feeble beginnings the great city has grown. Sixty years ago it was thus described by an eye-witness:—"The town of Melbourne, though only fifteen months old, consists of about one hundred houses, among which are stores, inns, a jail, a barrack, and a schoolhouse. Some of the dwelling-houses are tolerable structures of brick. A few of the settlers are living in tents or in hovels, till they can provide themselves with better accommodation. There is much bustle and traffic in the place; and a gang of prisoners is employed in levelling the streets." So rapid was the progress that in 1841 the number of dwelling-places had increased fifteen-fold; and at the close of the first thirty years of the town's life, land which originally had changed hands for £30, was eagerly bought for £40,000.

New Zealand begins a life of her own with the Victorian era, as a non-penal colony, although we learn from a

Growth of British-Australasian Colonies. 89

despatch sent by Sir James Stephen to Mr. Backhouse (Dec. 12, 1838) that the British Resident had been placed officially on the civil establishment of New South Wales, and was wholly under the instruction of the governor of that colony. Not until the close of 1840 was New Zealand recognized as a separate colony.

A great deal of interest attaches to the founding of Western Australia (1829) and South Australia (1836), because these colonies, not being penal settlements in the first place, illustrate two other systems of colonization of a somewhat peculiar and exceptional kind, the one by a government, and the other practically by an individual, Gibbon Wakefield. Western Australia was known, in the first place, as the New Colony on the "Swan River", the *Zwanen Rivière* of Vlaming, and the *Rivière de Cygnes* of the French. In reality the colony went beyond the Swan River valley in its territorial definitions, stretching from Cape Leeuwin northwards to lat. 30°, and from Cape Leeuwin eastwards to the latitude of King George's Sound. It was described as containing originally about five or six millions of acres fit for a population of 1,000,000 souls. A glance at the map will show that the Swan River Settlement, the nucleus of the present colony of Western Australia, was only the south-west corner of Australia. The latest measurements give the area of Western Australia as 975,920 square miles, or 624,588,800 acres, with a coast-line of about 3500 miles. These Australian communities, when first planted, were, naturally enough, merely little blocks of lands, separated from one another by enormous distances of ocean, and still more difficult spaces of continent. In order to realize how far, for instance, Swan River was from Sydney, it must be remembered that a distance greater than that between London and "the Canaries" had to be traversed. The best descriptions of the Swan River country were given by Captain Stirling, who commanded the *Success* frigate, and Mr. Fraser, a botanist, who seems to have done for the expedition what Banks and Solander did for Captain Cook's survey. The report of the whole sea-board was eminently favourable, both as to its climate and soil. From Cape Naturaliste northwards the land behind the coast-line was described as "fine undulating plains, thinly wooded", with a range of mountains behind, rising from 1200–1500 feet high. Across the mouth of the Swan River lay a bar with only 6 feet of water at low water, but this, in Captain Stirling's sanguine opinion, could easily be deepened. There were whales along the coast which would be a prize for the British whalers; and its geographical position was far more commanding than that of New South Wales, the voyage to the Cape being shorter by nearly a month, and the run to Madras and Ceylon taking a little more than three weeks at all times of the year. It was even thought that the Swan River Settlement might become a convalescent station for the numerous invalids from India, both of the military service and also of the East India Company's service. Certainly it is recognized now how important a place King George's Sound is from a strategic point of view and in reference to the lines of imperial defence.

It was with bright hopes of colonization that the Swan River Colony was inaugurated. The Government took the project up, and although they stated that they would not incur any expense in conveying settlers thither or in supplying them afterwards with food, still they would make free grants of land. Whoever took out labourers would be entitled, with a few reservations on some points, to 200 acres of land for the passage of every such labourer, over and above any other investment of capital. There was a clause also to indicate that uncultivated land, under certain conditions, would revert to the Crown. The most important clause, however, was that no convicts or other description of prisoners were to be transported to the Swan River Settlement.

One gentleman of the name of Peel spent £50,000 in bringing to the Swan River all that could be required for farming on a great scale, and he also induced 300 labourers to accompany him to this land of promise in the south. As the Government offered a bonus of 20 acres for £3 worth of goods imported, the colonists carried out a great quantity of furniture and impedimenta which proved to be of no possible service to them, and it is said that carriages and pianos and articles of rich furniture were left half-buried in sand and exposed to the inclemency of the weather. Captain Fremantle was sent out as the pioneer of the settlement in ships containing no less than 800 emigrants, and, in the course of a week or two, after narrowly escaping shipwreck on the reefs along the shore, Captain Stirling, the first governor, landed on a little wilderness called Garden Island. Here for a long time the first colonists remained, sheltering themselves as well as they could in tents and brushwood huts from the winds and storms of the ocean in winter time. The country was completely unsurveyed, and a closer inspection proved that it was not so fertile as represented at first; there was no port deserving the name, and the goods of the colonists had to be landed on an open roadstead and carried overland through miles of sand and scrub. In 1830 about 1000 new emigrants arrived, and, somehow or other, the whole Colony settled down, as best they might, in the town of Perth.

It was evident that there had been terrible mismanagement and want of foresight, and that the whole scheme was a clear violation of the rules of common-sense. As this was one of the few formal schemes of emigration and colonization inaugurated by the British Government, as such, it needs a word or two of criticism. In the first place, it was clear that the plan was not a statesmanlike measure for relieving the poor and distressed classes of work-people at home, the Swan River being a colony where a certain amount of capital was almost necessary to begin with. Then the land itself was squandered and wasted in a most culpable way. A few officials and wealthy speculators obtained tracts, close to the first settlements, of enormous extent, thus driving the small cultivator far afield for his freehold. Everything was paid for by land, and the governor, instead of a yearly salary, received a grant of 100,000 acres. In fact, the British Government, finding that they had an immense amount of Crown lands in Australia which cost them nothing, bartered them away to the would-be colonists, at the same time exonerating themselves from any kind of responsibility in keeping the colonists, or helping them to the country or back again. There was no proper survey, no adequate preparation, and no thought or care. From the first the whole scheme was predestined to failure. Mr. Peel's capital vanished away, like that of other capitalists, in the sands of Western Australia, and those individual colonists who were wise, went elsewhere, to Tasmania or New South Wales, and for forty years there was small prosperity for the Swan River Settlement. In 1848, at the request of the settlers themselves, who were then in great difficulties for want of sufficient labour, the colony became a penal colony, and its character was thus changed. Whatever its present prospects, it owes little to the wisdom of the Government at home which issued the first "Regulations" of 1829.

The disastrous failure of the Swan River Settlement was full of lessons to those who had the cause of British colonization at heart, and especially to Gibbon Wakefield. At the beginning of the Victorian era there was certainly no social problem which demanded such close attention as that of well-directed emigration. It was a State duty to supervise it, but where was the State? We have seen how terribly the Canadian and Australian immigration was mismanaged. The cry of 'Convicts for Colonies and Colonies for Convicts' obscured all other views of a sensible and humane system. In 1834 the government had granted £1600 as a bounty in aid of emigration, and £3360 was advanced as a loan to assist 168 men, chiefly artisans with their families, to New South Wales and Van Diemen's Land, and 864 females were assisted to migrate to the same quarter by a grant of £12 each, in all about £15,000. But a sum of a million might have been wisely and profitably spent in guiding and locating the thousands of poverty-stricken men and women. It would have been a wise measure to have spent this, or even more, every year, and to have given thought to this ebbing of our national strength. The disastrous evils of Chartism might have been avoided in part or whole, the struggle between classes might have assumed a less bitter form, and the untold forms of human misery and wretchedness diminished by the wise forethought of a fostering State Bureau of Emigration. Gibbon Wakefield argued thus upon that crucial Australian question of land which is always turning up in Australian politics: "Save land, that most valuable asset, from being wasted and misused; eliminate the convict system, and you will have the germs of a self-respecting community". In his *Art of Colonisation* (Letter ix.) the miserable inadequacy of the means employed on the Swan River caused him, he said, to elaborate the South Australian scheme. He proved that it was possible to raise a revenue, from the first sale of waste lands in a colony, more than sufficient to supply immigrant labour, and the opening cost of survey, and the roads. The lands should not be squandered, but bought and sold at a sufficient and uniform price. The system of free grants, which was proved to be a bad one in the Swan River Settlement, was abandoned, except for sites of public schools and buildings. The main difficulty was, of course, to discover what was *the sufficient* price, and whether it should be uniform or discovered at auction by rising from a minimum upset figure. Here, too, at land auctions, it was necessary to be careful, as "rings" could easily be formed in order to secure a monopoly. However, the land-price (whatever the "prairie value" was) became a labour-tax on purchasers, by which all might profit and be supplied with emigrant labourers. It was meant to prevent speculators from grasping lands they did not intend to occupy; it was a corrective of absenteeism; it helped the progress of land-survey and promoted concentration of settlement.

Earl Grey adopted the principle in the Land Act of 1842, which made lands alienable only by sale, and fixed the minimum upset price at £1 per acre, stipulating that the gross proceeds should be applied to the public service of the colony, and one-half always to emigration purposes.

Gibbon Wakefield's system has been criticised severely, sometimes hardly with fairness. Mr. Rusden has pointed out that the "sufficient price" was not always honestly sought, and that in South Australia itself illegal trafficking and speculation was followed by those very disciples of Wakefield who should have known better.[1] Others sought to prove that the setting apart of large funds for encouraging immigration brought far too many immigrants into the country; and it may be admitted that Wakefield's system was drawn up with too great rigidity.

In 1851, Wentworth, the constitutional reformer of New South Wales, fulminated against the "exploded fallacies of the Wakefield system"; but this was probably because the Australian Colonies were desirous of

[1] Rusden's *History of Australia*, vol. ii. p. 91.

having all waste or Crown lands and territorial revenues in their own hands. When this took place, the Wakefield system, as an emigration-scheme from home, ceased naturally to exist.

Nevertheless, the Wakefield system, with all its defects, and in spite of all the misinterpretations to which such a variable expression as *"the sufficient price"* of Crown lands was exposed, helped the Australian Colonies. It caused our statesmen at home to regard the matter of Australian colonization seriously, and to provide for the future. It was far better than the methods of the Swan River Settlement. As the Australian Colonies increased, and their desire for self-government grew, they became jealous of any source of revenue that the Home Government might raise for any purpose by the sale of Australian land, claiming for themselves the fee-simple of the continent. But there was the other view and the other question as to the *exact* time when a sovereign and colonizing power like Great Britain should be called upon to surrender absolutely all Crown and waste lands to the colonists. There was no doubt that ultimately Australia would belong to Australians, but for a long interval of probation it was necessarily a property held in trust for a nation. Here lay one of the vexed questions of Colonial politics.

The theory of Australian land-sales, upon which so much depended, was canvassed much by such writers as Colonel Torrens, Powlett Scrope, Elliot, and others. The name of Torrens is associated in South Australia with a land reform that, in its bearings upon the practical question of the transfer of land, deserves to be reckoned with Wakefield's scheme of securing a freehold in the Colonies, and has proved more lasting. The Torrens scheme facilitated the transfer of property by the institution in Adelaide of a "Land Title Office", where all transfers of land were to be registered, the purchaser's name to be recorded, and a certificate of title given. According to the English law, each time an estate was to be transferred a fresh deed had to be made out, and possibly there might be a flaw in any of the antecedent deeds upon which this was based which would provide a cause of litigation. The Torrens Act by its very simplicity swept away the possibilities of a wearisome Chancery suit. It has been adopted in many countries, and is one of the greatest reforms of the age. In 1879 no less than 7,557,700 acres in Victoria were subjected to its provisions.

But we must now recur to the foundation of South Australia. Whether in consequence of the "new art of colonization" or not, South Australia has always been a fairly flourishing Colony, and a great contrast to Western Australia, which, however, is making a great movement forward now in consequence of recent gold discoveries at Coolgardie.

While Batman was exploring for the first time the banks of the Yarra, the notice of the foundation of South Australia was published in the English Government *Gazette* of May, 1835. This important event was due to the initiative of the South Australian Company, which had been founded in London in 1834. The formation of the company was largely due to the enthusiasm aroused by Wakefield's writings; but the difficulties of the undertaking were very great. They were thus described by one of the directors, Colonel Torrens:— "South Australia was at that time an unexplored wilderness; the colony was not in existence. Before we could sell land in the wilderness, or raise a loan on the security of revenues which were non-existent, considerable expense had to be incurred in providing offices, engaging clerks, and in attracting the attention and confidence of the public."[1] Moreover, the terms of the

[1] Hodder, *Hist. of South Australia*, vol. i.

Incorporating Act of 1834 were strict; they provided that land should not be sold at a lower price than twelve shillings an acre, and no free grants of land were to be made. Indeed the act was not to come into force until £20,000 had been deposited as security with the Home Treasury. Probably these terms could never have been complied with but for the faith and dauntless energy of Colonel Torrens and Mr. George Fife Angas. The latter gentleman gave very large financial support to the undertaking, and lent to the company some of his offices in London as well as his whaling ships. He is, therefore, fitly termed the father of South Australia.

The first settlers left England in May, 1836, in the brig *Rapid*, of 162 tons; and others soon followed. These pioneers landed on Kangaroo Island, of which the explorer Flinders had given a promising account. It was well wooded and picturesque, but in many respects the site was not suited for the purposes of a large city. Colonel Light resolved to move the settlement to S. Vincent's Gulf, and here, about six miles from the gulf, he chose a broad plain beneath the steep hills of the Mount Lofty Range, and on the banks of a small stream, called the Torrens, marked out the site of the future capital. As Queen Adelaide was the wife of the reigning king of England, her name was given to the town. In December, 1836, Governor Hindmarsh landed, and beneath a spreading gum-tree near the beach read his commission to a small audience of emigrants and officials. Adelaide has now a population of 133,252, representing 41·58 per cent of the whole population. Although sufficiently prosperous, it cannot compare with Melbourne.

South Australia has never been a gold colony like New South Wales and Victoria. It is rather a land of corn and wine, and those who have tasted the products of the sloping vineyards of the valley of the Murray can recognize how great a source of wealth lies here in store for the future generation of colonists. In 1839 there were only 440 acres of South Australia under cultivation; in 1891 there were 1,552,423 acres of wheat alone, to say nothing of other cereals, and 12,814 acres of vineyards. South Australia, like Western Australia, is remarkable for its territorial extensions right across the Australian Continent. The growth of both these colonies has been northwards across the inner deserts of Australia. South Australia is knit from south to north by the transcontinental telegraph, completed successfully in 1872, and connecting Adelaide with Port Darwin. This latter port is only second in magnificence to Sydney harbour, and was named after Dr. Darwin, who sailed with King in his survey of the north coast in 1818–1822. The first British settlements had been made on Melville Island in 1824. But with the exploration of the interior and the opening up of the country South Australia was enabled to petition the Home Government for that part of the continent which lay between the 138th and 129th meridians of longitude and the 26th parallel of latitude and the sea, and this request was granted in 1863. This northern territory was formerly known as Alexandra Land, and is calculated to include an area of 523,620 square miles, and thus was another magnificent principality added to the British Empire.

By one of those extraordinary discoveries that live on the pages of history as the picturesque turning-points of destiny it was found that the Island Continent of Australia was a gold-producing land, and that to an extent unprecedented in the history of the world. We speak of immigration hordes turning the fate of Europe in past ages and laying everywhere the beginnings of new nationalities. But what of the descent upon Australia, within recent memory, of those thousands of miners and explorers! In 1852 no fewer than 100,000 landed at Melbourne, and the population of the colony was doubled at a bound. In 1852 no less than 174 tons of gold were raised, valued at £14,000,000, and from 1852-1862 the enormous total of £100,000,000 worth of gold was exported from Victoria. In its power to transform the destiny of a colony or of colonies, the enormous influx of immigrants into Australia forty to fifty years ago was much greater than the influx of English miners into the Transvaal, with which it has been sometimes compared.

The mining population of Australasia practically settled almost at a stroke the Colonial questions of Australasia. Had it not been for this influx the Board of Trade or the Colonial Office might have parleyed a little longer with the ambiguities of the convict question, especially as Western Australia, after having begun with a clean bill, had asked for convict labour, and was the last colony to discard it. Even now despatches might possibly have been bandied to and fro between Downing Street and the Pacific. But the flood of free immigrants settled everything. The capital that Gibbon Wakefield strove to import into Australia was found in the country itself in marvellous abundance, and capital is the motive power of all other industries. The lucky miner turned to pastoral and agricultural pursuits; he became a squatter; he kept huge flocks of sheep; he fenced in his land; he built houses and ranches, cities and villages, and a full-grown community arose, like Athena from the head of Zeus.

The story of the British occupation of New Zealand Islands at the beginning of the reign of Queen Victoria, when there was a chance of the French disputing our claims, has already been hinted at; also, the efforts of Gibbon Wakefield to found Otago and Canterbury. These islands were first made a distinct colony from New South Wales by letters-patent in 1840, under the authority of the statute 3, 4 Vic., 62. They consist of three islands, the North Island, or New Ulster, with an area of 44,467 miles, *i.e.* considerably larger than Ireland; the South or the Middle Island, or New Munster, with an area of 58,525 square miles, nearly as large as England and Wales; and Stewart Island, or New Leinster, on the extreme south, with an area of 665 square miles. In 1887 a proclamation was made declaring the Kermadec Islands part of the Colony of New Zealand.

It must be noted that the climatic and other circumstances of New Zealand differentiate it from Australia and give it a separate history. The serious part of its colonization begins, like many another British colony, with the formation of the [first] New Zealand Company in 1825. This Company was formed by several eminent merchants under the auspices of Lord Durham, and although its plans were ultimately suspended, it must be always regarded as leading to the more matured efforts to colonize New Zealand. For it can hardly be maintained that the annexation of these islands to the jurisdiction of New South Wales in the commission of Captain Phillip, or the appointment of four justices of the peace in 1814 at various points, constituted an effective occupation.

The *New Art of Colonization* was making its way in the minds of men both inside Parliament and outside it, the central figures being Lord Durham, Wakefield, Buller, and Molesworth, as we find in the Canadian crisis. From 1837–1840 the principles of the new school were being constantly asserted, and the New Zealand Company was formed. In 1839 it assumed a more definite character and published its first prospectus, and in May Colonel Wakefield was on his journey to New Zealand in the *Tory* to purchase land for the new settlement. Much confidence was felt in the scheme and its authors, especially in Devonshire; and on the

25th of January, 1840, the first public meeting was held in Plymouth to discuss the advantages of the colonization of New Zealand by the counties of Devon and Cornwall, and a "New Plymouth" was formed in the Pacific Colony. The pioneer expedition was sped on its way from Plymouth by an entertainment given by the directors, at which nearly 400 persons were present, the Earl of Devon being in the chair. A letter was read from Lord John Russell, showing that various objections to the colonization of New Zealand by the Company were now removed. In September of the same year an entertainment was given by the Company at Blackwall, to celebrate the departure of the Nelson settlers, at which the Duke of Sussex, and many influential noblemen and gentlemen, were present. This expedition carried nearly 800 souls in four ships.

The terms of purchase of land in New Plymouth and Nelson were carefully arranged beforehand. The town of New Plymouth consisted of 550 acres, subdivided into quarter-acres, exclusive of streets, parks, and public places. The suburban lands comprised a belt of 10,450 acres, subdivided into allotments of 50 acres each, and, beyond the suburban allotments, the rural districts. No colonist could buy more than 8 allotments, and the choice of town sections was fixed by lottery. Out of every £75 realized from purchases, £50 was expended on emigration to the Colony. There were certain other privileges allowed to those who brought capital into the country, such as the free passages of immigrant labourers. Somewhat similar arrangements were made at Nelson, where each allotment consisted of three sections—one acre in a town, 50 acres of accommodation land, and 150 acres of rural land. There were many other useful regulations on the subject of emigration, one of the conditions being compulsory vaccination of the emigrants themselves, a necessary precaution in those days.

The chief thing, however, to notice is the improved methods upon which these settlements of New Plymouth and Nelson were managed. It was a Company, not a State concern. Little, comparatively, was left to chance, and the colonists, even before they started, knew their destination. How different from the New Plymouth of Massachusetts! how dissimilar the lot of those who sailed in the *Mayflower*! how varied the picture of British colonization! how picturesque in all its incidents! There is many an historical contrast in the annals of our nation, but few more striking than that of the foundation of Plymouth in North America and Plymouth in New Zealand.

The Canterbury and Otago Settlements were yet to come in New Zealand. Archbishop Whately was a supporter of the Canterbury scheme, and, together with him must be mentioned Godley, Sir John Simeon, Bishop Hinds, Hon. Francis Baring (Lord Ashburton), Henry Sewell, and many others. In fact, the New Zealand Company, with its directorate in 1842 of such men as Viscount Ingestre, Lord Petre, Sir W. Molesworth, Hon. F. J. Tollemache, Sir John Sinclair, Stewart Majoribanks, and many others, proved how deeply the idea of British colonization had entered into the minds of men of capital and position at the beginning of the Victorian era. The West of England Board of this Company, with the Earl of Devon as chairman, and such directors as Sir Anthony Buller, J. Crocker Bulteel, Sir C. Lemon, E. W. W. Pendarves, Edward St. Aubyn, Lord Vivian, and others, comprised a representative group of the county families of Devon, perhaps the greatest colonizing county of England. The Canterbury Settlement is especially interesting as a colony in which, as Rusden states in his *History of Australia*,[1] there was a genuine effort to abide by Gibbon Wakefield's principle

---

[1] *History of Australia*, vol. iii. p. 609.

of a sufficient price. Auckland strove to produce prosperity by a low price of land, and Queensland, New South Wales, Victoria, tried to promote artificial settlement by squandering their inheritance of land. Contrasting, however, Canterbury with Auckland: when the former had sold 2,300,000 acres of land she had received £3,608,000; when the latter had sold 2,144,000 acres she had received £274,000. In agricultural prosperity no man, says Rusden, has ever asserted that Auckland could be compared with Canterbury, and he quotes Anthony Trollope's words (1873) that Canterbury was second in success to no colony ever sent out from Great Britain.

It was in New Zealand that Wakefield ended his life. Emigrating thither in 1853, he took up his abode at Wellington, a town so called from the Duke, who, when appealed to in England as to the practicability of Wakefield's schemes, said bluntly, "Let them be tried". Wakefield being virulently attacked at Wellington by some of his political enemies, defended himself in a long speech lasting over five hours. Driving back to his home afterwards in an open carriage in the teeth of a south-east gale, he caught a chill, and, lingering on some years, died in 1862, aged 66. Few men had led a more stormy existence, one in which there was more effort and more striving for the public good; but here was a fitting resting-place for him at last, in the "England of the South", which he had helped to call into being.

Together with New Zealand must be associated the Fiji group, added to our rule since the Victorian era began. The number of islands has been stated to be between 200 and 250, some of them mere rocks. The largest are Vitu Levu, with an area of 4112 square miles, and Yanua Levu, 2432 square miles. They are 1900 miles distant from Sydney and 1200 miles from Auckland. Discovered by Tasman in 1643, and visited by Cook in 1769, they were taken under British protection in 1874 by Sir Hercules Robinson (Lord Rosmead), the Governor of New South Wales. Lying in the warm waters of the South Pacific, the Fiji group enjoys a pleasant insular climate, and produces the best tropical fruits as well as sugar. It stands in the same relation to Australia as Mauritius to Africa. To the north-east lies Samoa, an island known to us in the world of literature as the abode for a time of R. L. Stevenson.

It will be convenient here to refer briefly to other settlements in the far East. There the growth of British influence since 1837 presents peculiar features of its own, different from those it displays in the continental developments in Canada, Australasia, and South Africa. Here, as at the Cape, we shall see that the idea of India overshadowed at first all other enterprises. Indeed, it was from headquarters on the Indian Peninsula that annexations were made in the far East. In the history of the Straits Settlements it will appear that Penang was occupied in 1786 by Sir John Macpherson, acting under the orders of the Indian Government. Malacca was taken in 1795 from the Dutch by an expedition sent from India; Singapore was acquired in 1819 by Sir Stamford Raffles, acting under the authority of the Marquis of Hastings, Governor-General of India. In 1837 all these places were still under the control of the Indian Government, and were not severed from it till April 1, 1867, when they were placed under the Secretary of State for the Colonies the same year, it may be noted, as that of Canadian Confederation.

In 1847 we acquired the island of Labuan, off the coast of Borneo. Its coal deposits are valuable, but, for various reasons, they have never been profitably worked. On the mainland of Borneo a British subject, styled "Rajah Brooke", acquired a considerable tract of land, which came under our protection in 1888. The

British North Borneo Company has also gained the control of an extensive territory in this vast island, though not without some opposition from Rajah Brooke. This territory, which is of considerable promise, was recognized as a British Protectorate in 1888.

Hong Kong, a desolate island fifty years ago, was ceded to Great Britain at the commencement of Queen Victoria's reign (1841). This cession was confirmed by the Treaty of Nankin in 1842. The site is magnificent, the hills rising up to the height of 3000 or 4000 feet, and the harbour is one of the finest in the world. The city of Victoria, named in honour of Her Majesty, has a population of over 200,000. There are few places in the world which have sprung into being so quickly as a naval depot and as a commercial centre as Hong Kong. From being a place where at the time of the treaty the simple object was only "to have a port to careen or refit our ships", Hong Kong has become a place which, in 1896, attracted 12,000,000 tons of shipping, both native and European. It is the chief *entrepôt* for the trade of the south of China, the Philippines, and French Indo-China. Originally a very malarious and unhealthy place, it is now just the reverse, and tramways up the mountain side convey Europeans to a wholesome climate on the top. With the aid of science and modern artillery Hong Kong has become a kind of Gibraltar of the Pacific. Right opposite, on the mainland, a strip of country called the Kowloon Peninsula has been ceded to England.

In connection with her eastern empire England has occupied, during the Victorian era, certain strong strategic positions which command the route thither. In January, 1839, Aden was attacked and taken by a British force acting under instructions from Bombay. This was the first addition made to the British Empire after the Queen's accession. In 1840 the Massah Islands and the island of Eibat, off the coast of Africa, were bought. Then, in 1854, the Kuriah Muriah Islands were ceded by the Sultan of Muscat. In 1857 Perim was finally occupied by a British force, and in 1868 the peninsula of Little Aden and the island of Sirah were secured by purchase. In 1882 the British bought a tract of land in Arabia, and in 1886 the island of Socotra was placed formally under a British Protectorate. In 1885 we occupied Diego Garcia, an important strategic position in the middle of the Indian Ocean. On the African coast there is the British Protectorate of the seaboard of Somaliland, south of the Gulf of Aden, and on both sides, therefore, of the Strait of Bab-el-mandeb England has strengthened her hold upon the approaches to the Red Sea. In the Mediterranean, the island of Cyprus, taken over in 1878 and administered under the terms of a defensive alliance between England and Turkey, is not exactly a British colony, but a strong post of observation. During the Victorian era, therefore, England has pursued the right policy of a maritime power, and has strengthened by many additions her lines of oceanic communication.

Chapter V.

The Growth of our African Colonies (1837-1897).

In 1620 two officers of the East India Company, Captain Andrew Shillinge and Humphrey Fitzherbert, took possession of Table Bay and the Cape in the name of James I., thinking "to entitle the King's Majesty thereto by this weak means rather than let it fall for want of prevention into the hands of the Netherlands"; also, by reason of the whale-fisheries there and the

The Growth of our African Colonies. 107

opportunities provided as a port of call. This annexation was never followed up, and the Netherlands East India Company stepped in and sent Riebeek out on his well-known expedition in 1651, taking the Cape over and building forts. The Cape, therefore, was a far older settlement than any of our Colonies in Australia, and it was from the Cape and Batavia that our first struggling Australian colonists sought food. The Cape also gave to Australia her first Merino sheep and her "golden fleece" of the Escurial breed, presented to the Dutch Government by the King of Spain. The Dutch Company held the Cape for nearly 150 years. Then finally the exigencies of war in Europe and the considerations of European diplomacy were destined to bring into prominence so commanding a post as the Cape. Indeed, the life-and-death struggle between Napoleon and Great Britain had rendered the speedy occupation of the Cape a necessity of war, and in 1795 Admiral Elphinstone and General Craig sailed from England with orders to seize it. They carried with them a letter from the Prince of Orange, dated at Kew, 7th February, 1795, to the following effect:—"We have deemed it needful by these presents to command you to admit into the Castle, as also elsewhere in the Colony under your command, the troops that shall be sent thither by His Majesty the King of Great Britain, and also to permit the ships of war, frigates, or armed vessels which shall be sent to you on the part of his said Majesty, into False Bay, or wherever else they can safely anchor; and you are to consider them as troops and ships of a power in friendship and alliance with their Mightinesses (the States-General), and who come to protect the Colony against an invasion of the French. (Signed) William Prince of Orange."[1] After some hesitation on the part of the Dutch officer, Commissary Sluysken, the forts and castle

[1] Judge Watermeyer's *Lectures*.

were given up. The British held the Cape first of all from 1795–1802, as legalized occupants rather than as conquerors, and then restored it to the Batavian Republic. Presently the same war-clouds and the same threat of French aggression overshadowed the world again, and necessitated a second and final occupation by the British. Castlereagh's instructions to Sir David Baird were to go to Madeira, delay as little as possible there, and then make a dash at the Cape and avail himself of probable neglect. He added: "As it is not impossible that two French ships of the line which sailed in May (1806) from Rochefort, which are not accounted for, may have thrown themselves into the Cape, with a reinforcement of from 1000 to 1200 troops, you will not rely with too much confidence on previous estimates. As I understand that the troops now in garrison at the Cape are mostly Germans and much disgusted with the Dutch service . . . take the earliest opportunity of inducing them to enter the 60th Regiment." These instructions reveal the prime motive and cause of the occupation, viz. fear of France and of the grasping power of Napoleon.

It was clear that the Cape was destined to be the prize of war to the strongest sea power. The crisis was to come in 1806, and General Baird captured the post with 4000 men, at a cost of 15 killed and about 190 wounded. The defence cost the garrison 700 men. This second occupation was legalized by the Convention of 1814, by which an agreement was made between the prince, sovereign of the restored and united Netherlands on the one hand, and his majesty the King of Great Britain on the other, that, in consideration of certain charges provided by the latter for the defence of the Low Countries and their settlement in union with Holland, the Colony of the Cape of Good Hope, together with Demerara, Essequibo, and Berbice, should be ceded

The Growth of our African Colonies.

in perpetuity to the British Crown. Technically, therefore, the Cape stands upon the unassailable position of an international convention, like the West Indian possession of British Guiana, Great Britain succeeding lawfully to the rights of the Dutch.

Egidius Benedictus Watermeyer, a well-known Cape judge of Cape extraction, has summed up the nature of the Dutch Company's rule in forcible words: "Their principles were false, and the seeds of corruption were sown early; for the last fifty years there was little to which the examiner of Cape records can point with satisfaction. . . . The most industrious race in the world, they repressed industry; one of the freest states, they encouraged a despotic misrule—utter anarchy was the result: some national feeling may have lingered, but, substantially, every man in the country, of every hue, was benefited when the incubus of the tyranny of the Dutch E. I. Company was removed." Elsewhere he notices that there was no education, no printing-press, no books, no roads, no bridges, at the Cape under Dutch rule. In other words, South Africa, before the British came to it, was little better than a primitive wilderness.

At first the Colony, both in the popular and official mind, was confused a great deal with our Indian Empire. The Suez Canal had not yet been cut, and all outward- and inward-bound ships for the east sighted Table Mountain and the Cape Peninsula. But it was only a halting-place, just as it had been to the Portuguese first of all, and the Dutch East India Company afterwards. In the words of Lord North, the Cape was considered to be an important place strategically, *i.e.* as "the physical guarantee of our eastern possessions". As a sphere of separate British colonization its time was not yet. It is difficult to realize now how the two spheres of Indian and Colonial administration overlapped one another. The Cape was regarded by Indian officers—for many years of this century—as an agreeable sanatorium where they could draw full pay whilst on furlough; there were inland stations where Government farms, as at Somerset East in the eastern districts, existed for the purpose of providing Indian remounts. In both countries there were natives, and in both countries risks from native wars, and the best class of governor to be employed seemed one of the military type. This confusion of the two spheres of administration, Indian and Colonial, was partly inherited from our predecessors in the eastern seas, the Portuguese and Dutch. One marked feature of the Victorian era has been the more exact apportionment of Indian and Colonial responsibilities, and the clearer definitions of huge tracts of territory. South Africa has widened out into a separate empire, with a domain reaching far up into the continent, and with a number of Colonies, States, and Protectorates possessing an individuality of their own in each case. It has long since ceased to be regarded as a stepping-stone to India, a sort of continental St. Helena or Ascension, where ships might pause and officers might recruit.

One of the first acts of the British Government calculated to extend the bounds of Empire was to send out a large body of 4000 State-aided emigrants in 1820 to Algoa Bay in 23 ships. There were 90,000 applicants in Great Britain for this form of State relief, which proves how willing the distressed poor were to respond to a scheme organized and carried through by Government. The original cost of settling these colonists was £120,000, but in the space of a generation their property was valued at 4½ millions sterling, whilst their numbers had reached 34,000.[1] The flourishing towns of Port Elizabeth and Grahamstown owe their

[1] Adderley's *Colonial Policy*, p. 171.

beginnings to these settlers. It is remarkable that this colonization experiment made by the State should not have been repeated elsewhere and under other circumstances, considering its success. It is true that the disbanded German Legion was planted in 1855 along Kaffraria, after the Crimean War, but this was a different scheme altogether. The 1820 "Plantation" ought to have been the commencement of a new and enlightened policy of emigration upon systematic and economic principles. After the Napoleonic wars there was terrible distress all over Great Britain; the poor-rate was advancing by leaps and bounds, as an examination of any parish rate-books will tell us, not the least distressed element being soldiers and sailors, who were driven to a life of vagrancy and crime by the sheer stress of circumstances. For these unfortunate men themselves this was an unworthy and undeserved lot, and here was an opportunity for Government to step in and utilize the vast prairies of Canada, the unlimited regions of South Africa, and the new Australasian territories, by helping them to emigrate. The British Government, short-sighted in its generation, preferred the convict system, a late and imperfect remedy in itself, to orderly and well-directed emigration. With regard to the Algoa Bay settlers and the German Legion in South Africa, is it too late to copy the methods shown by them of military and frontier Colonies? Might not colonization on easy terms in Rhodesia be held out to time-expired men as the reward of their services, and as an opening for their activity, and thus help to popularize military service in Great Britain?

The commencement of the Victorian era found the Cape at a crisis in her native policy. In December, 1835, Lord Glenelg had written in a despatch to Sir Benjamin D'Urban, the Governor of the Cape, that in his opinion the Kaffirs had ample justification for the last war (of 1834-1835), and that the claim of sovereignty over the new province of Queen Adelaide in the East could not be sustained. Reference has already been made to the reversals of policy (Chapter i.) to which the Cape has, from time to time, been exposed. It is pretty well agreed that Lord Glenelg was one of the most incapable Colonial administrators ever known, and even the Whigs of the day grew weary of him. "If the amiable Lord Glenelg were to leave us," wrote Sydney Smith, "we should feel secure in our Colonial possessions." Not only at the Cape, but also in Canada, the shadow of Glenelg maladministration rested upon our Colonial affairs. It cannot be alleged that Sydney Smith or the Whigs were much in favour of Colonial growth, such as it was, in South Africa, for the latter expressed himself thus in the *Edinburgh Review* (1836), in an article on the Kaffir war: "The first thing that strikes us is that the extraordinary advance of the Colony on the country of the Kaffirs always was, and is, a wrong". But whatever political essayists might think or say, or, indeed, however great the mistakes of Colonial secretaries, our empire in South Africa was bound to grow during the Victorian era. Another Kaffir war soon ensued, known as the "War of the Axe", arising from the theft of an axe by a Kaffir in Colonial territory in 1846. The result of this was that the Colonial territory was pushed still farther to the east and north-east, and all the frontier between the river Keiskama and Kei brought under direct imperial control. There was hard fighting and most difficult bush campaigning of a protracted character, extremely irritating and costly to Great Britain.

In the "thirties" the great trek or exodus of Boer farmers towards the interior took place, an event of great moment in the history of South Africa. The Emancipation Act of Great Britain had, in its application, angered the slave-holding Boers, who were not treated

The Growth of our African Colonies. 113

very fairly in the way of compensation. The money was made payable in London, and agents had to be employed to draw up the requisite forms to obtain it. Many of the Boers, who were very ignorant and unbusiness-like men, disposed of their claims to their agents for very small sums, and others, looking upon the whole transaction as a fraud, refused to sign the documents at all. This compensation grievance was at the bottom of the "trek". The Boers went forward and founded the Orange Free State and the South African or Transvaal Republics. It is curious how the seeds of states and communities are sown. Great Britain let the Boers go, and let them fight the savages on the north, the Matabele, and that native Attila, Moselekatze, making no real protest at the time to all these proceedings, which were manifestly irregular and fraught with mischief, till the Boers came to Natal and Port Durban and proclaimed the Republic of Natalia. Then in May, 1843, the British Government stepped in and declared Natal to be a British Colony, an extension of rule almost forced upon them. The whole situation, however, constituted a real turning-point in South African history, which took place, apparently, without an official realization of its gravity. Probably South Africa was not rich enough then to attract attention, its wealth being chiefly pastoral, and its exports chiefly hides, skins, and ivory. It was known best as a hunter's paradise, swarming with every kind of antelope and with elephant, rhinoceros, and hippopotamus, such a region as ardent sportsmen like Gordon Cumming have best described. There were no signs of mineral wealth in South Africa in 1837, nor were there any indications that, in sixty years, there would be an export and import trade of £26,000,000.

It may be noted as a fact of some interest as bearing upon the question of South African sovereignty, that when the Natal Boers appealed to the King of Holland for naval protection in setting up the "Republic of Natalia", his answer was decisive. "That the disloyal communication of the emigrant farmers had been repelled with indignation, and that the King of Holland had taken every possible step to mark his disapproval of the unjustifiable use made of his name by the individuals referred to." This answer was dated November 4, 1842.

But South Africa might long have continued to be the paradise of hunters if it had not been for the discovery of the Diamond Fields in 1867. This discovery resulted in the annexation of "Griqualand West", as the province was officially called, by Sir Henry Barkly in 1871, a farther and most decided extension of British authority. This was the real starting-point of modern South Africa, the wealth obtained from the diamond mines calling public attention to South Africa, and enabling capital to flow into the country, and to be employed upon such reproductive works as railways and telegraphs. The governorship of Sir Bartle Frere, clouded though it was with disaster and misfortune, led ultimately to a better understanding of the situation in South Africa. The Zulu power was broken once and for all at Ulundi, and thus the sole remaining native power, threatening any real danger to European colonists in South Africa, was destroyed. The home policy of Great Britain with regard to this especial period is difficult to follow, harder still to explain. There was a wish in more than one official quarter to draw back from South African responsibilities. Great Britain acquiesced in the occupation of Damaraland and South-west Africa by the Germans, although for many years English resident magistrates had been seen in the country, especially in the neighbourhood of Walvisch Bay. She was careless also on the east coast, and allowed German intrigue to go on there to an almost incredible extent. Finally, she made up her mind to take over the whole east coast littoral as far as the Portuguese possessions round Delagoa Bay, and presently Zululand. Meantime in the interior and along the Bechuanaland country immediately to the west of the Transvaal border, the tale of intrigue against British rule was more serious than the projects on the east coast. Boer raids were made across the frontier openly, and a period of unrest set in. Here was a critical moment in the history of South Africa. Two mock republics, called Goshen and Stellaland, had been called into existence by freebooters, and the object of England's enemies in South Africa—for she had many—was to cut her off from the interior. It was at this crisis that the Right Hon. W. E. Forster took up the South African cause, both on imperial and philanthropic grounds, and the result was the Warren Expedition of 4000 men, by which the key to the interior was secured at once and for all time. It was on September 30, 1885, that the Colony of British Bechuanaland was officially proclaimed. This was one of the most important extensions of territory yet made in South Africa, and Great Britain proved also that she had not forgotten the Bechuanas.

The Charter of the British Imperial South Africa Company, dated October 29, 1889, was a sequel in a sense of the Warren expedition, and it had illustrious patronage, more illustrious indeed than that of the New Zealand Company sixty years ago. It claimed amongst its supporters the Duke of Abercorn, the Duke of Fife, Lord Gifford, Cecil John Rhodes, Albert Beit, Albert Henry George Grey, and George Cawston. The history of the expansion of our South African colonies northwards is recent and well-known. It is a sufficient commentary to say that Buluwayo, the seat of Lobengula, and a native power within the last four years, has now been linked by rail with Kimberley and Capetown. It is probable that the Zambesi Valley and the heart of Africa will soon be brought into direct railway communication with the Cape Colony and the ports on the south. The Cape railway system is a marvellous proof of the enterprise of our race. Forty years ago there was no railway in South Africa, the first soil of the first railway being turned in 1859; in 1878 there were 328 miles of line; in 1879, owing to the progress of the diamond mines, 937 miles, and in 1885 1600 miles. The goldfields gave the railways a fresh start, and in 1897 the total of government lines was 2253 miles, exclusive of 300 miles worked by private enterprise,[1] the earnings of these lines reaching £4,078,561, and the number of passengers being 8,000,000 during 1896. The speed with which the last sections of the main railway in South Africa have been made is remarkable, no less than 335 miles having been constructed between October, 1896, and October, 1897, or a mile a day for every working day. The advantages of a railway in a land of slow communication by ox-wagon, and where the rinderpest destroys even this mode of progression, are obvious. From a strategic as well as a commercial point of view it is absolutely invaluable. In South Africa it must be again and again noted how vacillating the policy of the British Government has been, and, on the contrary, how firm the spirit of individual Britons. Had it not been for the efforts of a well-known band of men and capitalists in South Africa, of whom Cecil John Rhodes is the chief figure, it is doubtful whether Great Britain would have been able to uphold her paramount position as the sovereign power in South Africa, a title she had justly earned, justly inherited by formal agreement and persistently kept for nearly 100 years by the costly expenditure of millions of money in Kaffir wars, and the continual sacrifice of British lives. At the critical moment some

---

[1] See Paper by Sir David Tennant, Nov. 1897, before the Royal Colonial Institute.

The Growth of our African Colonies. 117

counselled a retreat in all seriousness to the Cape Peninsula, and there was more than one power in Europe willing to take England's place.

Let us review in brief the tale of territorial expansion in South Africa during the Victorian era. First, there was the original birthplace of the settlement at Capetown, the feeble centre of Dutch authority. The two outlying districts were at Graaf-Reinet and Swellendam, which scarcely acknowledged any allegiance to the tyrannous old Dutch Company with their effete placaats or proclamations, old-world customs, and monopolist principles. When the flag of the old Dutch Company went down, the British took charge of the Cape, as they might of a derelict at sea, of no value in itself, and a great harm possibly to other people. About 500 or 600 miles to the eastward the British Government placed a British crew in charge of the Cape, viz. the Algoa Bay settlers of 1820, who peopled Albany and founded Port Elizabeth. Eastward and northward the course of Empire took its way. One by one the Kaffir chiefs fell, Makana, Macomo, Kreli, Sandili, and the rest, and their territory was absorbed. For some time the expansion was round Griqualand West and the New El Dorado, thence it shifted to Zululand and the east. But the true course is northwards in spite of the inertia of the Dutch States, and onwards to Bechuanaland, Mashonaland, and Zambesi. The base from which Great Britain attacks the heart of Africa is on the South. Europe looks upon the progress of civilization in Africa as flowing south from itself, Great Britain reverses the picture and feels that her mission is pushing her northwards from the Cape. If the rival nations of Europe meet in Equatorial Africa, Great Britain will not be backward in the race, as her colonizing exploits best prove.

The West African Colonies cannot show the same tale of progress as in South Africa, although they have been the scene of British colonization for a much longer space of time, the Gambia disputing with Newfoundland the honour of being the oldest colony of Great Britain, dating back to 1588, the year of the Elizabethan patent. Besides the Gambia there are the colonies of the Gold Coast (1622), Sierra Leone (1787), and Lagos, the youngest settlement, dating no further back than 1861. In addition to these is the Niger Protectorate, the most important sphere of British influence and the most extensive of all. The West African Colonies were important to the British on account of the slave-trade, especially after the Peace of Utrecht (1713), when, by the Assiento Contract, an English company obtained the monopoly for a certain number of years of supplying slaves to Spanish America. The prosperity of the West African Colonies was bound up closely with the fortunes of the West Indies and the sugar industry, English captains taking slaves from the west coast to Jamaica, the principal mart of slaves. The abolition of the slave-trade in British ships and the Slave Emancipation Act meant a destruction of this nefarious traffic, and a period of decadence ensued. The duty of the British Government was thenceforward to suppress slavery, and do coastguard duty at the various unhealthy stations of the west coast of Africa. The cost in British lives and in British treasure, in the execution of this duty, was excessive. The right of search for slave cargoes in ships that hoisted false flags was a vexed international question, and brought Great Britain into constant friction with France and the United States. As long as there was a demand for slaves in Cuba there were always ruffians ready to run the blockade, and Great Britain found it best to give Spain £400,000 to stop the Cuban trade. It was also calculated that the West African squadron cost a round £1,000,000 every year.

It is not altogether surprising, therefore, to learn

that in official quarters there was a desire in the "sixties" to limit the responsibilities of Great Britain in this part of the world. In 1865, as already noted (Chap. ii.), a Parliamentary Committee, especially appointed for the purpose, with Lord Norton as chairman, recommended that we should withdraw ultimately from all our West African possessions, except, perhaps, Sierra Leone.[1] The *Quarterly Review*, in an article on "Our Colonial System" (July, 1863), advanced the theory that it was "difficult to defend the occupation of territory on the coast of Africa—settlements like Sierra Leone and the Gambia—by any just economical argument". It was more than doubtful whether the policy of settling liberated West African negroes in our Colonies was a good one. Nor was it clear that a negro republic like Liberia, founded on the west coast by philanthropic Americans in 1822, and declaring itself an independent and self-governing community in 1847, was anything more than a travesty of the model it professed to copy. It has been already noted that the West Indian negroes have no desire to leave the West Indian Islands. It is strange that, although Lord Norton advised retrocession from West Africa, Earl Grey did not exactly share his views. His reason was a curious one, and may have been coloured by the fanciful experiment in Liberia, by which it might have been thought negro colonies could become self-governing, the true policy in West Africa being, in Earl Grey's words, to keep constantly in sight the formation of a regular government on the European model, and the establishment of a civilized policy, taking care that each successive step should appear to the people themselves the natural mode of providing for some want, after the example of our own institutions. This was, at any rate, a very sanguine estimate to take of the

[1] *Colonial Policy*, by Lord Norton.

possibilities of our West African Colonies and of their population. Our merchants, however, were constantly pushing ahead in spite of the Government, and the Commission of 1865 found that in reference to Sierra Leone itself there were no less than 82 treaties with native chiefs. It was the Ashanti expedition of 1872, when "King Coffee" was taken and deposed, that marked a new era of official interference, although it certainly did not ripen into any great activity. France has of latter years pushed forward in West Africa more quickly than Great Britain, and by her activity in the interior has limited the scope of British enterprise behind the Gambia. "This is a great pity," Sir H. H. Johnston remarks, "because at the beginning of this century our influence on the Gambia extended very far inland, as may be easily understood by any one who reads the travels of Mungo Park and other African explorers eighty or ninety years ago."[1] West Africa, no less than Central Africa, Central Australia, and the Great North-West, boasts of its epic of adventure and exploration, beginning first with Mungo Park, sent out by the "African Association", the forerunner of the "Royal Geographical Society", which, under the guidance of such enthusiasts as Sir Joseph Banks and Barrow, took up with zeal the cause of geographical exploration. The Niger problem was, in the opinion of Mungo Park, writing to Lord Camden, "a problem second only to the circumnavigation of the Cape of Good Hope, and in a geographical sense the greatest that remains to be made in the world". After Mungo Park came Captain Tuckey, who had explored in 1802 the coasts of Australia and made a survey of Port Phillip. Next came James and Bowdich, lured on to Ashanti by rumours of a wonderful El Dorado at Coomassie, whence the problem of the Niger could be best

[1] *Proceedings Royal Colonial Institute*, vol. xx.

assailed. Beyond, in the mysterious interior, lay the mysterious Timbuctoo, the bourne of all explorers, and described first by the adventurous Frenchman M. Caillie (1824). The expedition of Oudney, a naval surgeon, Clapperton, a naval lieutenant, and Major Denham, an old Peninsula hero, who set out from Tripoli, and, marching southwards, reached Lake Tchad, now the meeting-place of the rival interests of France, England, and Germany, is remarkable, because, in this instance, the Government and Lord Bathurst had interested themselves with the Bashaw of Tripoli, who undertook to escort the British expedition as far as Bornou (1822-1823). Nearly thirty years afterwards, Dr. Richardson, accompanied by Dr. Barth and Dr. Overweg, two Prussian gentlemen, started from Tripoli also with a view of reaching Bornou, "under the orders and at the expense of Her Majesty's Government". This mission is instructive, as it is one of the few set on foot by official orders, and, curiously enough, Great Britain, contrary to her usual custom, has neglected these Tripoli and Saharan adventures, stepping aside in favour of France. Dr. Richardson died on his journey, but his German companion, Barth, achieved great triumphs of exploration around Lake Tchad and in the kingdom of Bagirmi. He chanced upon the Benué, the great Niger affluent, at Tepi. The Niger Valley was destined to be known from end to end and the problem of its curious tortuous course explained. The Niger was not a tributary of the Nile, nor was it the Congo, nor did it vanish in the sands of the Sahara, all of which propositions were seriously entertained for many years of this century. It was a great river by itself, destined to be the civilizing agency and commercial artery of "Nigeria". The West Africa of the Victorian era was no longer the West Africa of Ptolemy and the old geographers.

There is one agency in the Victorian era which has helped to extend the boundaries of our Empire in many quarters of the globe, and this is colonization by trading ventures and chartered companies. The history of all trade companies is most interesting, but in the annals of British colonization it will be seen to reflect in a particular degree the versatility and individualism of the race. One of the most remarkable of these companies in its history and inception is "The British North Borneo Company", arising in the first instance from the trading venture of "Rajah" Brooke of Sarawak, who, in 1838, sailed in his yacht to the east, and in 1841 obtained a concession of land in the west of Borneo from the Sultan of Brunei. Subsequently, in 1846, he obtained for the British Government the cession of the island of Labuan, with a view of creating a coaling station and a naval depôt, and was himself nominated as governor by the British Government. About the same time Singapore became the official centre of government in the Straits Settlements. After these preliminaries, and especially when Mr. Alfred Dent obtained, in 1877-1878, from the sultans of Brunei and Sulu, concessions in land in the north of Borneo, the way was paved for the creation of the British North Borneo Company by royal charter in 1881. In this charter it may be observed that the sovereignty of the sultans was left unimpaired. With regard to trade—and here was the great difference between the old-fashioned charters, such as those of the East India Company and the Hudson Bay Company—the Borneo charter expressly stipulated that there should be no monopoly.

The Royal Niger Company stands on a different footing from previous chartered companies in our history. There is free navigation of the Niger for peaceful commerce, but there are saving clauses against the transport of articles destined for belligerents. The Hudson Bay Company was a close monopoly, but the case of the Niger Company is different. There are two acts which modify the policy of any trading company in Africa: (1) the Act of Brussels, relating to the suppression of the slave-trade, and the exclusion of arms of precision and spirituous liquors for native consumption; (2) the Berlin Conference, by which the navigation of African rivers is thrown open to the commerce of the world. A great sphere for British industry has been found in "Nigeria", as that part of West Africa may be conveniently termed, covering an area equal in extent to half of British India, and forming the germ of an empire in itself.

It was in 1841 that a cession of land was obtained at the confluence of the Benué and the Niger, where Lokoja, the present military capital of the Niger Company, is situated. We must associate West African expansion with the names of Captain Allen and Sir George Goldie and the West African Company (1881). This company was the forerunner of the Royal Niger Company (1886), now a predominating influence far into the interior, over Hausaland and the kingdom of Sokoto. On the west is the empire of the French Sahara, and on the east Lake Tchad, and on the south-east Germany, esconced at the Cameroons. Nigeria has become so important a sphere of influence, especially if taken in connection with its possible position as a controller and civilizer of the Hausa States, the most promising native material in West Africa, that in a short time we may expect to see it taken under the direct control of the Colonial Office, due compensation being given to the directors and shareholders of the company. This may be the formal beginning of our West African Empire.

The British South Africa Company owes its origin to the natural expansion of the British Colonies and Protectorates in the south, also, in a great measure, to the rivalry of Germany. Unlike "Nigeria" and "Ibea", a large portion of the territory annexed by this company is situated in subtropical regions, and may, therefore, be better suited to the purposes of European colonization, especially in the highlands. The principal field of the operations of the British South Africa Company is, according to the charter, the region of South Africa lying immediately to the north of British Bechuanaland, to the north and east of the South African Republic, and to the west of the Portuguese dominions. The land thus falling under the control of this Company is one of the latest, and certainly not one of the smallest acquisitions of the Victorian era. According to article 20 there is nothing in the charter to authorize any monopoly of trade, and a free passage and intercourse over and through the Company's territories are reserved for British subjects. The bare recapitulation of these Victorian charters will at once prove how entirely they differ from the old charters. As an instrument of government they are provisional. The merits of these companies are obvious. They have effected a patriotic work by means of private enterprise and the exertions of public-spirited directorates. The triumph of Nigeria lies in the opening up of large portions of barbarous lands to trade and trade influences as far as Lake Tchad, that meeting-place of rival interests; of Rhodesia, or the South Africa Company, that it has formed a most valuable connecting link between the Cape Colony and Zambesia and the Equatorial Lakes.

There is no name that will live longer in South Africa than that of David Livingstone. Little by little this great missionary was led to explore the valley of the Zambesi, about which even the Portuguese themselves knew little. Upon his well-known second expedition, in which he went out as consul under the auspices of the British Government, he reached Lake Nyasa, the existence of which he was the first European to discover. Upon his third and last expedition he discovered the south end of Lake Tanganyika, Lakes Mweru and Bangweolo, and the course of the Upper Congo. The death of Livingstone, and his pathetic message to "heal the open sore of Africa", led to the Livingstonia Mission, and to an increased interest in the lake country of Equatorial Africa. Presently there sprung up the "African Lakes Company" and the coffee-planting industry, and in course of time British Central Africa. A portion of this country was organized as a protectorate, and part became a sphere of British influence, administered under the charter of the British South Africa Company. There are therefore two separate spheres of administration in British Central Africa north of the Zambesi, one a protectorate governed directly from London, the other managed by the British South Africa Company. "Nyasaland" is not a wide enough term to express the whole of British Central Africa. Sir H. H. Johnston took over the protectorate in 1891, aided in his task by a small standing army of 200 Sikhs from the regular Indian army, and 600 well-trained natives of British Central Africa. Sir H. H. Johnston gives some interesting figures to show the progress of the protectorate. In 1891 the annual trade of Great Britain with British Central Africa scarcely reached £30,000; in 1896 it rose to £100,000. In 1891 the local revenue was £1700; in March, 1896, it exceeded £22,000. In 1891 the Europeans in the protectorate were barely 90; in 1896 they reached 300. In 1891 there were 3 steamers on Lake Nyasa; in 1896 there were 8, with 16 large steamers and 46 barges and cargo-boats on the Zambesi and Shire Rivers. A survey for a railway from the Portuguese frontier on the Ruo to the Upper Shire has been completed, and extensions are in view.[1]

[1] *Proceedings Royal Colonial Institute*, vol. xxviii.

The Imperial British East Africa Company, or "Ibea", includes another large sphere of Central Africa on the east coast, from Wanga to Kismayu on the south, as well as inland west across the Victoria Nyanza, to the extreme limit of the Congo State, thus including Uganda and Unyoro within British jurisdiction. The Juba is the northern frontier, to be prolonged, in agreement with Italy, to the western watershed of the Nile Valley. The native rulers of this part of East Africa were the Viceroys of Zanzibar, formerly nominated by the Sultan of Muscat for the collection of revenue. Muscat lies in the Province of Oman, on the western entrance to the Persian Gulf. About thirty years ago the kingdoms of Oman in Arabia, and of Zanzibar in East Africa, were separated, and two brothers placed as independent rulers on their respective thrones. This was due to Lord Canning, the Governor-General of India, in 1861, and by this award, the Sultanate of Zanzibar, being the richer kingdom of the two, was bound to pay the annual subsidy of £6000 to the ruler of Muscat, a payment subsequently undertaken by the Indian Treasury. The influence of Great Britain was paramount along the whole of the east coast, no less than nine-tenths of the trade resting in British hands. Slavery was abolished as far as possible, and upon the slave market of Zanzibar rose a Christian cathedral, the seat of an English bishopric. In 1878 a concession was actually offered to Sir William Mackinnon by Seyd Burghash, the enlightened ruler of Zanzibar, of trade throughout the length and breadth of his sultanate, calculated to embrace 590,000 square miles, and including Lakes Nyasa, Tanganyika, and the Victoria Nyanza. Had such a concession been secured to England and English enterprise, "how changed", to use the words of Mr. George Mackenzie, the Governor of "Ibea", speaking in 1890–1891, "would have been the whole situation at Khartoum and along the whole valley of the Nile, as well as in Abyssinia!"[1]

The late Sir Bartle Frere, upon the occasion of his well-known mission in 1873 to Seyd Burghash, was one of the first to point out that Great Britain through India and the Indian coast traders had really a great interest in East Africa.

The Germans began first of all to interfere in East African affairs in 1880–1885 with the result finally of the present delimitations. As Great Britain, no doubt because of her imperial burdens elsewhere, has retired from Western Africa before France, so she has left a field, once exclusively her own, in East Africa open to German colonization. There is no doubt that with such pioneers as Sir John Kirk and Sir William Mackinnon, her influence was absolutely supreme twenty years ago in these regions. "Ibea" possesses a splendid harbour in Mombasa, and there are two navigable rivers, the Tana and the Juba. One of the most important engineering projects in view for "Ibea" is a railway connecting Mombasa with the lake country and Uganda and the sources of the Nile. The Nile problem itself has been solved mainly by the efforts of Speke and Grant, and other British explorers during the Victorian era, and if British occupation and colonization follow in the wake of British exploration this is only a natural sequel. "Ibea" may be, and probably is, an "undeveloped estate", but by the Anglo-German Convention it remains, for a permanence, a part of the British Empire, and a field for British enterprise. In connection with our Indian Empire this slice of Africa must be more useful to Great Britain than to any other power. Arab traders will be our loyal subjects along the coast in a hundred bazaars, whilst the Sikhs will

[1] *Proceedings Royal Colonial Institute*, vol. xxii.

continue to garrison the country as they do now, under the leadership of British officers.

It may be well to close the chapter of Great Britain's expansion in Africa by recalling the part that Britons have taken in opening up its remote regions and wildernesses, and this is given with some force by Sir Harry Johnston, one of the most active of African explorers and administrators.[1] All the great rivers and lakes of Africa, he remarks, have been made known to the world by the explorations of British subjects. Englishmen, Irishmen, Scotchmen, or Welshmen first discovered and gave the approximate dimensions of Lakes Tchad, Victoria Nyanza, Tanganyika, Rukwa, Nyasa, Chilwa, Bangweolo, Mweru, Mantumba, Lake Leopold, Ngami, Lake Tana, and Lake Debu. The name of Livingstone is connected with the mapping of the Zambesi from its source to its mouth. Other Englishmen first explored and mapped the Orange River and the Limpopo, the Ruvuma, the Rufiji, the Juba, the Webbe, the Gambia, the Senegal. Mungo Park is acknowledged by all men to have been the first to place the Niger river accurately on the map. Stanley is the hero of the Congo, whose most important affluent, the Ubangi, was discovered and mapped by Grenfell. Englishmen were the first to report the existence of the Shari, the principal affluent of Lake Tchad, while as regards the Nile and its system what geographical work done by other Europeans can be compared with the researches of Bruce, Petherick, Baker, Speke, and Grant? Who were the first to turn the alfa grass of North Africa to the practical use of making paper? Englishmen. Who first created palm-oil as a trade product, now being sold annually for millions of pounds? Englishmen. It was Englishmen like Sir John Kirk, Sir Alfred Moloney and others, who started or developed the trade in rubber

[1] *Proceedings Royal Colonial Institute*, 1896-1897.

and gum on the east and west coasts of Africa. Englishmen, first of all, have developed the cultivation of cotton in the Zambesi countries and in Egypt, and indigo on the Niger. Who first discovered diamonds and gold in South Africa? Englishmen. And the nitrates, which it is hoped may yet add to the exports of Egypt? An Englishman, Mr. Floyer. Who first stimulated the cultivation of the ground-nut in Gambia, which now produces nearly all our finest olive-oil, quietly manufactured at Marseilles? Englishmen. Who first introduced the tea plant into Natal, and created what is likely to be a most flourishing trade in tea in that gallant little colony? Englishmen. And last on this list of agricultural products, who were the first coffee-planters in Central Africa? A dogged little band of Scotchmen. Who constructed the first railway in Africa, which brought prosperity to Egypt and turned Cape Colony from a little red patch on the southern extremity of Africa into a vast empire? Who encircled the whole continent with telegraph cables and conceived the carrying out the bold project of traversing Africa from south to north by telegraph wires? Who put the first steamers on the Niger, on the Zambesi, on the Congo, on the Nile, on the Gambia, on almost every navigable African river? Englishmen. And, it may be added, nearly all this colossal work has been done within the wonder-working years of the Victorian era.

Chapter VI.

The Growth of Colonial Constitutions—Canada.

From the previous survey of our Colonial Empire it may be gathered that the Colonies themselves fall, generally speaking, into two large groups:—(1) Crown Colonies—under the direct administration of the Crown—where, as in the West Indies and the West African Settlements, the executive government is not responsible to the people who are governed; (2) those large groups of Colonies in Canada, Australasia, and South Africa, which, under the circumstances of a wide franchise and a broadly-based constitution, enjoy "responsible" government. It is evident that representative government is not always responsible government, for in the Crown Colonies themselves there are upon the councils many persons elected or nominated to represent certain public interests, but without the power in the last resort to make any change in the government, their position being that chiefly of an advisory body. It is to the "responsible" or self-governing groups that we look with the greatest interest, as they present to us a picture of a civic and social life similar to the home life, and, in many of its phases, a simple replica of it.

The first fact that strikes the eye of the observer is the marvellous and exuberant prosperity of these responsible Colonies, especially during the last few decades of this notable Victorian era; and if we trace carefully the true operating causes of this prosperity, we shall assign much to the favourable conditions of soil and climate in which the colonists have made their homes, much also to the immunity enjoyed, in Australasia especially, from external dangers, much to the inherent pluck and colonizing aptitude of the British race, and, last but not least, much to the free character of the institutions under which the colonists have lived. Political freedom is a wonderful quickener of vitality; political responsibility, falling upon strong and capable shoulders, is an incentive to extraordinary efforts; and responsible government, as the legitimate issue amidst favourable surroundings of representative government, is nothing more nor less than the embodiment of the supreme ambitions of nationhood. Each group of our "responsible" Colonies, without sacrificing its natural allegiance to a constitutional head in the Crown of England, has a nationhood of its own, of the kind indicated by Sir Wilfrid Laurier in French Canada. In the history of the world, communities of people have reached their ideal type only through the *sturm und drang* of life by ceaseless rivalries, by desolating wars, and by terrible life-sacrifices. In Canada, Australasia, and South Africa there has been, generally speaking (for wars have not always been absent), a political evolution, on peaceful lines under the protecting ægis of the British flag. The type that will ultimately be evolved will be the product of the peculiar influences of the country, but it will owe much to the form of government under which it has been able to flourish. The public arena is the training-school of the individual, and in the arena of our Colonies there breathes a free spirit of full manhood and emancipation. The gradual development of this life to ripeness and maturity affords a most interesting study in our current political annals, and its history is that of the merging and welding together in the bonds of the *Civitas Britannica* many races of men. Indeed, it will be found—and we shall have frequent cause to notice it—that political principles are stronger than race. Lord Norton, in his able *Review of our Colonial History and Policy*, points out that there have been three distinct periods in the constitutional history of our Colonies, speaking in its broadest and most general sense, and including our "first" as well as our "second Colonial Empire". In the first we left Colonies, which were at that time remote from the seat of government, to govern themselves in the way they thought best, but at the same time we attempted to make them subservient to our interests at home by means of commercial regulations. All business with them, being chiefly of a commercial character, was referred to the Board of Trade and Plantations, and this very association proves the main aspect in which they presented themselves to the eye of the British Government. It was an age of monopolies, and Great Britain was at first a strictly monopolist trading power. When we read of British "dependencies" in the last century we are to understand that they were dependent more especially in the commercial sense. Let us illustrate this from the case of Newfoundland. This island, the oldest of British Colonies, was resorted to annually by British sailors, who came thither in the wake of the great Cabot, and caught fish for Catholic Europe. Many Englishmen wished to settle in the island and become colonists in the true sense of the word, but the British Government actually discouraged colonization, as it seemed to interfere with the monopolist character of the industry. In 1660 the Star Chamber declared that "no master or owner of any ship should transport to Newfoundland any persons who were not of the ship's company, nor such as were to plant or settle there". This was the principle of protection with a vengeance, all the more inexplicable because the stakes were high at Newfoundland at one time, and, amidst the rivalries of European nations, whose sailors came thither to fish, British immigrants were best calculated to settle the question of sovereignty at once. Edmund Burke described the fisheries as being "mines richer than Mexico or Peru".

When it was impossible to check the flow of immigration wherever a local industry grew up, as in the West Indies, then the home government gave the community ample self-governing powers. The West Indian and New England Constitutions were a case in point. There were always trade restrictions, and as long as these were not violated the colonists could manage their own local and municipal affairs. This complaisance went on for a long time, and practically there was little to prevent a tolerably smooth working of both Imperial and Colonial administrations. We availed ourselves largely of the services of the New England colonists in naval and military warfare, and perhaps the question of general imperial defence was better and more fairly understood then than it is at the present moment. Great Britain was helped largely by American levies in the struggle against France for Canada.

In the second period, by tampering too much with the self-government conceded to the American settlers, we lost the American Colonies. Then, suddenly seized with alarm at the result of their rashness, our Colonial administrators, thinking too much internal liberty a dangerous thing, sought to check colonization and impound liberty altogether, taking no service from our Colonies, but all their expenses of defence upon themselves. This was reverting to a state of tutelage, the result of our fear or of our incapacity to realize the true state of things, and it could not last. But it lasted almost to the accession of Queen Victoria. Sir G. C. Lewis wrote in 1841 that since the close of the American war it had not been the policy of England to vest any portion of the Legislative power of the subordinate or Colonial government in a body elected by its inhabitants.[1] The only partial exception, he remarked, existed in the Canadian provinces. It is here we must first look for the true germs of Colonial emancipation. In the third period was inaugurated the principle of Colonial self-government, when representative government, as a preliminary process in itself, ended logically in the full grant of responsible government, or government by party. Legislation then proceeded according to the will of the colonists

[1] *Government of Dependencies*, p. 160.

themselves. Under these circumstances the term "Dependency" is hardly the right word to use in a constitutional sense, as it implies direct control and government by "orders in council". The veto of the Crown exists, for instance, in the matter of Colonial loans, but it is seldom exercised: the power of taxation has long since been surrendered, and, as we shall see, their own fiscal policy is in the hands of the colonists. If the colonists elected their own governor, it would be difficult to say what constitutional tie existed between them and the mother-country. In achieving this position of constitutional freedom, so nearly akin to practical independence, yet differing widely from it, there have been steps and processes of growth, diversified occasionally with the incidents of an acute crisis.

It is very often thought that what is known in Canadian history as the Papineau Rebellion was mainly the uprising of one nationality against another in the valley of the S. Lawrence, and a long-concerted plot on the part of the French Canadians to throw off the British yoke and set up a republic of their own. By others the religious grievance was alleged to be the most prominent exciting cause of the rebellion, and the establishment by Governor Sir John Colborne (Lord Seaton) of thirty-seven rectories in Upper Canada is quoted as being the spark that set the whole country on fire. If this were really the case, there must have been a good deal of smouldering discontent and a large amount of inflammable material at hand; otherwise we can scarcely imagine that a single act of administration of this kind would have had such a disproportionate effect upon the minds of the Canadian people.

Let us review in outline the circumstances of the case, *firstly*, as they actually were in Canada itself; and, *secondly*, as they were represented to be in the parliamentary debates at home, especially those in March, 1837, when

Growth of Constitutions—Canada. 135

the Canadian crisis was at its height and its political aspects exposed to the keenest criticism. After the conquest of Canada the political history of the country had been as follows:—(i.) From 1760-1774 there had been a period of military rule. As soon as the articles of surrender were signed at Montreal, General Amherst became Governor-General of Canada, and he divided the country into the three districts of Quebec, Three Rivers, and Montreal, the distinction between Upper Canada (Ontario) and Lower Canada (Quebec) not having arisen. General Murray was appointed to Quebec, with the title of Lieutenant-governor over Canada; Colonel Burton to Three Rivers, and General Gage to Montreal. To each of these officers was assigned a council consisting entirely of military officers, who decided all cases. The English language was made the sole medium of official communication; all public offices were given to British-born subjects; there were no regular salaries, the officers being paid by fee; and all the laws, customs, and judicial forms of the old French colony overthrown. It was found, however, that this administration, considering the preponderance of the French population, could not last, and when complaints arose in the natural course of events, it was recommended: (1) that it was not advisable to insist upon the English language as the sole medium of official communication; (2) that it was unwise to abolish all French usages and customs, especially those relating to land and the law of inheritance; (3) that Canadian advocates should be permitted to practise in the courts. These recommendations paved the way for the second period of administration.

(ii.) On May 2, 1774, a bill, known as the Quebec Act, was brought into the House of Lords by the Earl of Dartmouth, and passed without opposition. It was sent to the Commons for their concurrence. By this act all the provisions of the royal proclamation of 1763 were repealed, the commissions of officers revoked, and new boundaries established for the province, which now embraced all ancient Canada, Labrador, and the countries west of the Ohio and Mississippi. At this date it must be remembered the United States did not exist on the map of North America. The Declaration of Independence was not made till 1776, nor the Peace of Versailles signed till 1783. Further, the Quebec Act released all Roman Catholics in Canada from penal restrictions, and renewed their dues and tithes to its regular clergy, and confirmed all classes in the possession of their properties. When it is considered that the Catholic relief measures in England itself were not passed until 1829, after many discussions and much party fighting, this concession in Canada strikes us as being well in advance of the spirit of the age. In the domain of law the French laws were declared to be the rules for decision relative to property and civil rights, whilst the English criminal law was established in perpetuity. Both the civil and criminal codes were, however, liable to be altered or modified by the ordinances of the governor and a legislative council. This council was appointed by the Crown, and was to consist of not more than twenty-three and not less than seventeen members. Its power was limited to levying local rates, the British Parliament reserving to itself the right of internal taxation, a reservation which throws some light upon the policy which led to the taxation of the American colonies in the south and brought about their rebellion. However, the act was looked upon as a concession to French Canadians, the "Custom of Paris" becoming the law of French Canada. The Quebec Act remained in force until 1791, a period of seventeen years.

(iii.) The third period was inaugurated by the Canadian Constitutional Act of 1791, which was prepared by William Grenville, and laid before Parliament by Mr. Pitt. A great deal had happened since 1774, and the

American Rebellion, ending in the autonomy of the Thirteen States, had not been without its influence on Canada. In the first place a large number of "United Empire Loyalists", who had adhered to the cause of Great Britain, were settled in Canada. West of the Ottawa lay a noble country inclosed by the S. Lawrence and the lakes. A list of the Loyalists was made, and in 1784 the country round Niagara and Amherstburg, and along the S. Lawrence and the Bay of Quinté, was surveyed for them. A grant of £4,000,000 of public money was voted for them; field-officers were allotted 5000 acres each, captains 3000, subalterns 2000, and private soldiers 200 each. It is estimated that 10,000 emigrated to Upper Canada. At the same time Nova Scotia, the maritime province, took 20,000 colonists.

The importance of this element in Canadian history can scarcely be over-estimated. Here was a nucleus of a new colony, British to the backbone, and the champions of the cause of the Crown in North America. They had sacrificed a great deal for this cause, and demanded a hearing on all Canadian questions from that time forward. By the Act of 1791 Canada was divided into two Provinces, the Upper and the Lower, with the boundary of the Ottawa, and a census of the whole country showed that out of the whole population of 150,000 only 20,000 belonged to Upper Canada. Pitt had no desire to blot out the French nationality. On the contrary, it has been suggested that his object in dividing Canada into two provinces was to create two communities, separate from and jealous of one another, so as to guard against a repetition of that rebellion which had separated the Thirteen States from the Empire. There was no great official desire for the extension of the British Colonial Empire. With regard to the government of the provinces, each province was to have a governor of its own and a parliament consisting of two houses, namely, an

Assembly elected by the people, and a Legislative Council nominated and not elected.

A few words on the subject of this nominated council may be of use here, as a great deal turned subsequently upon its position and privileges. Because it was nominated it became the *bête noir* of all Canadian reformers. In giving Canada a constitution it was the intention of the English legislators to reproduce roughly the outlines of the British constitution, and a nominated Legislative Council seemed likely to supply the position of a House of Lords and a privileged aristocracy. In the debate on Canadian affairs[1] Mr. Labouchere (Lord Taunton) observed that "admiring Fox as he did, he never admired him more than when, in 1791, he saw with prophetic sagacity the result of giving Canada a Legislative Council upon an aristocratic basis. He warned the Parliament of those days, and Pitt's argument was simply expressed in these words, 'I will not answer now, it is only an experiment'." Nevertheless Pitt thought that there was something efficacious in this Upper House, and is reported to have said that he thought the want of a titled aristocracy had accelerated the separation of the former American Colonies, being convinced that an aristocracy derived from the Crown of England would materially strengthen the connection between the colony and the mother-country.[2] There is no doubt that all British statesmen were in in search of a certain balance and a certain element of stability in the growing Colonies. They wanted, ready-made if possible, a constitution in which monarchy, aristocracy, and democracy were blended and united, nor would any government be really acceptable to British subjects unless they had what Madame de Stael expressed in her work on the French Revolution as the saving

[1] Hansard, March 8, 1837.
[2] Tomline, vol. iii. p. 222-226, and *Quarterly Review*, No. lxxxiv. p. 317.

quality of the English Constitution, " la réunion graduée des divers états de l'ordre social ". There was a proper poise of the constitution, which both Pitt and Fox could appreciate as, theoretically, the best " which equalized and meliorated the powers of the two other extreme branches, and gave stability to the whole". It is possible that in our Colonies (perhaps we may see it most in our Australian Colonies) we are still in search of a " poise ", a kind of self-righting apparatus in itself, preventing the violence of one chamber and the anarchy of individual ministries, and thereby holding a shield over the true liberties of all the people. In the case of Canada, in 1791, finding this "balance" was not easy, and Fox leaned towards an elective council, Pitt to the aristocratical and hereditary council. Pitt's idea savoured a little of feudalism and of the old-world spirit, not so dead last century as this. In Canada, the bit of old France and the old-world spirit, which struck De Tocqueville in the way it peeped out in habits of life and modes of expression he met with himself, for example, when he heard Canadian nuns speaking of " Notre bon père, George Quatre", as the ladies of S. Cyr might have done of Louis Quatorze, or when he heard on the Sagenaw a Canadian Indian singing a song of old France as he sculled him down the river—this, and much more, favoured an old-world experiment. There were the French seigniors already planted along the S. Lawrence, and an institution in the land. Could they not be utilized as a graft? Old John Locke had drawn up certain Constitutions of Carolina in 1669, and could not a feature of his Utopia be revived in Canada? It was symmetrical, to say the least of it. There were lords-proprietors, seigniories, baronies, precincts, and colonies, where land was to descend from father to son in a strictly-preserved line; there were state-functionaries, admirals, chamberlains, chancellors, constables, chief justices, high stewards, treasurers, landgraves, cassiques, and all kinds of outlandish names and artificial distinctions, sinning against the very first principles of British colonization. The "fundamental Constitutions of Carolina" fell still-born, but it is extraordinary how long the idea of importing a ready-made aristocracy prevailed, and how it coloured conceptions of colonial life. Mr. Merivale, in his *Lectures on Colonisation*, reminds us (p. 109) that in 1766 the Earl of Egmont, of Enmore Castle in Somerset, then a Lord of the Admiralty, proposed to have the proprietorship of Prince Edward Island settled on himself, on a feudal plan, with power to erect a certain number of baronies, each baron to build a castle, and to employ so many men-at-arms to do feudal suit and service. This plan also came to nothing, but it reflects, doubtless, in some way the ideas that were current even at this late date, in certain circles, about an imported aristocracy; and although neither Pitt nor Fox indulged in mediæval dreams, or were really in favour of a scheme that would have been more in consonance with the transatlantic ideals of Cardinal Richelieu and Colbert than those of practical Britons, still the notion of introducing privilege into a colony, and making class-distinctions in colonial society, was evidently present in their minds. The history of Canada, like the history of our other Colonies, proves that there could never have been any room for fanciful and unreal constitutions. In Canada the old battle was carried on with somewhat the same war-cries and by somewhat the same methods as the constitutional battles at home. The popular and elected assembly had the power over the purse, and fought with this, and no aristocracy could have prevented them. Lord Durham, in his report of 1839, observes that the Constitution of the House of Lords was "consonant with the frame of English society"; but the attempt "to invest a few

Growth of Constitutions—Canada. 141

persons, distinguished from their fellow-colonists neither by birth nor hereditary property, and often only transiently connected with the country, with the power of the House of Lords, seems only calculated to ensure jealousy and bad feeling in the first instance and collision in the last ".

Speaking from a later and wider experience, and from a somewhat different standpoint, in 1850, Mr. Lowe, who had sat himself as a nominated councillor for New South Wales, and had experienced himself the conditions of political life in our Colonies, observed: " If there be any one institution which tends to bring the Home Government into collision with the Colony, to disturb the action of the Constitutional system, to throw discredit upon public men, to introduce discord into the public councils, and to create every disturbance which it is desirable to exclude from the deliberations of a Legislative Assembly—it is the institution of Crown nominees. They represent nobody; they have not the slightest affinity with aristocratical institutions; the scapegoats of the Constitution, the target for every attack, the butt of every jest."[1]

The honours that are granted now to distinguished Colonists, especially those of the Order of S. Michael and S. George, and their admittance to the Privy Council, differ *in toto* from the Colonial honours recklessly bequeathed by the Stuarts, and proposed to be continued in our Colonial Constitutions. Charles I. created a remarkable order of Baronets called "The Knights Baronets of Nova Scotia", numbering 150, each of whom was entitled to receive a large grant of land on the condition that he would settle emigrants on it. This was privilege with a vengeance, and it is difficult to see how these baronetcies were deserved, either in the promise or the execution of the task

[1] See Mill's *Colonial Constitutions*, p. lix.

allotted them. It is in keeping with the fact that the Governor of Maryland used to have power to grant patents of nobility. In Victorian days Colonial honours are upon a different plane, and are given for merit, generally the merit of successful work and of a long service in building up the Empire. Men win their spurs, if not on "the tented field", still in the hard campaign of colonization. The reward comes after deserts, not, as in the case of the Nova Scotian baronets, in anticipation, and it is rarely grudged by fellow-colonists. That such honours come from the hand of the ruler of the most ancient monarchy in Europe, and from the head of a constitution broadly based upon the will and affections of the people, is no small additional source of pride and gratification to the recipients. It is possible in this way to plant the acorn, as it were, of a colonial aristocracy, whilst it is impossible to transplant the venerable oak.

By the Act of 1791 the Crown Lands of Canada were still in the possession of the Crown, and it was enacted that an allotment in each province should be made for the support and maintenance of a Protestant clergy, and such an allotment was to be, as nearly as possible, equal in value to a seventh part of the lands granted. The king empowered the governors in each province to erect parsonages and to enclose them, and to present incumbents of the Church of England, subject to the authority of the Bishop of Nova Scotia. These ecclesiastical lands were known as "The Clergy Reserves", and became a great bone of contention. The Act of 1791 left with the Colonists the power of directing the assessment and the levying of taxes, and also of appropriating them. This was a most important power, and was the same lever wherewith the Commons of England had worked the protection of their liberties against the Crown. The occasion was destined to arise in Canada when the Canadian colonists would use it in the same way.

The Act of 1791 was the first attempt at an organized constitutional government, and by some Canadians the 16th of July, 1792, when the first Assembly met, is remembered as the birthday of representative government. It was a long way yet to responsible government, but here was the first instalment. There was a precise, almost a loyal, imitation of old-country institutions in small things as well as great; and of the nineteen counties into which Upper Canada was divided, no fewer than eight bore the names of English counties, and eight were called after eminent English statesmen. The Canadian County of York was divided into two ridings, and so was the County of Lincoln.

The constitution, however, proved to be unworkable. From the year 1818 began a series of disputes and misunderstandings, partly arising from race animosities, partly from religion, partly from land questions, partly from patronage questions, and partly from the inherent defects of the constitution. In the year 1828, after a number of petitions had been sent home from the Colony for the redress of grievances, Canadian affairs formed the subject of a parliamentary inquiry, in which the reality of the grievances was affirmed. Still nothing was done, and in 1833 the Canadian Assembly fell back upon their power of stopping supplies, and judges, public officers, and the ordinary officials were left without salaries. Consequently there was a deadlock in the government, which lasted until 1837. In 1834 the Canadian grievances were considered formidable enough to be embodied in a series of ninety-two resolutions, "some of grievance, some of eulogy, some of vituperation, some directed against individuals, and some against the government at home, but all of them amounting to a long and vehement remonstrance, and in framing that remonstrance they consumed the whole session, and separated without voting a single vote of supply at all ". This is the criticism of Lord John Russell,[1] and it is interesting to note that the ninety-two resolutions concluded with a grateful message to Daniel O'Connell, whom the gratitude and blessings of his countrymen had proclaimed the Great and the Liberator. With his name was coupled that of Joseph Hume, whose "constant devotedness, even under a Tory Ministry and before the reform of Parliament, was partially successful in the Emancipation of Ireland from the same bondage and the same political inferiority which menaced the people of Lower Canada". This passage is instructive, because it shows how, not only with reformers at home, as already noted, but even with the Canadian reformers in Canada itself, the cause of Canada was inextricably bound up and associated with Ireland. But could the one cause help the other? Was it not wiser to keep them separate?

It was the desire of Sir Robert Peel in 1834 to redress these grievances, and to entrust the task of arbitration to Lord Amherst, but his brief administration fell, and the experiment was not carried out. Still, the sores remained.

It may be convenient for the understanding of the whole question to point out more particularly and *seriatim* what some of these Canadian grievances were, how they arose, and how they were aggravated. In Upper Canada we had to deal with a fairly homogeneous Anglo-Saxon population; but in Lower Canada, where the greatest mischief was brewing, we had to face the problem of a preponderating French-Canadian population attached to the Roman Catholic Church. Now, one of the grievances, first and foremost, was that of the "Clergy Reserves", as left by the act of 1791. Of the lands

[1] London *Times*, 17th January, 1838.

Growth of Constitutions—Canada.

granted in Upper and Lower Canada, upwards of 3,000,000 acres consisted of Clergy Reserves, in lots of 200 acres each, scattered over the townships. The stipulated proportion of one-seventh was exceeded in Lower Canada, 673,567 acres having been granted instead of 446,000, being an excess of nearly 230,000 acres. These lands went to subsidize more especially the Episcopal Church in Canada. In the House of Commons at home it had already been stated by the Select Committee of 1828, that these reserved lands, as at present distributed, retarded more than anything else the improvement of the Colony, lying, as they did, in detached portions, . . . intervening between the occupations of settlers. In addition, the whole land question was managed badly Land was squandered away in useless grants to absentees, or sold for a small sum. The difference in the management and economy of land was visible along the American frontier, and even a traveller could tell as he travelled in and out the Maine frontier, in which territory he was, that of Great Britain or that of the United States, from the superior condition of the latter. The average difference, as between Upper Canada and the States of New York and Michigan, was "notoriously several hundred per cent".[1] The comparatively ancient city of Montreal could not compare with Buffalo, the creation of yesterday, and the painful truth was reiterated again and again along a frontier of 1000 miles. In Upper Canada the land had been kept mostly in English hands, a grievance to the French-Canadian colonists. In addition to 3,200,000 acres granted to United Empire Loyalists in 1787, there had been the grants of 730,000 acres to militiamen, 450,000 to discharged soldiers, 136,000 to executive councillors and their families, 255,000 to magistrates and barristers, 36,900 to clergymen as

[1] Lord Durham's Report.

private property, 92,526 to officers of the army and navy, 264,000 to persons contracting to make surveys, and many other grants.[1]

In Lower Canada, Nova Scotia, and Prince Edward Island, the land question was, if anything, in a more unsatisfactory state.

An additional source of complaint was found in the fact that the government of Upper and Lower Canada had found its way into the hands of a clique banded together by a "family compact", which soon fell into almost purely national lines. It was gall and wormwood for the French-Canadians in Lower Canada to have no part or share in government or in the patronage of office. They were not completely denationalized, and "the sunny France" of their fathers was still the cherished country of the Canadians' memory. Thither their young men who sought distinction made summer pilgrimages, and there they drew inspiration or instruction from the pages of its literature. The men of the "habitans" or peasants took their mental impress from their priests or their leaders; but "all the intellect of Lower Canada was French exclusively".[2] Thus two populations were facing one another in Canada, the French and the English, hostile and sullen, with all the irritating grievances of religion, race, and caste to provoke them against one another. Lord Durham said in his report that "social intercourse never existed between the two races in any but the higher classes", and on one occasion, when Papineau, the French-Canadian Speaker of the House of Assembly in Lower Canada, gave an entertainment to the governor, Lord Aylmer, only two Englishmen were present besides the governor and his suite. Things had been going from bad to worse, and although during the first period of the possession of the Colony intermarriages were frequent, they were rare in

[1] Lord Durham's Report. [2] Macmullen's *History of Canada*.

1837. The two parties "could combine for no public object or harmonize even in associations of charity. ... In Montreal and Quebec there were English schools and French schools, and the children of these were accustomed to fight nation against nation".[1] It may be asked whether, considering the presence of the United States Republic across the border, there was any really deep sympathy with Republicanism felt by the French Canadians, exercising a centrifugal force and luring them into the arms of the Republic itself. For there was much intrigue going on, and many demonstrations of American sympathizers across the border. To the French "habitans" or peasantry it would appear that the Republic on the south presented few real attractions, whatever might be the case with the smaller party of professional constitutional agitators. For generations the "habitans" of the old semi-feudal seigniories, divided into strips along the banks of the S. Lawrence, with their narrow river frontage, had lived on peacefully, comparatively uneducated, and content with a quiet routine of life. Longfellow has drawn an imperishable picture of the French-Canadian peasantry, satisfied with their lot, devoted to their priests, and conservative in thought and habits.

Such men were not the revolutionists of society nor the victims of random democratic impulses with the watchwords of Liberty and Equality and Fraternity: their society constituted a remnant of picturesque old France. Very different were these settlers from the English colonists of the Atlantic sea-board, where Puritanism had its refuge. With the New Englanders political and social emancipation was a powerful, sometimes an absorbing, motive. The minds of their nascent society laboured to give shape and colouring to colonization, and such men as Sir H. Vane succeeded in impart-

[1] Lord Durham's Report.

ing some of their own spirit to the Parliament at home. The ordinary French Canadians were not men of this stamp, and, reckoning up the powers and forces at work in the Canadian Rebellion, it is well to remember that we had not to contend with such strong opinions and violent prejudices as existed in New England. Discontent was rife, but it had not ripened into the irreconcilable spirit.

Such were some of the Canadian grievances, and such the attitude of the parties there. The Government at home were evidently at a loss what to do, and, not facing the question boldly, resorted to a Commission, and sent out Lord Gosford, Sir Charles Grey, and Sir George Gipps. These men effected little real good, and Roebuck thus spoke of them in the Canadian debate of March, 1837: "Sir George Gipps has a leaning towards liberality, Sir Charles Grey is a high Tory, and as for poor Lord Gosford, he seems to have led a disagreeable life between the snarling Whig and the arrogant Tory". It may be noticed also, that before he set out on his somewhat difficult diplomatic errand, Lord Gosford was the recipient of a peremptory message from King William IV. on the subject of Canada. "I will never consent to alienate Crown lands," said the king, "or make the Council elective."[1] The question of making the nominated Council an elected body was the ambition of Papineau and the Canadian reformers. The Constitutional question, now being pushed to the forefront by French and English colonists alike, gave them a common platform upon which they might sink their differences of race and creed. In Upper Canada William Lyon Mackenzie was working together with Papineau in Lower Canada. Mackenzie, who was known as the Canadian correspondent of Joseph Hume, the leader of the Radical section of the House of Commons, was

[1] *Edinburgh Review*, vol. cxxxiii. p. 319.

originally a pedlar-lad who emigrated from Scotland and became a shop-assistant in Toronto. He rose by degrees to the management of a Canadian newspaper. He undertook a mission to England, and was successful in obtaining an audience at Downing Street, and laying some of the Canadian grievances before the authorities, amongst them Lord Goderich and Lord Howick. Papineau was a somewhat different character, and agitated upon different lines, " formed by nature for the eloquent agitator, but not for the wise and prudent legislator. . . . In height he was of the middle size, with features of a Hebrew cast; whilst his large dark eyebrows shaded, in a higher arch than common, keen lustrous eyes, quick and penetrating. Deeply read in general literature, familiar with the old Canadian lore of Hennepin, Charlevoix, and the other learned Jesuit fathers, who had written of La Nouvelle France in bygone days, he appealed to all the feelings and prejudices of his countrymen with irresistible effect, and carried them captive by the force of his oratorical and conversational powers."

In March, 1837, the interest shifted to London. Lord John Russell, during the Melbourne administration, brought forward ten resolutions on Canadian affairs, which are instructive in themselves, and also in the debate they evoked. We might have expected that the Whigs would have settled the Canadian question offhand and in a liberal spirit, but they had played with it and evaded it so long that it appears as if they had made up their minds to do as little as possible. Upon this occasion the philosophical Radicals, supported by a few members, figure as a distinct section in opposition to Lord John Russell, and put forward Mr. Leader, member for Bridgwater, an unknown man, said to have been a carriage-builder at Putney, to attack him. Lord Russell argued against any very great material concessions to Canada.[1] Since the 31st of October, 1832, no provision had been made by the Legislative Assembly of Lower Canada to defray the expenses of government; there were many arrears, and these it was incumbent upon the Canadians to pay, even if pressure were used. With regard to the request for an elective Legislative Council, it was inadvisable to grant it, although, at the same time, it might be possible to improve the system of nomination and make it fairer for both races. As to the repeal of a certain Act passed by the Parliament of the United Kingdom in favour of the North American Land Company, it could not be thought of, and the title of the Company should remain inviolate. On the question of the net proceeds of His Majesty's hereditary, territorial, and casual revenue, it might be expedient to place them at the disposal of the colonists if the Legislature of Lower Canada thought fit to grant a civil list. As Lord Russell is reported to have brought forward his resolutions "with considerable reluctance",[2] it is uncertain how far he spoke his own sentiments, and how far he was guided by others, possibly the Court party.

Mr. Leader then criticised Lord Russell's resolution. He stigmatized this as equivalent to a Coercion Bill, and considering that the noble Lord represented a Liberal constituency, he was not surprised at his reluctance in bringing it forward. The present confusion was caused by "the conduct pursued for the last twenty years by a nominated council going against the wishes of the Canadian people, and supported by the bad policy of the Colonial Office." The noble Lord, he argued, had said that if the Legislative Council were made elective, the interests of the people would predominate. "But what a sentiment to come from the noble Lord!" exclaimed

[1] Hansard, March 6, 1837.
[2] Mr. Leader's Speech, Hansard, March 6, 1837.

Mr. Leader. On this, as well as upon other occasions, Lord Russell, in his desire to keep the nominated council as a counterpoise in the Colonies, was hardly logical. He rested the Colonial case upon compromise, and exposed, therefore, a vulnerable side. Upon the question of the payment of arrears, Lord Russell was desirous of stepping in between the Executive and the Legislative Assembly, and appropriating revenue in an unconstitutional manner. Should this be allowed, Mr. Leader said that "the constitution of Canada was a mere parchment, the Assembly nothing more than a debating club". The principle he affirmed was that as long as the Canadian people had a Constitutional Assembly of their own, it was beyond the right of the House of Commons to interfere with their concerns or to make any change in their financial affairs. Mr. Leader maintained that it was "not a contest between English and French, as many of British and American descent were found to agree with those of French descent". This statement can hardly be reconciled with some paragraphs of Lord Durham's report, in which he certainly emphasizes the existence of the race feeling, but it serves to put the whole question in the light of a constitutional struggle appealing to all alike. After alluding to the opinion of Fox, expressed in 1791, that the nominated council was "a semblance, and not a substance", and proving that unless constitutional concessions were made, it would be "impossible for the Whig Government, or any other government, to rule Canada except by force of arms", he moved as an amendment "that it is advisable to make the Legislative Council of the province an elective council". Mr. Leader's peroration was somewhat remarkable, as he connected the cause of Ireland with that of Canada, and thus dragged a trail across the scent, somewhat impairing the undoubted force of his criticism of the constitutional deadlock in Canada. "I appeal", he said, "to honourable members from Ireland to do justice to Canada. In political conditions Canada may be considered the miniature of Ireland. The Irish members demand justice for Ireland; I demand justice for Canada."

Mr. O'Connell spoke and protested against Lord Russell's resolutions, and in support of Mr. Leader. "In short, the Court party, if he might so call it, the British party, was the Orange party in Canada." Roebuck, the member for Bath, added, "We have a case before us in all its leading features parallel to that of Ireland. Canada and Ireland have both been conquered by England, and the majority of people in both countries are Roman Catholics." He spoke more sensibly when he said that Canada's grievances could be summed up in two words, "Bad government", and that the complaints related to finance, the administration of justice, the Jesuit estates, and the land grievances. The result of the adoption of Lord Russell's resolution would be a deep and lasting enmity. In America, England would be held up as an oppressor, Canada would join the States, the standard of independence would be raised, and "we shall for ever leave the shores of America amidst the hootings, revilings, and exultations of many millions of her people". Roebuck was not wanting in the power of warm and vigorous invective, but his influence was somewhat discounted by the fact that he was Canada's paid parliamentary agent, a fact which, in the course of debate, was thrown back upon him by Mr. Gladstone, who, upon this occasion, supported what Mr. Leader termed "The Coercion Bill" of Lord John Russell, in a particularly vigorous speech. At this date Mr. Gladstone was the rising hope of the "stern unbending Tories".

More interest attaches to the speech of Mr. Labouchere (Lord Taunton), member for Taunton, who appears to have struck the *juste milieu*, although he did not possess the courage of his convictions. It is curious to note that the case of Canada was most warmly taken up in the west of England, by Buller and Molesworth in Cornwall, and especially by the members for the three Somerset constituencies of Bridgwater, Bath, and Taunton. Mr. Labouchere said that he had often to urge upon the House what appeared to him the real and well-founded grievances inflicted upon the Colonies of Upper and Lower Canada. He had often to express opinions extremely contrary to the Government of the day with regard to the policy pursued in Canada, and he thought that it was our duty and our interest to leave them the direction of their own affairs, and to interfere as little as possible with them.[1] He gave his support to Lord Russell "with reluctance", and saw no reason, at the same time, against the principle of an elected Upper Chamber.

The shades of opinion in this memorable debate are worth noticing. According to Leader, Lord Russell was reluctant, and many of his supporters, no doubt, like Mr. Labouchere, were reluctant also. In reality there could not have been any very great margin of determined opposition in the Whig party itself. However, the dissentient party of Colonial reformers and philosophical Radicals in opposition to Lord Russell were outvoted by very large majorities of combined Whigs and Tories. As above hinted, the cause of the Canadian reform may have suffered by its advocacy. For the time it was hardly worth while to break up the Whig party, or any other party in the State, for its sake. After all, in the programme of the advanced section Canadian politics was only one of the numerous odds and ends.

On November 6, 1837, seven months after this debate, the first disturbance occurred in the streets of Montreal.

[1] Hansard, March 8, 1837.

Warrants were issued for the arrest of the leaders, and Papineau fled to the United States. In December, about 400 rebels gathered near Toronto, in Upper Canada, and endeavoured to gain possession by night of the arms which were stored in the City Hall, but the alarm-bells were rung and the attempt was frustrated. Sir Allan M'Nab hastened to Toronto, and defeated the rebels in a pitched battle; their leader Mackenzie was outlawed and a price put on his head. Mackenzie had taken possession of Navy Island in the Niagara River, and held it with a force of 1000 men, and hoisted a flag with two stars—one for each of the Canadas—in imitation of the United States. Mackenzie issued a proclamation declaring Canada a Republic.

Into the particulars of the insurrection it is not intended to enter here. The rebels were crushed with comparative ease, the country was held by our troops; the constitution was suspended, and martial rule prevailed, as in 1774. At home there was much perturbation, and a good deal of recrimination. Some were inclined to draw the reins of government from home tighter, others to relax them. It was not easy to decide upon the right acts to take and the right man to choose. Sir Francis Head, Governor of Upper Canada at the time of the rebellion, had characterized the agitation in the country as "the work of an insignificant band of conspirators". But he was somewhat feather-brained and untrustworthy, and was recalled. Writing at leisure many years afterwards a work called *The Emigrant*, he showed the unalterable bias of his mind and policy when he spoke of "the baneful domination of what they called responsible government in the United Provinces of Canada perpetuated by Lords John Russell and Sydenham".

This was a critical moment in the history of our Colonial constitutional history. Had the attractive power of the great Republic across the border been greater at that time, or had Upper Canada itself been influenced to a greater extent than it was by the spirit of the Nonconforming element in the religious world (for there were many Nonconformist protests against Episcopacy there), or had, indeed, the representatives of British official authority been more violent and more masterful in their treatment of the rebellion, lasting harm might have been wrought to Canada, and perhaps she would have drifted away altogether from British control. As it was, there was a strong party in England, which, instead of yielding to the demands of Lower Canada, would have withdrawn the representation it already possessed and governed the province indefinitely by the more direct power of "The Queen in Council".

It was fortunate that at this date Lord Durham was available. His father, William Henry Lambton, of Lambton Castle, near Durham, descended from an ancient family, had been a friend of Fox and a staunch Whig. The son is described as being of somewhat an emotional and uncontrolled temperament, quick to resent an indignity but quick also to sympathize. He had long taken an interest in Colonial affairs, and especially in schemes of New Zealand colonization (1825), and was favourable to "the ballot", a test question in those days amongst advanced politicians. Lord Durham appears to have stood by himself in the political world, and, to use Justin M'Carthy's phrase, was posing just at that time as "a kind of unemployed Cæsar". He took with him, however, on his errand to Canada, Charles Buller and Edward Gibbon Wakefield, men of ripe colonial experience, and, as already indicated above, full of the right sort of enthusiasm. Roebuck, in his plan for the government of some of our Colonies, says that Lord Durham made overtures to him to assist him in his work in Canada in a kind of secret and unofficial way. But this was not to Roebuck's liking. The commission issued to John George, Lord Durham, Viscount Lambton, was a wide one. During the suspension of the Canadian Constitution he was "High Commissioner for the adjustment of certain important questions depending in the Provinces of Lower and Upper Canada, respecting the form and future government of the said Provinces". "He was entitled also Governor-General, Vice-Admiral, and Captain-General of all our Provinces within and adjacent to the Continent of North America." *The London and Westminster Review* (6–28), under the inspiration of Mill and Molesworth, sped him on his errand. "To a people thus calumniated it will now be for Lord Durham to do justice. The whole institutions of two great provinces are prostrated before him, and Canada is a tabula rasa . . . in itself the dictatorship which has been assumed, and of which Lord Durham is the immediate depository, admits of justification. When a country is divided into two parties, exasperated by the taste of each other's blood . . . an armed umpire, with strength to make himself obeyed by both, is a blessing beyond all price." Lord Durham landed at Quebec, May 27, 1838, and left again on November 1, 1838. His investigations into the state of the two Canadas, Nova Scotia, New Brunswick, were embodied in his famous Report, dated London, January 31, 1839.

The general lines of Lord Durham's Report are so sound that we can willingly award him the palm of the highest statesmanship. Amongst other suggestions, he recommended, in 1838: (1) First and foremost, a Federal Union of the provinces of Lower and Upper Canada; (2) an Inter-Colonial Railway; (3) an Executive Council responsible to the Assembly. That the advantages of a railway should be advocated at such an early date, when prejudices against them were strong in England herself, is a striking proof of the foresight and perspicacity of Lord Durham. Railway development has been the watchword within recent years of Canadian progress, and the extraordinary achievement of the Canadian Pacific line has been instrumental in bringing East and West together, and making the confederation of the provinces a reality. In the political world Lord Durham saw that the obstructive expedient of stopping supplies in all the provinces created an intolerable deadlock. "We are not now", he says, "to consider the policy of establishing representative government in the Colonies. That has been done irrevocably. . . . The Crown must consent to carry on the Government by means of those in whom the representative members have confidence." Again: "The matters which concern us are very few. The constitution of the form of government, the regulation of foreign relations, and of trade with the mother-country, the other British Colonies, and foreign nations, and the disposal of the public lands, are the only points on which the mother-country requires a control. Municipal management, local government, and the privileges, carried to their logical conclusion, of representative government, will do the rest, and make even the apathetic *habitan* alert and progressive." This was counsel worthy of being written in letters of gold. This was striking at the very root of the constitutional difficulty. The cry of "La Nation Canadienne" meant ruin; but political reform, that would meet the wishes and direct the policy of the *habitan* no less than the English immigrant of advanced views in Upper Canada, meant consolidation and political unity. Above all, the union of the two provinces was a move towards political consolidation, and was the prelude of greater things. It forced the political yoke-fellows both of French and British extraction to understand one another.

Upon the general constitutional crisis throughout Canada Lord Durham writes: "It is but too evident that Lower Canada, or the two Canadas, have not alone exhibited repeated conflicts between the executive and the popular branches of the legislature. The representative body of Upper Canada was, before the late election, hostile to the policy of the Government; the most serious discontents have only recently been calmed in Prince Edward Island and New Brunswick; the Government is still, I believe, in a minority in the Lower House in Nova Scotia, and the dissensions of Newfoundland are hardly less violent than those of the Canadas." Lord Durham, tracing the causes of the discontent, rightly observes that they were mainly constitutional. Representative institutions had been given, but although the Assemblies could pass laws they could not exercise any influence whatever on the nomination of a single servant of the Crown.

The way out of the constitutional deadlock was not difficult. Lord Durham pointed out that every purpose of popular control might be combined with every advantage of vesting the immediate choice of advisers in the Crown, were the Colonial Governor instructed to secure the co-operation of the Assembly by entrusting its administration only to those who could command a majority . . . and if he were given to understand that he could count on no aid from home in any difference with the Assembly that should not involve the deeper and more permanent relations between the mother-country and the Colonies, such cases, for instance, as those of trade and sovereignty. This change might be effected by *a single despatch* from home to the Governor (surely no document would have heralded in a more momentous and far-reaching constitutional change); and if any further enactment were requisite, it would only be one that would render it necessary that the official acts of the governor should be countersigned by some local functionary. Here, indeed, was the reform in a nutshell! With regard to the reserved questions relating to all foreign affairs, and those touching trade and trade principles, and those affecting the disposal of public lands, it must be borne in mind that the old commercial policy was still in vogue, and the principles of Free-trade were not yet asserted. When once they were, it was no long step for the Colonies themselves to inaugurate their own system and place tariffs for revenue even upon the manufactures of the mother-country, as they do now. The disposal also of their public lands has long been in the hands of the British Colonists.

Upon the more purely philanthropic side of his mission Lord Durham was a public benefactor in the way he treated the emigration question, pointing out the criminal negligence of the whole system, its want of supervision, and the horrors of the ship accommodation, to which allusion has already been made. It was no unusual thing for 30 or 40 deaths to take place from typhus fever in the course of a single voyage out of a passenger-list of 500. Many were invalided at the hospitals at Quebec, and as to the healthy remainder, they were often turned adrift without a shilling in their pockets to procure them a night's lodging. The vessels themselves were overcrowded, ill-found, and ill-ventilated. This was the way the Government of Great Britain was treating that vast national exodus from her shores, and it was this inhuman treatment of the human chattels that fired the indignation of Gibbon Wakefield and Charles Buller.

Considering the enormous amount of good that ensued upon Lord Durham's printed report, it is somewhat melancholy to record that, in some respects, his administration in Canada was ruinous to himself. It has been said with a considerable show of truth, that in saving Canada he spoilt his own career. Armed with full powers he proceeded at once to take those stringent measures which, in a precautionary sense, were in his judgment absolutely necessary for the peace of Canada, and, among other acts, condemned some of the leaders of the rebellion to transportation to Bermuda. This was seized upon by his enemies at home, of whom he had many, and made a weapon against him. Although Lord Durham maintained that, according to his commission, he could hand the rebels over to the commanding-officer at the naval station at Halifax, and thus deport them to Bermuda, his critics asserted that the Bermudas lay beyond his *venue*. With regard to himself, in his despatch to Lord Glenelg (28th Sept., 1838) he boldly said: "My acts have been despotic because my delegated authority was despotic, and I do not blush to hear that I have exercised despotism". At the same time he notified his intention to resign, his innate pride urging him, no doubt, to this decision. Moreover, the criticism in Parliament of his acts was particularly hostile and bitter. Lord Melbourne and the Whigs were placed in a difficult position, and here, again, party politics at home, with their usual malignant persistency, helped to cloud and obscure the true state of Colonial affairs; and, besides, Lord Durham had a particularly incompetent man to deal with in Lord Glenelg. However, he passes out of sight, amidst the storms of those turbulent times, a strong, commanding, and somewhat pathetic figure. No greater praise could be given him than that implied in the words of Lord Norton, that his policy "would be a starting-point from which a free, natural, and vigorous attachment would spring up between the Colonies and the mother-country".[1]

[1] *Colonial Policy*, p. 22.

Chapter VII.

The Growth of Colonial Constitutions—Canada.

By the mission of Lord Durham, Canada had won a great deal, and the advocates of Colonial reform had secured the main strongholds of constitutional freedom. Much, however, was still to be done. In England herself the idea of these Colonial liberties was new, in spite of all the teachings and warnings of past times. The Whigs were not very enthusiastic; and with regard to the Tories, their attitude at the time might be summed up in the words of the Duke of Wellington, "A constitution for Malta! I should as soon think of elections in an army, or a parliament on board ship." No doubt this idea of the incapacity of the Colonies for self-government arose from their unfortunate association so long with the War Office. But the Tory pamphleteers of the day had no sympathy with representative assemblies, if we may judge from the pages of the "Tory three-decker", the *Quarterly Review*. In April, 1829, the *Quarterly* had put the case strongly against the idea of Colonial representative government, and its remarks gather additional force and significance when it is remembered what a political force the *Review* was in the days of William Gifford and John Lockhart, and how the great organ was associated with the name of Canning. Not that the Tory party has ever been out of sympathy with Colonial expansion and the doctrine of widening the Empire, as the *Quarterly* itself teems with suggestions for "fresh fields and pastures new" for our trade and emigrants, as a panacea of ills at home; but representative government, to say nothing of responsible government, in the Colonies themselves was a new and abhorrent idea. In 1829 New South Wales was clamouring for a legislative assembly and trial by jury, and the very request seemed outrageous. The Cape of Good Hope, with its 55,000 white colonists, was also asking for an assembly, but it was argued, perhaps not altogether without reason, that it was hard to find qualified jurymen at the Cape. To crown the absurdity of it all, "the cod-fishers of Newfoundland are sighing after a representative government: we imagine that we shall next hear of the liberated negroes of Sierra Leone petitioning to be represented by a black House of Assembly". The preposterous demand, however, of New South Wales for a legislative assembly and trial by jury induces the *Quarterly Review* to moralize thus: "In truth, it is pretty much with Colonies as with children: we protect them and nourish them in infancy, we direct them in youth, and leave them to their own guidance in manhood: and the best conduct to be observed is to part with them on friendly terms, offer them wholesome advice and assistance when they require it, and keep up an amicable intercourse with them. ... As to granting to this or to any other Colony a legislative assembly, we conceive that His Majesty's Government, with the examples of Canada, Jamaica, and some other of the West Indian Islands before its eyes, will hesitate in giving way to any such clamorous demand."

In 1831, upon the occasion of more colonial difficulties, allusion is made in the *Quarterly Review* to the stoppage of supplies in the Legislation of Jamaica by the colonists, which was no doubt an extreme measure. "Even in the petty island of Dominica it has been found necessary to dissolve the Assembly in consequence of its withholding the supplies. And it is but very recently that, in the course of a protracted struggle between the House of Assembly of Lower Canada and His Majesty's Government, the former had recourse to a like course of proceeding." The argument the reviewer draws is that these Colonial legislatures are all exceedingly incapable, and that they are a *reductio ad absurdum* of popular government. What mischief they did do was not great because of their insignificant and insubordinate position, but what might not have ensued if such assemblies had occupied the high and commanding position of a British Parliament? How vain therefore was the wish to broaden the base of our Parliament in England if we had such bad examples on a small scale even in our Colonies!

The effect of Lord Durham's Report upon the Tory party was that of the proverbial red rag to a bull. The outcry was that it should be utterly rejected, together with "its pompous absurdities, its puerile pedantry, its distorted facts, its false reasoning, and its monstrous inconsistencies" (*Quarterly Review*, March, 1839). It was said that every uncontradicted assertion of that volume would be made the excuse of future rebellion, and if that "rank and infectious Report did not receive the high, marked, and energetic discountenance and indignation of the Imperial Crown and Parliament, British America was lost". It was seldom that the Tories of that day displayed greater *animus* than on this occasion. Fortunately, after the heat of party had somewhat worn off, wiser counsels prevailed at the helm, and it was decided to lighten the strain in Canada, not by destroying the machinery of government, but by mending it, and, with this purpose in view, it was advisable to send out, as quickly as possible, the best constitutional governor available, and not the military man with the resources of war.

The position of governors of a truly constitutional order was defined on a past occasion by the late Lord Rosmead, the governor of Cape Colony, in a speech at Kimberley, as resembling "the little figure in a Dutch weather-glass, which only comes out under an umbrella when the barometer points to stormy "; or, as Lord Dufferin, a man of great colonial experience, puts it, he is "like the fustian-clad man whom we see tending a complicated piece of machinery, going about with a little tin can of oil, and pouring in a drop here and there, in order to secure the easy working of the whole". He must be a careful man with delicate perceptions and a conciliatory disposition. This is the picture of the latter-day governor when the machinery presents the aspect of a complex and organic whole, requiring the smallest possible interference from outside.

In our own constitutional history there has been nothing corresponding to the checking influence of a governor invested with almost absolute power, standing, it may be, between the people and their desires. This moderating and guiding force, dependent upon the character of an individual, and exercised continually upon the working machinery of the colony, has had its weakness, and, it may be added, its redeeming quality of strength. It was bad when the personal element predominated, and when an affair of state was reduced to the level of a disputatious quarrel between two or three or more individuals. In the Canadian crisis, especially during the governorship of Sir Francis Head, there was far too much recrimination and far too little sound sense. The main issues were blurred in the partisan attempts to blacken individual characters, and to undermine individual reputations. The age of acrimony has passed, and we now have the calm and impartial verdict of history. Like the kings of Israel and Judah, some governors are good and some are bad, some are wise and some foolish. It was fortunate for the destiny of Canada that from 1839-1841 Mr. Powlett Thompson, elevated to the peerage as Baron Sydenham of Kent and Toronto, was "the man in fustian". He appears to have been an extremely able man, who "held the balance between lingering Tory prejudice on the one hand, and extreme Reform expectations on the other", thus illustrating in his own person that admirable spirit of compromise which, considering the different races of Canada and the unfortunate irritation which then existed there, was one of the first essentials of peaceful constitutional progress. He was termed the merchant-pacificator of Canada because, in addition to other strong qualities, he was a good man of business, and had dealt successfully with the financial difficulties of the time. A Canadian historian has thus summed up his beneficent reign: "He found Canadians suffering from recent intestine rebellion and foreign lawless aggression, their exchequer empty, their inhabitants mistrusting one another; and left them in enjoyment of peace, with mutual confidence established and credit restored".

Lord Russell's instructions to Lord Sydenham (October 14, 1839) laid down the general lines of Colonial policy to be pursued in the future. His Excellency was reminded that there was no surer way of earning the approbation of the Queen than by *maintaining the harmony of the executive with the legislative authorities.* "The Queen's Government had no desire to thwart the representative Assemblies of British North America in their measures of reform and improvement, nor did Her Majesty desire to maintain any system in policy among her North American subjects which opinion condemns. It was Her Majesty's gracious intention to look to the affectionate attachment of her people in North America as the best security for permanent dominion. There must be mutual forbearance between the various parts of the government, and in this respect the example of England might well be imitated. The Governor must only oppose the Assembly when the honour of the Crown and the interests of the Empire were at stake, and the Assembly must be ready to modify its measures for the sake of harmony and from a reverent attachment to the Crown." This Lord Russell endeavoured to communicate to the Canadian reformers, in the very throes of their struggle, the spirit of wise compromise. There is a sense of proportion in political constitutions as in everything else, and the exaggeration of one part means the corresponding depression of the other. The Canadian constitution is not exactly a copy or transcript of the British constitution, but it has needed, especially at critical times, that saving quality of compromise in the midst of jarring creeds and interests which was so wisely advocated by Lord Russell. Once the deadlock was passed, Canadian reform ran smoothly on.

There was another point which Lord John Russell cleared up in his despatch of October, 1839. Hitherto the people of Canada had been deprived in great measure of the places of trust and responsibility under Government, but in the future, if Canada was to govern herself she should depend upon her own native-born administration. The Queen's Government, wrote Lord John Russell, have no wish to make these provinces the source for patronage at home. They are earnestly intent on giving the talent and character of leading persons in the Colonies advantages similar to those which talent and character employed in the public service of the United Kingdom obtain. Throwing open the public offices to Canadian-born men of all classes was a necessary corollary of giving them responsible government. "Govern yourselves, and use your best men" is practically what is meant by this despatch. The sequel has not disappointed the expectations of the Colonial reformers of 1830-1840, and French-Canadian ministers are amongst the most loyal of Her Majesty's subjects.

The battle that was fought in Canada at the beginning of Her Majesty's reign is really, therefore, a most important one in our Colonial annals. It was a triumph of principles. To the majority of Englishmen at home the struggle was unintelligible, because unknown. How much hung in the balance we care not to speculate, for if a different spirit had animated the ministry of the day, and a policy of repression, violence, and intolerance had prevailed, it is hardly likely that we should be looking upon a confederated Canada now. Moreover, the lesson of Canadian unity has spread to the rest of our Colonies in South Africa and Australasia. The principles that were taught in Canada in the "thirties" were taught again in our Colonial Empire wherever representative government was destined to be carried out to its logical sequel.

The Union Bill of 1840 must be reckoned amongst the actual first-fruits of Lord Durham's Report. It provided for the Union under the name of the Province of Canada, and for the constitution of one Legislative Council and one Legislative Assembly, under the title of the "Legislative Council and Assembly of Canada". It was a Reform Bill and a Redistribution Bill. Although the question of elected councillors falls out of sight, and the supreme desire of so many Canadian reformers, upon which they rested so many hopes, was not satisfied, still, in other ways, a great advance was made in self-government. This bill took effect on February 10, 1841. It was really a Reunion Bill, and lasted until the Confederation Bill of 1867. This constituted the *fourth* great change in the government of the Colony.

In 1841 the new era began when the first Parliament of the united provinces of Upper and Lower Canada met at Kingston. This was, practically, the beginning of the present Canadian confederation. One of its first measures was to develop a system of municipal government, by which each township, county, village, or city was enabled to manage its own affairs locally, and to levy taxes for local government. In England we have discovered that local government follows very naturally upon the heels of parliamentary reform, and it has been somewhat slow in coming. But, generally speaking, it may be said that municipal government in our Colonies has come to maturity more quickly than in the mother-country, and so far as the township is the school and nursery of higher politics, it has been a fortunate thing for the individual colonist to be trained. The sense of local responsibility has been one of the most quickening influences of Colonial life, and it is this influence which chiefly differentiates the British Colonial system from that of other nations. In Canada there was a special reason for the speedy application of local and municipal government, considering the character of the population, which was chiefly French in Lower Canada and British in Upper Canada. Each race left to itself could manage its minor problems best without clogging the machinery of government.

In spite of many great and real concessions to popular feelings, and the general desire for more constitutional liberty, the Governor of Canada still retained, by the Union Bill of 1840-1841, a great deal of real power. He was the nominee of the Crown, and held the right of initiating appropriation bills, his services being paid for out of the Colonial exchequer. The judges also held their briefs direct from the Crown, although paid for by the colonists, and the Imperial Government still retained a tight hold over the Crown lands. Lord Metcalfe (1843-1846) gave it out as his individual opinion that "while he recognized the just power and privilege of the people to influence their rulers, he reserved to himself the selection of the executive"; in other words, he carried in his pocket the key of the constitution.

The history of Nova Scotia throws a side-light upon the nature of the constitutional struggle in Upper and Lower Canada. During Lord Elgin's governorship (1847) a constitutional crisis occurred in the maritime province. Sir John Harvey, acting as Lieutenant-Governor, had several vacancies in his Council to fill up, and, deserting the existing ministry, he put himself in communication with the opposition. They advised him to dissolve the Assembly, which he had a constitutional right to do, *proprio motu*, in the hope of securing a majority. This he did, and, so far, he proved that his own wishes were able to override the majority of the members of the House of Assembly. Such decisions simply show that in the struggle for a constitution there were occasional lapses back into the *régime* of autocratic governors, which may or may not have been warranted by the actual circumstances of the case. We are dealing with a transition state in which no definite rule is laid down, and the *lex scripta* of the constitution is at variance with the *lex non scripta* of governors. Perhaps these incidents show that the progress of Colonial constitutional liberty, like that of our own at home, was destined to be slow and cautious. The crisis has really gone by, the danger point passed, and it mattered not much what these little delays meant. To use the words of Wordsworth:

> " It is not to be thought of that the Flood
> Of British freedom, which, to the open sea
> Of the world's praise, from dark antiquity
> Hath flowed, with pomp of waters, unwithstood,
> Roused though it be full often to a mood
> Which spurns the check of salutary bands,
> That this most famous stream in bogs and sands
> Should perish ".

For it was essentially British freedom that was being given to all the inhabitants of Canada of whatever nationality. If technical points of authority were not given up at once, still the whole spirit of Canadian administration had undergone a complete transformation.

In Lord Elgin's governorship the Canadian Government gained entire control over the civil list (1847) and post-office, and other departments generally filled by home nominees were afterwards thrown open to colonists. Here, indeed, is one of those radical differences between the British methods of colonization and those of Spain, Portugal, or indeed France. Spain has lost her magnificent transatlantic empire, and has been engaged in a life-and-death struggle to maintain her footing in Cuba. The causes of her decadence are many, and they are written in history, often in letters of blood. But had Spain ever possessed a school of Colonial politicians at any time in her history who would have given local autonomy to her colonists, and trusted them to have worked out their own destinies in loyalty to the Spanish flag, she might still have held a noble Colonial heritage. But the Spanish Colonies were often regarded as simply the official preserves of Spanish grandees, the dumping-ground of political adventurers, and the receptacle of governors of the worst possible type. So Cuba wishes now to be rid for ever of the shadow of direct Spanish control. The secret report of the Spanish travellers Ulloa and Juan, who visited the Spanish Colonies in South America about the middle of the eighteenth century, throws a lurid light upon Spanish maladministration. The jealousy between Peninsular Spaniards and the Creoles, or Spanish colonists born in the colony, presents a picture of a country divided against itself. It was quite enough to be born a Spaniard to secure the bitterest hatred of every Creole, and to be born a Creole to be obnoxious to a Spaniard. Every appointment, whether in the church, judicature, or revenue, or indeed every civil and military nomination, issued from Madrid. The ecclesiastical posts, from the bishop to the prebendaries, were all filled by Spaniards, who were always nominated at Madrid. The exclusion of Spanish colonists from Spanish Colonial appointments was a matter of course, and this home monopoly was made worse by the character of persons sent out to rule the colonists, who were often mere hangers-on, sycophants, and valets. The rule of the home-appointed "corregidors" or magistrates was absolute, and was exercised without scruple or remorse.

Or turn to the Portuguese Colonies, and we have a still more striking instance of the inability of a European nation to hold a transatlantic Colony. The Portuguese Colonies were a gigantic monopoly kept up for the benefit of the higher classes of Portugal and their dependents. An Auditor-general of the Province of Bahia once wrote home to his government: "Men return to Portugal full rich, who came out full poor". When John VI. fled to the magnificent Colony of Brazil he was accompanied by 20,000 needy adventurers, who all sought office and remuneration in Brazil, like a swarm of locusts. Although a decree was promulgated in 1815 declaring Brazil an integral part of the United Kingdom of Portugal, Algarves, and Brazil—a curious precedent in the history of dependencies—there was nothing lasting about the arrangement. The tone of the Cortes towards Brazil was always harsh and domineering, and in due course of time Brazil fell away from the parent-country by revolution. But had the Portuguese been wise, it is possible that we might still have been reading of the United Kingdom of Portugal, Algarves, and Brazil.[1]

John Stuart Mill observes that the best equivalent the statesman can offer to the small community that sinks its individuality in a large empire is to open to the inhabitants of this community the service of the government in all its departments, and in every part of the empire. Here is an admirable *quid pro quo* for the loss,

[1] *Quarterly Review*, vol. cviii.

perhaps, of wounded dignity, and it really is a first-rate measure of justice. Who ever hears a complaint, Mill exclaims, from the natives of Guernsey or Jersey? The Ionian Islands were then under the power of the British Crown, and their grievance was that the highest posts of government were shut against them, although Corfu had given a minister of European reputation to the Russian empire, and a president to Greece itself before the arrival of the Bavarians. Then he quotes the enlightened policy of Sir W. Molesworth, who had appointed Sir F. Hinckes, a leading Canadian politician to a West Indian governorship.[1] Sir F. Hinckes (1807-1885), an Irishman by birth, had emigrated to Canada in 1831, and in 1837 had been a strong supporter of the Liberal cause. In 1838 he had started the *Examiner* newspaper with the motto of Responsible Government and the Voluntary principle. His appointment, therefore, proves how little the spirit of rancour and persecution was allowed to show itself in Canada. After the Canadian rebellion was once put down and the causes of dissatisfaction removed the home government let matters rest. Even Papineau and Mackenzie, the leaders of the rebellion and the most responsible conspirators of all, were suffered to return to Canada, and, strange to say, both were elected to seats in the Canadian Assembly. The spirit of amnesty was abroad, and a great revulsion of feeling took place in England itself, showing itself in certain measures of almost unexpected and uncalled-for reparation.

Such a measure was that known as "The Indemnification Bill", which created a great stir in Canada and not a little interest at home, mainly because of the constitutional issue raised. As a result of the Rebellion of 1837 there had been a great deal of pecuniary loss suffered by French Canadians in Lower Canada, and in

---

[1] *Representative Government*, p. 328.

some quarters, now that the conflict was all over, there was a desire to indemnify them, especially, no doubt, because there were many victims who had been unwillingly drawn into the vortex of civil war. The question assumed the serious aspect of a race question between Upper Canada, which was chiefly British, and Lower Canada, which was chiefly French. The cry of the British section was "No pay to rebels", and Lord Elgin had to face the conflicting claims of both parties. If there was any error about the measure at all it was an error on the side of political generosity, the hearty approbation of the Queen and her Ministers being given to it. The clauses were discussed in the House of Commons and raised a great debate, Mr. Gladstone condemning the Bill, and arguing that, as it affected imperial honour, it should have been thrashed out at home before it had become a matter of discussion in the Colonial Assembly. Lord Russell replied that the best judge of the question to be referred to the home Parliament was the Colonial governor, and in this case his judgment had been good. Lord Russell thus indicated in no uncertain way how great an amount of responsibility he conceived *still* attached to the office of a Colonial governor. The indemnification, however, was passed, and may certainly be quoted as an instance of the wisdom of Lord Elgin. No measure, indeed, could have been more calculated to soothe the feelings of the French Canadians. Sir F. Hinckes was a very prominent supporter of this bill, and in the excitement of the time his house was burnt down at Montreal.

Another bill, which also has a strange sound in English ears, and grew out of the special circumstances of Canada, was the "Seigniorial Tenure Act", passed towards the end of Lord Elgin's *régime*. We have to go back to the early history of French Canada to understand this Act, and the very mention of the seigniors recalls a remarkable phase of French colonization. When Richelieu formed the company of "One Hundred Associates" in 1627, after cancelling the charters of all other companies, he desired to create, under the French crown, an aristocracy in Canada, consisting, in many instances, of the younger branches of the old French families. They held control over a vast extent of country from Florida to Hudson Bay, and claimed the sole right of trading and fishing, except the cod and whale fisheries. The leader of these associates was the famous Samuel Champlain, and the association itself was an emigration society as well as a commercial venture. It was just one of those magnificent transatlantic ideals that led astray the imagination of European statesmen, and sinned against the stern practical spirit of colonization. In reality it was a cumbrous piece of feudalism imported into America, and could not be expected to live. The seigniors were a caste in themselves, like the landgraves and cassiques of John Locke's Carolina Constitutions, and obtained their land in the first place by means of Court favouritism. They were not allowed to transfer property unless they paid excessive fines, so as to keep up a landed class. They were given the power of holding judicial courts, and of trying all kinds of offences, murder and treason excepted. It was a picture, somewhat sobered down, of baronial privileges, such as prevailed formerly in England. The censitaires or vassals had to appear before their seigniors without sword or spurs, with bare heads and one knee on the ground. The censitaire was bound to grind his flour at the lord's mill, bake his bread in the lord's oven, give one fish in every eleven, and work for his lord one or more days in the year. It has already been noticed how badly the land system worked in Canada, and how the free flow of capital and emigration was checked, and how indeed the French Government never wished really for any great continental expansion. It was hard to win a freehold, which is a great inducement to all colonists. The best thing to do was to buy out the seigniors at a reasonable figure. This was done, and the value fixed by a commission. Thus the Seigniorial Tenure Act may be regarded as a Landlords Compensation Act, and also a popular enfranchising act, as it set the *habitans* free, who were really not much better than serfs or *villani*, and gave them an opportunity to become freeholders. But that such a system as that of the seigniorial tenure should have commended itself to French statesmen in the beginning of the seventeenth century is certainly instructive. The Jesuit missionaries, who followed in the wake of French colonists and soon went far afield as explorers and geographers, did a great and beneficent work, and the Lake District of Canada became the scene of the labours of the Huron Mission; but the "Viceroyalty of Canada, Acadie, and the adjoining territories" had this inherent defect, viz., that it never attracted a sufficient number of *bonâ-fide* colonists.

It was about the same time that the "Clergy Reserves" question received its final settlement. In Canada all legislation concerning church and schools, religion and education, has, under the circumstances of a mixed population with many creeds, to be carefully framed in the spirit of restraint and moderation. In a certain and very definite sense the sale of the "Clergy Reserves", together with the handing over of the proceeds to the municipalities for the purposes of education, constituted a process of disestablishment, in the sense of undoing what was already done and taking away what was already given as church endowment, although we are reminded by Lord Norton[1] that the real result of the Colonial Act of 1854 was to invest a large portion of a realized fund securely for the Protestant denomina-

[1] *Colonial Policy*, p. 33

tions, and was not a very stringent measure of disendowment. Without raising the question of the policy or impolicy of establishments in a general sense, or discussing the difference between a religion endowed by generations of founders and benefactors and that subsidized and supported by the State for a specific purpose, it is clear that the case of an established church in a new country must be very distinct from a similar establishment in an old, and that it is almost hopeless to argue from one case to the other. Historically speaking, the first church established in Canada was the Roman Catholic, when in obedience to the plans of kings and cardinals the old forms of Church and State were transplanted bodily into the valley of the S. Lawrence. In the charter of "The Hundred Associates" (1627), three priests were "established", in the technical sense, for each settlement, and were endowed with lands. Canada was a colony where two races met and two systems met, and it might be argued, at any rate with a show of justice, that if the Government of France had established a church in Lower Canada in her own way in the seventeenth century, the Government of Great Britain was entitled to do the same thing in Upper Canada in the nineteenth century. However that might be, it was destined that the Protestant Reserves should disappear and a grievance should go, whether it was because Protestants disagreed amongst themselves about "Protestantism", or because they wished to conciliate the Roman Catholics in their midst. In all these questions the population test is a factor in the situation, and it is instructive to realize the proportion of creeds in Canada. According to the census summaries of 1891 we find that the Roman Catholics composed 41·46 per cent of the whole population; Methodists, 17·65 per cent; Presbyterians, 15·73 per cent; Episcopalians, 13·41 per cent; Baptists, 6·33 per cent. It is probable that, forty or fifty years ago, the Roman Catholics constituted a still larger proportion, the Protestant element having been more largely recruited by immigration than the Roman Catholic.

In 1854 a Reciprocity Treaty was concluded between Canada and the United States which lasted till 1864. Canada conceded to the United States free imports of natural products, inshore fisheries of mackerel and herring, and the opening of the S. Lawrence and its canals to their trade. At the same time the Canadians gained many concessions from their neighbours, and their commerce rose from £1,600,000 to £4,400,000. If this policy had been persisted in on both sides it is more than probable that the relations of Canada with the United States would have improved immensely. This Reciprocity Treaty was the first instance of a British Colony negotiating a trade treaty with a foreign power independently of the mother-country, and proves clearly how the old commercial system had broken down in 1854. The United States, in a fit of what appears to be somewhat impulsive legislation, closed the treaty in 1864, hoping to bring Canada on her knees, and to ask, possibly, for the boon of annexation. But their protectionist policy defeated its aim, and only served to throw Canada on her own resources. With the aid of her mercantile marine she built up new markets for herself in the West Indies and also in Brazil. The question of Canadian reciprocity with the United States has received a blow lately by the policy foreshadowed by Sir Wilfrid Laurier; but the question has always created two parties in Canada herself, one of them asserting that such a reciprocity would mean ultimately the peaceful absorption of Canada by the Great Republic; the other denying this political sequel, and maintaining that the interchange of products would mutually benefit all. It is impossible, however, to shut our eyes to the danger which might ensue, commercially, to the British Empire if Canada were bound hand and foot to an American continental policy, which, from the Arctic Ocean to the Gulf of Mexico, would be rigidly protectionist against Great Britain and all the world outside the North American continent.

In 1858 a constitutional crisis arose in Canada, during the governorship of Sir Edmund Head, which indicates in itself how completely different the state of society is in the Colonies from that which is usual in older and more settled countries. It arose from the choice of a capital and of a seat of government. In our Colonies, where the provinces cover a large extent of territory in themselves and are widely separated from one another, the question of the seat of government is really a difficult one to decide. In the Cape Colony, where there existed two provinces only, the eastern and the western, it was always a moot point as to where the seat of government should be, whether at Cape Town, the extreme west corner of the Cape Colony, or at some more central point in the interior. Indeed, the problem is not settled satisfactorily even yet in South Africa. In Canada, in 1858, no fewer than five cities, amongst them Quebec, Toronto, and Montreal, claimed the distinction, but the Queen's choice fell upon Bytown or Ottawa. In a colony more depends upon the choice of a capital and of a seat of government than at first sight appears. As Herman Merivale points out in his *Lectures on Colonisation and Colonies*, one of the worst inherent embarrassments in working a free constitution in thinly-peopled communities, especially where a liberal franchise prevails, is that the power of the few great towns is exorbitant. Their representatives are at once strong in numbers, and, what is more important, always on the spot. Distant sections of the province are virtually disfranchised, and finish by succumbing to the loss of

Growth of Constitutions—Canada. 179

political influence, contented if they are only treated with moderate justice. In the case of Canada, Bytown or Ottawa, occupying a comparatively obscure but at the same time fairly central position, as modes of travelling then existed, was a good choice.

In 1860-1870 Canada was on the eve of greater things. It was, moreover, in Lord Monck's governorship (1861) that, according to Lord Norton, the true influence was found of a constitutional governor. There was practically a dead-lock between the Upper Canadians and the Lower Canadians, and Lord Monck held the balance between the two. The question to be presently before the country was that of a Federal Union of all the provinces. New Brunswick and Nova Scotia could not well hold aloof from the Lake Provinces of Upper and Lower Canada, and, in the nature of things, union or confederation was inevitable.

Before entering upon this entirely new phase of Canadian politics, it may be convenient to recapitulate what had already been achieved. Great principles had been vindicated since 1774, the date of the Quebec Act, and great social and material advantages gained. Let us take the burning question of religion in Canada.

(1) By the Quebec Act it must always be remembered that the Roman Catholic religion in Canada had been freed from all penal restrictions. It was in 1801 that Pitt gave his pledge to King George not to revive the question of Catholic Emancipation, or to carry out his proposals of the previous year. So far, therefore, the cause of Catholic emancipation had advanced more quickly in Canada than at home.

(2) Life and property were secure for all classes in Canada; there was trial by jury, and the right of every subject to the protection of the writ of Habeas Corpus.

(3) To the French Canadians their own laws relating to property and civil rights were preserved, and so the

hand of an alien jurisdiction was laid as lightly as possible upon them. To this day the French civil law prevails in the province of Quebec.

(4) Representative institutions are placed on a sounder footing by the Act of Union in 1840–1841, and from this concession began

(5) The initiation of money grants in the People's House, formerly in the hand of the governor and the Crown.

(6) Provincial control over all local revenue and expenditure.

(7) The beginning and perfecting of municipal institutions, as a corollary of political enfranchisement.

(8) The opening of all the services of the country to colonial men, and the control of the civil list, post-office, &c.

(9) The gradual adoption of the principle of responsibility to the legislature, under which a ministry can only retain office while they have the confidence of the people.

In addition, it may be noted that the abolition of the seigniorial tenure of Lower Canada, and the removal of what may be called feudal and old-world customs, cleared the ground for the enterprise of the French Canadians themselves, and helped them on their way to an independent, free, and self-respecting political life. Further, the position of the judiciary was vastly improved, and the independence of the judges emphasized in every way as an axiom of state. The danger of overriding a judiciary by the haphazard vote of a popular assembly is being illustrated in the Transvaal Republic, where the Grondwet or rule of the constitution is left to the uncertain interpretation of political parties, and does not rest with the judges. Lastly, the Reciprocity Treaty entered into by the Canadian Government with the United States (1854–1864) indicated a new departure in trade principles, the freest possible liberty being given

Growth of Constitutions—Canada.   181

to the Colonies to make their own trade agreements apart from the mother-country.

The confederation of the River and Maritime Provinces of Canada may be regarded as a great triumph of representative government in the country. Lord Norton observed that the progress of events had left but one escape for all the British North American provinces from the fate of absorption into the neighbouring states across the border, and this was confederation. There is no doubt that in many ways the propinquity of the United States hastened on the confederation of Canada. There had been actual war between the two countries in 1812–1814. There had been frontier disputes since then, Fenian scares, the Oregon war-cloud, and threats of annexation for many years. The United Empire Loyalists had parted from the States once and for all in 1783, and were a solid phalanx in themselves, bound to the British Crown. The French Canadians shrank from contact with republican principles, and had an individuality of their own, which was more free under the British Crown. They did not like to be called French, as the German traveller Reisen noted in his *Canada*, but they called themselves Canadians. They were as simple and primitive a folk as Virgil might have painted in his *Georgics*. Their tie with France was broken many years ago. It is estimated that the original settlers never numbered more than 8000 altogether, although they had increased to 65,000 in 1763.[1] They constituted in reality a bit of old France, with its monarchical, orthodox, and religious traditions. With De Tocqueville, who stood on American soil and looked back upon the scenes of republican France with sorrow and pity, reflecting how democracy had overturned some ancient institutions and shaken others to their foundations, the French Canadians would sympathize, if they turned their thoughts to France at

[1] Bryce's *Short History of the Canadian People*, p. 221.

all. There was a great gulf between their past and the modern life of France. If any of their seigniors or priests went from Canada to French seminaries to be taught, they brought back sad, rather than welcome, news of the break-up of society. Union with modern France was out of the question, even if it were practicable at any time. Upon American soil there was nothing very attractive in the Republic on the south to draw them to itself. Under British rule they lived a free life, with their protection guaranteed and their lands and religion preserved to them. Under a federal system they would lose no substantial privilege, and would gain in importance if they looked beyond the present to the future.

The idea of Federalism had long been in the air. In 1849, as we have seen, Roebuck had sketched the lines of a policy in his *Plan of Government*, and if we take Roebuck as an example of English Radicalism of the day, the school was not particularly attached to American institutions. William Cobbett, who had sought an asylum there, on Long Island, was not in love with our "Yankee" cousins. However that may be, there was not discernible in English Radicalism that indifference to the destiny of Canada which was a marked feature of the Goldwin Smith school. Amidst the colonists themselves there was a desire to be united together in a confederacy. It was a policy deserving the careful attention of all serious politicians, and as early as 1827, before Lord Durham's Report, several resolutions were placed before the Legislative Assembly of Upper Canada with a view to combining Upper and Lower Canada. In 1849 the North American League was formed in Toronto on the same lines as Roebuck's suggestions. It may be noted that in 1857 the province of Nova Scotia, which for some time had also taken an interest in the question of the closer union of all the Canadian provinces, addressed themselves to Mr. Labouchere (Lord Taunton), who was then Colonial Secretary, and whose part in the memorable Canadian debates of 1838 may have been remembered. Here was an almost unique opportunity for Lord Taunton to take up the work which Lord Carnarvon so successfully carried through afterwards, but his spirit or inclination was not equal to the occasion. He declined to help forward the cause, thinking that the Imperial Government ought not to interfere in the matter, but should leave it to the spontaneous action of the colonists. This was a cautious, and possibly correct, view, but in the case of Canada, which seems a little different from that of Australasia and South Africa to-day, it may well be doubted if confederation would ever have been carried if individual enthusiasm and individual initiative had been lacking and things had been allowed to go their own way.

The confederation of Canada is one of those events of which, even at the space of thirty years, we cannot judge the full significance. It is great in itself, and it is great in what it promises to lead us to in the future. Looking beyond Canada, the framing of the famous Dominion Act of 1867 appears to serve as a precedent for other developments in other portions of our Colonial Empire. What has been done in Canada may be done, surely, in South Africa and also in Australasia, whether they follow it exactly or not in general principle and in details. Especially in South Africa it is argued by the partisans of a Britannic confederation that if there is opposition there now amongst the Dutch and Boer population to British rule, this may be mollified, and in fact overcome, in the same way and by the same means that French Canadian opposition in the valley of the S. Lawrence was met in 1837 and the following years. Race differences have been proved not to be an insurmountable obstacle in a wide question of confederation; for principles of political and social freedom, once established in their breadth and tolerance, go a long way to obliterate racial feuds and racial distinctions. If the French Canadians refused to sing a "Te Deum" in the valley of the S. Lawrence in 1837, upon the occasion of the Queen's accession, they are willing to join now in 1897 in the universal jubilation of the Empire, upon the occasion of the sixtieth anniversary of her reign. True it may be that there is not, either in South Africa or Australasia, a powerful and possibly inimical neighbour to hurry on and consummate political events, but there may be no less cogent reasons of another description. The States and Colonies themselves may feel the necessity of cohesion in these days of large measures, and of a uniform policy in tariffs and railway policy. It does not pay to have an everlasting battle of rates and routes, as in South Africa. It is a folly to be so independent as to have different gauges for railways. As a standing proof of statesmanship of a far-seeing kind, what is more convincing than that magnificent engineering enterprise—the Canadian Pacific Railway, which has linked all the provinces together with a bond of steel?

The confederation of Canada, or, as it is legally styled, "The British North America Act, 1867", is the fifth change in the history of the Canadian Constitution, and provides that the Dominion of Canada shall be divided into four provinces, viz. (1) Ontario, formerly Upper Canada; (2) Quebec, formerly Lower Canada; (3) Nova Scotia; (4) New Brunswick; the existing limits of each to remain undisturbed. Provision was made for the admission of Newfoundland, Prince Edward Island, British Columbia, Rupert's Land, and the North-West Territory in case of application from the legislatures of these provinces. Manitoba joined in 1870, British Columbia in 1871, and Prince Edward Island in 1873. The history of confederation is, indeed, the history of a vast and far-reaching plan, which engrossed the attention and called forth the energies of some of the best men of the age, and amongst them Sir John Macdonald, that grand figure in recent Canadian politics. Great events were unfolding themselves in Canada, and, as is generally the case throughout the British Empire, men were found worthy of any crisis that might arise. In the destiny of human affairs there is probably no limit assignable in reason to the influence and personality of individual minds once seized with the enthusiasm of a cause and devoted to it with absolute whole-heartedness. Their example is contagious, their zeal is catching, and their words are regarded almost as prophetic. In building up the framework of the United States how much is due to those individuals who, like Alexander Hamilton and the writers in *The Federalist*, sketched the outlines of a wonderful instrument of government! And how much is due to the commanding personality of Washington we all feel and know after the lapse of a hundred years. The task that men do in this case lives after them, and the political task of that administrative kind that binds men together in wide and enduring concert is perhaps the most wonderful human achievement we know. There is room in Greater Britain now for such builders of States.

But it is necessary that they should bring to their task some of the requisite divine afflatus, and not too hard-and-dry a spirit of political economy. How often in the history of the world has the clay been ready for the potter's hand, but the master artificer has not passed that way! How often have ears been strained to catch some perfected expression of what was passing in the minds of all, but the talismanic voice that would make it universal has never come! How often have the hands been ready to strike or work, but the order to do so has never fallen from the lips of a born leader of men! In the British Empire there are many elements, fluid and unstable in themselves, perhaps more elusive than water and more fickle than air, nevertheless, at the right time and at the right moment, they may be called to flow together, as tributaries to one great stream, and they will obey and descend along the channels prepared for them. Chemistry teaches us how the presence of one element, distinct from the others, and of a completely different parentage in the great laboratory of nature, will nevertheless cause them to meet and coagulate in one definite mass. Can no modern Rosicrucian arise and exercise the spell of political transmutation? The life of Sir John Macdonald bids us hope that in this wonderful work of consolidating the British Empire we need not despair of leaders in the colonial world itself.

When Sir John died his body was laid in Canadian soil, like another great worker in the cause of Canadian unity, Charles Powlett Thompson, Baron Sydenham of Kent and Toronto, but it was thought right that there should be a memorial bust erected to his honour in S. Paul's Cathedral. Upon the occasion of the unveiling of this bust by Lord Rosebery, on November 16, 1892, there was a striking demonstration of sympathy. Some willingly gave Macdonald credit for having saved Canada from political absorption into the United States, and this, in the future history of the world, may mean much to England without detracting from the greatness of the United States. Lord Rosebery rose, on this occasion, to a high level of enthusiasm, and the epitaphium was worthy of the dead. In the dark crypt of S. Paul's, in the very heart of that great workshop of London, a link, stronger than iron or steel, like Burke's invisible, yet all-powerful bond, seemed to have been forged. "One by one", said Lord Rosebery, "we are collecting within this cathedral the lares and penates—the household gods—of our commonwealth. Up above them sleep Wellington and Nelson, the lords of war who won the Empire; below here we have the effigies of Dalley and Macdonald, who did so much to preserve it. We have not, indeed, their bodies. They rest more fitly in the regions where they laboured; but here to-day we consecrate their memory and their example. We know nothing of party politics in Canada on this occasion. We only recognize this, that Sir John Macdonald had grasped the central idea that the British Empire is the greatest secular agency for good now known to mankind; that that was the secret of his success, and determined to die under it, and strove that Canada should live under it. It is a custom, I have heard, in the German army, that when new colours are presented to a regiment, the German Emperor first, and then his princes and chiefs in their order, drive a nail into the staff. I have sometimes been reminded of this practice in connection with the banner of our Empire. Elizabeth and her heroes first drove the nails in, and so onward through the expansive eighteenth century, when our flag flashed everywhere, down to our own times, when we have not shrunk or quailed. Yesterday it wrapped the corpse of Tennyson; to-day we drive one more nail in on behalf of Sir John Macdonald. This standard, so richly studded, imposes on us, the survivors, a solemn obligation. It would be nothing if it were the mere symbol of violence and rapine, or even conquest. It is what it is because it represents everywhere Peace, Civilization, Humanity. Let us then to-day, by the shrine of this signal statesman, once more remember our responsibility, and renew the resolution that, come what may, we will not flinch or quail under it." To Lord Rosebery we might say: Utinam semper talis esses!

Appended to this book is a brief sketch of the

Canadian constitution as it is now presented to us for study. In the first place, it closely resembles the British constitution, and is founded on the same system of charters, statutes, conventions, and usages. This constitution was first fixed in its essential features by the Canadian statesmen who met in Quebec in the autumn of 1864, and it derived its sanction as a law from the consent of the Queen, Lords, and Commons. The late Professor Freeman has pointed out that Canada, although very far from being purely English in blood or speech, "is pre-eminently English in the development of its political institutions", and more English than that of the United States. Mr. Bourinot, an acknowledged authority on Canadian constitutional history, goes further than this, and has broadly asserted in a well-known essay, published first in the *Contemporary Review*, that while there is a distinct element in Canada which is not English, it is the influence and operation of English institutions which have, in a large measure, made French Canada one of the most contented communities in the world. The language, the law, and religion of " 'eternal Rome' still remain in all their old influence in the province; but it is, after all, the political constitution, which derives its strength from English principles, that has made this section of Canada a free and self-governing community, and given full scope to its civil and local rights. In its political development French Canada has been, and is, as essentially English as the purely English section of the Dominion."

A marked feature of the Canadian constitution is the Privy Council, which, by sections 11 and 12 of the British North America Act, was established as a power in the country. Its creation is a proof of fidelity to the British model, such an institution being impossible in a republican federal system like that of the United States. Consisting of well-tried and able men of every department in the State, they constitute in themselves an element of stability, and are, moreover, a link with the Crown. On the occasion of the Diamond Jubilee, several of the Colonial representatives and premiers were admitted as members of Her Majesty's Privy Council, a very distinguished honour, and, in the case of Canadian members, following most naturally upon their position as members already of the Canadian Privy Council.

The question of education, considering the component parts of the population of Canada, has been one of the most trying to deal with, but as the religious difficulty was met in the spirit of tolerance and compromise, so has it been with education. The consciences and religious liberties of Protestants and of Roman Catholics in the provinces are specially safeguarded. There is an appeal to the Governor-General in Council from any act or decision of any provincial authority affecting any right or privilege of the Protestant or Roman Catholic *minority* of the Queen's subjects in relation to education. In a colony like Canada secularism was never likely to be popular, at any rate in Lower Canada or amongst the Roman Catholics of any province.

Perhaps the most serious hitch in the working of the "Dominion" Government has arisen from "The Manitoba School Question". In its different stages it has been particularly illustrative (1) of the difficulties of adjusting religious difficulties in a composite population of Protestants and Roman Catholics, (2) of the difficulties incident, from a constitutional point of view, upon the working of the federal and provincial authorities, when the question of sovereignty and the right of veto are tested. The case is as follows. In the province of Manitoba the great majority of the immigrants were Protestants, and an agitation was set on foot to abolish the Roman Catholic separate or denominational schools.

In 1890 the Provincial Legislature of Manitoba passed two Acts, one of them creating a Department of Education and an "Advisory Board", with power to authorize text-books and to prescribe the form of "religious exercises to be used in schools". The other Act, called the Public Schools Act, was framed with a view to establishing a system of public education on a "non-sectarian" basis, no religious exercises being allowed except those conducted according to the regulations of the "Advisory Board". The consequence was that the Roman Catholic minority lost the legal right of collecting money for their separate schools, and were compelled to contribute to the new system, which came under a Department of Education and an Advisory Board. By experience we know in Great Britain itself what a thorny path is that of educational reform, and the question cannot be said to be finally settled even now, and we can easily imagine how many prejudices would be aroused and how many susceptibilities would be wounded in Manitoba. There were the three proverbial courses open to the Roman Catholic minority: (1) they could ask the Dominion to disallow the Act, (2) they could resist the operation of the Act and test the case in the law-courts, (3) they could petition the Dominion Government (the Governor-General in Council) to issue some remedial order.

They determined to test the validity of the acts in the law-courts, and an application was made to the Court of the Queen's Bench of Manitoba, on the ground that the School Acts of 1890 were *ultra vires*, and prejudicially affected a right or privilege the Roman Catholic minority possessed by law or practice at the time of the union. The Manitoba Court refused the application on the ground that the acts in question were *intra vires*, and therefore constitutional. This decision was reversed by the Supreme Court of Canada, and an appeal being made to the Judicial Committee of the Imperial Privy Council, this decision was reversed again and the validity of the Manitoba School Acts of 1890 established.

But the matter did not rest here. The Roman Catholic minority, having failed in this particular course, appealed to the Governor-General in Council, in November, 1892. The case was again taken before the Supreme Court of Canada, and, finally, before the Judicial Committee of the Imperial Privy Council, and judgment was delivered in January, 1895. This judgment dealt with every conceivable aspect of the case, and unanimously sustained the contentions made on behalf of the Roman Catholic minority. Finally, a "Remedial Order" was despatched to the Manitoba Provincial Legislature requesting them to supplement the educational legislation of 1890 by such act or acts as might be necessary to restore to the Roman Catholic minority certain rights and privileges connected with the establishment of separate schools. The Provincial Government sent an answer practically refusing to obey the order, and the Dominion Government decided to enter into further correspondence with the Manitoba Executive. An appeal to Rome has elicited from the Pope a harmless opinion in support of the principle of religion being recognized as part of the natural curriculum of education. But the question can hardly be said to be finally set at rest. The appeal to Rome, curiously enough, was made by the Liberal wing of the Roman Catholic party, who thus proved that they came into conflict with their own hierarchy, who seemed to be too zealous. But can Rome, under these circumstances, be a successful moderating power?

Another collision which threatened to be serious arose between the Province of Manitoba and the Dominion authority on the subject of railway extension. The Provincial Legislature were desirous of developing their local trade by means of a railway run to the United

States border in spite of the monopoly of the Canadian Pacific Railway. This railway, in its general character, was an exceptional undertaking, requiring exceptional support and exceptional privileges, otherwise it would never have been constructed. As a national work of the utmost importance it was upheld in its privileges by the Dominion Government, and the Manitoba Railway Acts were vetoed again and again. As the Manitoba Legislature re-enacted them, the Dominion Government had to give the Canadian Pacific Railway certain privileges in consideration of its consent to remove these restrictions which were objected to by the Manitoba Provincial Government. It will be seen, therefore, that Manitoba has, so far, tested severely the power of the federal tie that links all the provinces together, but so far this tie remains unbroken.

Chapter VIII.

The Growth of Colonial Constitutions—Australasia.

In the history of our Colonial constitutions, as worked out and finally elaborated in Australasia and South Africa, it may be truly said that Canada afforded the true guide and example. Before any of the Australian and Cape settlements were really in a position to don the *toga virilis*, the great principles of Colonial emancipation and Colonial government had practically been conceded. The Canadian field of politics attracts, if it does not entirely engross, the attention of all students of Colonial life as an arena where, once for all, great issues were decided. If it occupies almost an inordinate space, this is no more than its due, and the eye rests

Growth of Constitutions—Australasia.

upon its various crises as it may, to compare small with great, upon one of Creasy's decisive battles of the world. It is the encounters of the giants in Canada, and, although it may not be quite true to say that at the Cape and Australia it is the fight of the pigmies, still the nature of the contest was infinitely less bitter and obstinate, the home Government being often more willing to bestow constitutions of a liberal type than to withhold them.

The seven Colonies of Australasia provide us with a sevenfold picture of Colonial development, and also of Colonial constitutional history, and it is impossible here to do much more than to indicate certain general features of the whole movement, and mark certain transitional periods. Broadly speaking, it might be useful to remember that the penal colonies are somewhat different, by virtue of their peculiar circumstances, from the rest, as we shall see, and that New Zealand has a history of its own which is insular in its peculiarities. For the 1200 miles of the Tasman Sea that roll between it and the great island-continent of Australia have been enough to give it a very distinct development. Amongst the Australian Colonies, New South Wales, as the radiating centre of all British administration in the early days, naturally arrests our attention first of all. A brief recapitulation of the stages of its constitutional growth may give us a general idea of the kind of growth that took place, with more or less variation, in the rest of the Colonies.

(1) First, there was the necessary rule of autocratic governors from the day when Captain Phillip landed with his batch of convicts in 1788. (2) No change took place till 1824, when, in the governorship of Sir Thomas Brisbane, the first Legislative Council, consisting of six gentlemen, was appointed to advise the governor, amongst them John Macarthur, the founder of the wool

industry and one of the greatest benefactors of Australia. Four more members were added by Governor Darling, and additions were made from time to time, so that the governor had at his elbow the men best qualified to advise him in all Colonial affairs. Proceedings were, however, conducted in private until 6th June, 1838, when the public and the press were first admitted. (3) From 1824-1842 the members of this council were all nominated by the governor, but in that year the principle of election was adopted, six being elected and six nominated. This composite council was therefore partly official and partly non-official. (4) This representation, however, did not keep pace with the wants of the Colony. In 1842 New South Wales received a constitution by the 5, 6 Vict., 76, which widened its first government, and although representative to some extent, it was evidently an introduction only to fuller privileges and not to responsible government. It consisted of a Legislative Council of 36 members, one-third of them nominated by the governor and two-thirds elected by the people. To this stage of freedom of government to which New South Wales had arrived, it was proposed, by the act of 1850, to admit Van Diemen's Land, South Australia, Victoria, and Western Australia, with *power to reform themselves*. This in due course of time led to complete self-government or responsible government,—the fifth stage of constitutional progress. But before this was finally adopted, it may be instructive to allude briefly to some of the public discussions of the whole subject in the British House of Commons and elsewhere. For just at this particular turning-point there was a great deal to be cleared up, and much to be considered.

The attitude of Lord John Russell in the historic Colonial manifesto of February, 1850, in the House of Commons, is far more advanced than his position in March, 1837, when he introduced his ten resolutions on the Canadian crisis alluded to above (chapter vi.), calling down upon himself the vehement expostulations of Roebuck, Hume, and Leader, and the milder remonstrances of Labouchere and Lord Howick. Practically, Lord Russell, although he did it "with reluctance", refused to consider the case of the Canadians in 1837, and to satisfy their claim to self-government. Very different is Lord Russell's position in 1850. After a review of our Colonial history from the days of the Stuarts, and after alluding to the proposition of parting from our Colonies only to dismiss it, he comes to the question of the mode of governing the Colonies. "I think", he said, "that, as a rule, we cannot do better than refer to those maxims of policy by which our ancestors were guided. It appears to me that in providing that wherever Englishmen went they should enjoy English freedom and have English institutions, they acted justly and wisely—they adopted a course which enabled those who went out to distant possessions to sow the seed of communities of which England may always be proud."[1] There lay before the House a declaration of Colonial Policy, signed by 13 or 14 members of parliament and 3 or 4 peers, asking for Colonial and Australian emancipation. Lord Russell said that this declaration was not unlike his own programme. Indeed, it had been actually carried out "in respect to Canada, Nova Scotia, New Brunswick". Lord John quoted a conversation which he had many years ago with Baldwin on Canadian reform, and the result was that he found himself in no great disagreement with this Canadian reformer. In the "fifties" of this century Lord Russell, therefore, had a very open mind about the question of Australian reform, and certainly, as far as professions went, could not well say more.

His Australian Bill, which he introduced on this

[1] Hansard, Feb. 8, 1850.

occasion, is a movement forward, and indicates a departure of an original type. "We do not intend", he said, "to go on the principle of having a council and assembly, as hitherto, in imitation of the government of this country, . . . but we propose that there should be but one council, a council of which two-thirds should be formed of the representatives of the people, and one-third nominated by the governor, . . . but when we propose this form of government, I should add that we propose to give the colonists the power of altering their own constitution, and that if they should prefer government by Legislative Council and Assembly, there would be no difficulty on the part of the Crown." The choice lay between the bi-cameral and uni-cameral form of government. It was proposed also that the popular element should be introduced into Van Diemen's Land upon the same principle, and that in South Australia similar changes should be made. There were suggestions, also, that on the proposition of two of the Colonies there should be an assembly of the different Australian Colonies to frame the same tariff for all, and to deal with the waste lands. It was proposed also to separate the Port Phillip district from New South Wales. "I have stated enough", said Lord Russell, "to show that both in the North American Colonies and in the Australian Colonies it is our disposition to introduce representative institutions, give full scope to the will of the people of these Colonies, and thereby enable them to work their way to their own prosperity, far better than if they were controlled and regulated by ordinances that went from this country."

Lord Russell's resolutions were: (1) that provision be made for the better government of Her Majesty's Australian Colonies; (2) that the governors and Legislative Councils of H.M. Australian Colonies be authorized to levy duties of customs on goods, wares, and merchandise imported into such Colonies. Sir William Molesworth, in a speech made upon the occasion, criticised severely the methods of the Colonial Office, where heads "changed so often", and were "generally misinformed". But he reserved his heaviest artillery for the nominee system in the government, which was incongruous. Mr. Lowe (Lord Sherbrooke), who had been an Australian colonist and politician himself, was strongly opposed, as we have already pointed out, to the nominee system in Colonial politics as a disturbing and embarrassing factor. In Australia itself it appears that, however admirable the spirit of Lord Russell's speech and correct the sentiments expressed, in February, 1850, they were not regarded as equivalent to a full instalment of practical wants. William Charles Wentworth, who, in the words of Sir Henry Parkes,[1] had been "saturated with Lord Durham's report on the constitutional grievances of Canada, and stimulated to activity by his intercourse with liberal-minded men at home", moved, on May 1, 1851, more than a year after Lord Russell's manifesto of Colonial policy, a declaration and remonstrance, considered by Sir Henry Parkes as one of the foundation-stones of the fabric of Australian constitutional liberties. Many of the complaints have a striking family likeness to those of the Canadian protests. They turned upon the administration of the waste lands, the civil list, the territorial revenues, and the employment of Colonial-born men in public offices. They ran as follows:—

"We, the Legislative Council of New South Wales, do hereby solemnly protest, insist, and declare as follows:—

"1. That the Imperial Government has not, nor of right ought to have, any power to tax the people of this Colony, or to appropriate any of the monies levied by the authority of the Colonial Legislature; that that power

[1] *Fifty Years of Australian History*, vol. i. p. 29.

can only lawfully be exercised by the Colonial Legislature; and that the Imperial Parliament has solemnly disclaimed that power by 18 George III., cap. 12, sec. 1, which act remains unrepealed.

"2. That the revenue arising from the public lands, derived as it is *mainly* from the value imparted to them by the labour and capital of the people of this Colony, is as much their property as the ordinary revenue, and ought, therefore, to be subject only to the like control and appropriation.

"3. That the customs and all other departments should be subject to the direct supervision and control of the Colonial Legislature: which should have the appropriation of the gross revenues of the Colony, from whatever source arising; and as a necessary incidence to this authority, the regulation of the salaries of all Colonial officers.

"4. That offices of trust and emolument should be conferred only on the settled inhabitants, the office of governor alone excepted; that this officer should be appointed and paid by the Crown; and that the whole patronage of the Colony should be vested in him and the executive council, unfettered by instructions from the Minister of the Colonies.

"5. That plenary powers of legislation should be conferred upon and exercised by the Colonial Legislature for the time being; and that no bills should be reserved for the significance of Her Majesty's pleasure, unless they affect the prerogative of the Crown or the general interests of the Empire."

It will be remembered that in Canada one of the sources of irritation was that Crown nominees were paid partly out of territorial revenue, and that patronage was confined too much to the "family compact" and a small governing clique. All this was remedied as early as 1839, when Lord Russell, in his instructions to Powlett

Thompson, had promised the throwing open of offices of public trust to men of Colonial birth (chapter vii.). With regard to the question of imperial taxation, raised by Wentworth, his theory apparently would be that for the Imperial Government to levy revenue, even from sales of crown lands, was unfair to the colonists. This is a different question from raising revenue at the ports, and in this case Wentworth was surely somewhat in advance of the times in claiming for the comparatively small population of New South Wales the fee-simple of enormous portions of Australia.

For there was the very important question of *how* society was constituted in New South Wales in the early days. From the very beginning the convict question was always hindering the cause of constitutional progress in this and other colonies. Wentworth himself must have known and felt it, as he and Lowe had been selected in New South Wales as the champions of anti-transportation. In Tasmania, which had originally received the sweepings of New South Wales, there existed a distinct cleavage of society, even to a greater extent than in any other colony. "Was it not enough", asked the free settlers of Tasmania, "to send out the felons of Great Britain to become Tasmanian bushrangers, without asking us to feed and clothe them after the completion of their sentences?" Lord Stanley answered that Tasmania always had been a convict settlement; but that did not clear the ground very much. Then "The Patriotic Six" of Tasmania sprang into existence, with the programme of "No Convicts for Tasmania". However much sympathy we may feel inclined to give to all anti-transportation men, struggling for purification of their civil life, it is impossible at the same time to ignore the fact that a convict colony was rather an unfavourable seed-plot for sudden and complete gifts of enfranchisement. Lord Russell, in his proposal of a one-third crown nomination in his Australia one-chamber system, showed a not unreasonable distrust of the convict element, and wished to reserve a good deal of direct control. The best sort of colonists probably felt all this, and knew that when they were asking for self-government they ought to wipe out their stain first. Sir Henry Parkes wrote a protest against the landing of convicts from a ship called *Hashemy* (June, 1849), and an Anti-Transportation League, formed in 1850 at Sydney, united the Colonies (except Western Australia) in the work of constitutional resistance, and finally led to the abolition of the convict system. We shall see that in South Africa there is a similar crisis, with a similar result, viz., that the colonists had their way after having shown the most unmistakable bias of their minds. One of the most remarkable features of the whole struggle is the slowness of perception shown by the official mind at home. In his Colonial manifesto of February 8, 1850, Lord Russell simply observed that with regard to transportation he "had no great leaning towards it", and after alluding to the feeling at the Cape as one which he "highly commended in itself", thought it founded on "exaggerated apprehensions". To use his own words, transportation was not a question that pressed immediately, but emigration did. The colonists thought differently; so did statesmen like Sir Charles Adderley (Lord Norton).

A short review, however, of the convict system will explain its importance, and perhaps show how all progress in constitutional reform rested upon its proper solution. To plant a convict colony in a country like Australia was to plant the seed of inevitable discord. A prison colony might have been carried out according to the original plan on the Bermudas or some island where, by the decree of nature, the settlement was confined to the geographical limits of an island. But when any other kind of life is suffered alongside of the prison colony, the tendency will always be on the part of the free part of the population towards self-purgation. Indeed, it was perfectly clear that a colony which was only a convict station, represented under the most liberal conditions a state of supervision and nonage. Whilst the stigma lasted there could be no political freedom and no civic enfranchisement. The mixed communities of free men, ticket-of-leave men, half-indentured men, and the worst kind of criminals as well, were most difficult to rule, and particularly troublesome to the governor. Upon the great question of convictism in our Colonies it is necessary to consider what was the popular and official opinion at home. In 1841 Earl Grey pointed out that the House of Commons —which, by the way, was a reformed House of Commons—had declared its objection by a formal vote against the retention in Great Britain of any large proportion of the offenders sentenced to transportation. A similar opinion was expressed in 1847 by a Select Committee of the House of Lords. Transportation, therefore, seemed to both Houses to be the principal secondary punishment known to the law. The Select Committee of the House of Lords, on the motion of Lord Brougham, had based its conclusions upon the evidence of judges and of "persons most experienced in the administration of the criminal law and in the charge of convicts". There were a great many specious arguments to prove that transportation was a beneficial process both for the mother-country and the colonies, especially under certain conditions and modifications.

To begin with, there was the economical argument. The first expense of transportation per head was reckoned at about £30, but this was the beginning and end of it. Mr. Cunninghame, in his *Letters from New South Wales* (1827), put the whole case thus: " Every rogue whom you retain at home to labour takes the bread out of the mouth of the honest man; as long, therefore, as England cannot keep her honest poor, so long will it be her interest to turn all her roguish poor out from her bosom to work and thrive elsewhere". In 1828 there were upwards of 4000 convicts on board the hulks, employed in the dockyards and other public works, at an annual expense of £60,000; the whole of whom would be turned loose on society in seven years. If these 4000 rogues took the bread out of the mouths of 4000 honest poor, another £60,000 would require to be spent, if not more, on this army of unemployed. Local and parish rates would go up indefinitely. To send the rogues out to New South Wales would cost twice £60,000, but then all further expenses would be saved. Abroad, and especially in France, where the " French Imperial Institute " watched British colonization narrowly, this New South Wales experiment was watched with the keenest interest.

From the ethical point of view, there was the attractive picture of men and women turning over a new leaf in a new country. Granted that an offender had served much of his time at Pentonville, could he not go out to Australia as a ticket-of-leave man, and with new opportunities and with fewer temptations build up a better fortune for himself? In the Colonies themselves a large number of the settlers who were anxious to employ labour were glad to receive " expirees " from Tasmania, men of the worst stamp very often, and ticket-of-leave men from home. Earl Grey (1846) was quite convinced that when New South Wales refused to take convicts there was a large minority of the most enterprising and most intelligent members of society in favour of receiving them. Personally, he thought that the Colonies were unwise not to avail themselves of the labour supply thus given to them. It is curious that so little was thought of the moral aspects of the whole question. Yet it was not for want of better knowledge.

The weaknesses of the whole system of colonization by transportation have been exposed in parliamentary committee, in pamphlets, in books, and by every kind of argument, but it is strange to note how long the fallacies of it survived. Briefly, no one could or would understand that crime ought to be treated on a scientific as well as a moral basis. Indiscriminate punishment does as much harm as indiscriminate charity. The punishment of transportation, as it was carried out, might be either too great or too little for the individual offender. It was far too clumsy and cruel to tear a man from his home, perhaps a bread-winner of the family, upon a first conviction for a simple larceny, and thrust him amongst the worst class of criminals. There was no regular principle of segregation by means of which those who were convicted of minor delinquencies could be separated from others, at any rate for a long time, and so all the evils incident upon contamination with crime were preserved by the system itself. What prisons were in England we may realize from our novelists and writers. Far too much was made of the possible benefit to be derived from change of circumstances and of surroundings, and very plausible were all the arguments. But moralists know that, as a matter of fact, nothing is more true than the old Latin saying, "Coelum non animum mutant qui trans mare currunt". The future of a man lies in his previous training and disposition, and if he is inclined to be idle, profligate, and thriftless at home, he will be the same abroad. And Colonial life, in the beginning, requires especial patience and restraint, and temperance on its industrial sides. Those who wish to obtain the riches of the

Indies must take the riches of the Indies with them, which will be a more or less trained mind, faculties for observation, readiness of resource, and a practical wit. When Governor Phillip landed his convicts at Port Jackson, it was discovered that, as soon as the land was cleared and made ready for ploughing, few convicts of the large number transported knew anything about farming.

It is more than doubtful whether transportation acted as a real deterrent of crime. It was stated once to a police committee by the ordinary of Newgate that the generality of those transported consider it as a party of pleasure and rejoice in it. "I have heard them," he said, "when the sentence of transportation has been passed by the recorder, give thanks for it, and seem overjoyed at their sentence."[1] Sydney Smith, in one of his smart essays, wrote that "no felon will hear a verdict of 'not guilty', without considering himself cut off from the fairest career of prosperity"; and elsewhere, "the chances of escape from labour and of manumission in the Bay are accurately reported and perfectly understood in the flash-houses of S. Giles, and while Earl Bathurst is full of jokes and joy, public morals are sapped to their foundation". The Dean summed up Botany Bay as follows: "If considered as a place of reform for criminals, its distance, expense, and the society to which it dooms the objects of the experiment are inseparable objections to it".

Justin M'Carthy has reminded us that in 1837 a Committee of the House of Commons was appointed to consider and report upon the convict system. Lord John Russell, Sir Robert Peel, Charles Buller, Sir W. Molesworth, Lord Howick (Earl Grey), being members of it. The evidence they procured "settled the question in the minds of all thinking men". The Rev. W. Clay, son of

[1] *Quarterly Review*, December, 1820.

the famous prison chaplain, says in his memoir of his father, that probably no volume was ever published in England more loathsome than that of the appendix to the committee's report. After this it is somewhat wonderful that Lord Russell, as one of the Select Committee, did not see the depth of the evil, and express himself even more strongly in favour of the Cape Colonists when they decided, once and for all, to have nothing to do with convictism. Lord Russell often spoke fair on these Colonial questions, but when it came to action he often drew back, and proved that he could not go to the length of his spoken opinions.

When Earl Grey proposed to remedy matters by assisting free emigrants out to the Australian Colonies, he was simply providing the material for resistance to the whole theory of penal colonies. In course of time each free emigrant was bound to come into collision with the system itself. It was part of his civil, moral, and indeed his constitutional life to do so. For a time there was an *impasse* at home; but the true remedy for the whole convict system was to be found in better prison discipline at home, in the institution of reformatories, in the Discharged Prisoners' Aid Societies, and in the influence of an improved popular education. It is worth noting that the colonists of Great Britain, in compelling the reformation and cleansing of their own society, forced the statesmen of Great Britain to make certain great and well-known reformations at home, and a protest based originally upon the theory of the dignity and self-respect of Colonial life ended by helping, indirectly, to raise the conceptions of mistaken political economists at home.

It is clear that the agitation of the colonists against the convict system meant more than appeared on the surface, and was never clearly understood. In the constitutional history of Australia the movement was really the first step towards the attainment of self-government. Free citizens of Great Britain could not endure to be ranked as *déclassés* as soon as they had set foot on Australian soil. In a convict station of the strict and orthodox type the principles of the "Magna Carta", the "Bill of Rights", and even the dearly-bought privileges of the "Habeas Corpus" and "Trial by Jury" seemed to be lost sight of in the presence of the military governor and his officers. Between martial law on the one hand and fully-conceded liberties on the other there seemed to be no possible halting-place where the two systems might meet and the two opposing principles might be harmonized. A constitutional governor of the Canadian type, like Lord Elgin or Lord Monck, could not grow out of the surroundings of a convict settlement. Here was the deadlock of the whole political situation.

The way, however, to full representative and responsible government in Australia was paved not only by the change of public opinion at home on the whole subject of colonization, but especially by the influx of miners and the growth of the gold industry. When Hargreaves claimed £1000 from the New South Wales Government as the reward for the discovery of a gold-mine, Deas Thompson, a Victorian colonist, said to him, "If what you say is correct, Mr. Hargreaves, we have got a goldfield. It will stop emigration to California, and settle the convict question", and, he might have added, solve our constitutional difficulties. Not that the miners were always model franchise-holders themselves, as they needed martial law, as we have seen when they proclaimed the "Republic of Victoria". The diggers were almost as embarrassing a factor to begin with as the convicts. Nevertheless, with the acquisition of property and generally improved state of trade everywhere—for the public revenue of the Colony of Victoria alone was twelve times greater in 1853 than in 1850, before the discovery of gold took place—a new epoch was destined to arrive. That great problem which had puzzled Gibbon Wakefield and his school, viz. how to bring capital into a colony, was solved by the discovery of mineral wealth in the Australasian Colonies themselves. The general question also of the disposal of Crown lands was approached more easily, now that, instead of a few feeble centres of colonization, there were many to consider. If it was unreasonable that a few thousands of colonists should ask for the fee-simple of a vast domain of Colonial territory for themselves alone, the case was altered when the great tide of free emigration swept over and invaded Australia. There was no longer any doubt that the Australian colonists would ultimately hold the whole of the continent as their own.

Responsible government came to New South Wales in 1856 with a nominated upper house, called the Legislative Council, and a Legislative Assembly. The first Australian Parliament was opened at Sydney by Sir William Denison on May 22, 1856. Upon the 21st November, 1856, the first Victorian Parliament was opened under responsible government, consisting of two houses, the Legislative Council and Legislative Assembly, both elected, thus differing from the New South Wales Legislature, in which the Council was nominated. On 2nd December, 1856, Tasmania opened her first Parliament with two houses, the Legislative Council and Assembly, both elected. On 22nd April, 1857, South Australia followed suit with a Council and an Assembly, both elected; and Queensland came next with a Legislative Council nominated by the Governor, and a Legislative Assembly elected by the people. The first Parliament was opened at Brisbane on the 29th of May, 1860. Western Australia was the last of the group to enjoy the privilege of responsible government, and this did not come until the end of 1890, owing to exceptional causes. However, between 1856 and 1860 all the principal Australian Colonies were in harmony as to the general outlines of their government on the bi-cameral principle.

The two-chambered system was not, however, adopted without some questionings in official quarters. In 1850 Lord Russell distinctly stated in the House of Commons[1] that the new constitutions for the Australian Colonies were "not to be on the principle of having a Council and Assembly as hitherto, in imitation of the Government of Great Britain". It was proposed that there should be but one Council in all the Colonies, of which two-thirds should be formed of representatives elected by the people, and one-third nominated by the Governor. The revolution that underlay this new maxim of Colonial government was really very great. In the celebrated Canada Bill of 1791 the idea was, as we have seen, to reproduce the main features of the British constitution with its various balances of power, the King being represented by the Governor and an Executive Council, the House of Lords by a Legislative Council named by the Crown for life, and the House of Commons by an Assembly of the representatives of the people. By the single-chamber system this time-honoured division of government disappeared, and with it the check upon hasty and impulsive legislation. The kind of arrangement proposed by Lord Russell may be roughly imagined by supposing the House of Commons and the House of Lords sitting in the same chamber, and voting together on the same questions, the only difference being that the Lords were nominated by the Crown instead of being elected by the popular vote, and that they comprised one-third of the whole Assembly. A composite chamber sounds an anomaly in British ears, but it was thought that it might work

[1] Hansard, Feb. 8, 1850.

in the Colonies. Earl Grey was in favour of this composite single chamber, as considerable advantages, he thought, would arise from the presence in the Legislature of a certain proportion of members who did not owe their seats to popular election, but, being only one-third of the body, could never prevent the passing of measures which were strongly supported by public opinion, but only secure their being fully discussed. The mistaken demands of an excited and ill-informed popular feeling might also be carefully reconsidered, and the proper check placed upon too zealous reform.[1] The idea that it was possible to find within the walls of a single chamber a self-righting balance and a wholesome leaven of administrative caution continued to be a lasting one with Earl Grey. In a letter to Sir Henry Parkes, dated May 4, 1874, he adhered to his opinion that the single chamber given to New South Wales in 1842, partly elected and partly nominated, was better than that which was substituted for it a few years later. To restore it was, of course, impossible, and he only referred to it in order to point out that it deserved to be considered whether the principle on which it was founded might not be adopted to the extent of dispensing with the second branch of the Legislature, *i.e.* the Legislative Council, and of introducing into the Assembly a limited number of members who should not owe their seats to popular election. These might be selected by the Assembly itself, and might hold their seats for life, or till they resigned them. By this arrangement the ablest and most experienced men of different political parties would obtain seats in the Assembly, and, holding them for life, would be able to act with independence. The want of a stable element of this kind, he added, has been much felt in the House of Commons since the Reform Bill of 1832, and even to

[1] Adderley's *Colonial Policy*, p. 101.

a greater extent since the 1867 Reform Act. The rotten boroughs, faulty as that system was, provided an avenue which enabled some of the best men to enter Parliament on a system of virtual nomination.

Sir Henry Parkes[1] gave it as his deliberate opinion that if a constitutional controlling force were wanted, it was best to have it in a second chamber rather than in a second class of legislators in a single chamber. A single legislative chamber, composed of different classes of members, would be "distracted by inherent antagonism peculiar to its formation, and the work of its hands would be often more perverse and ill-considered than would be that of a single chamber on a level elective basis". Lowe gave it as his decided opinion, as we have seen, that the nominee system would never do in the Colonies, and from his experience at home and in the Colonies he was supposed to take the place of an *amicus curiæ*. When, however, the question of the form of their constitution was put before the Australian Colonies, they preferred, in 1850–1856, the two-chamber system. Lowe revealed his own opinion on the general crisis thus in 1850. Speaking in the House of Commons on the 12th March, 1855,[2] he said that it had been the pleasure of the House of Commons to delegate to the Australian Colonies, unversed as three out of four of them were in the ordinary functions of self-government, the powers of forming their own constitutions. This was premature, and likely to work mischief. Further, the home Government had expressed a wish for some form of the nominee system. If there were to be two chambers in the Colonies, the Secretary of State had addressed a despatch to the Governor-general that the Upper House should be nominated by the Crown. Indeed he had gone so far as to say that he would give the

[1] *Fifty Years of Australian History*, vol. i. p. 320.
[2] Hansard Reports.

Colonial Legislature absolute dominion over the waste lands of their Colonies if they would consent to the Upper House being nominated. Lowe was perfectly right in objecting to the bribe and to the way it was put, for if it was deemed advisable, as he himself thought it was, that the colonists should have their waste lands, they ought to have them, but not on such conditions. What, however, is most instructive about Lowe's remarks in 1855 is the opinion emphatically expressed by him, that the home Government, instead of being behindhand with constitutional reform, actually precipitated it with undue haste. In New South Wales itself, when the question of the form of their constitution was before the colonists, and a select committee were taking in hand the draft of a new constitution, it was advised that the form of government should be based on the analogies of the British constitution. The committee stated that they had no desire to hazard the experiment of an upper house on a general elective franchise. Curiously enough, William Charles Wentworth and his friends went back to the Imperial Act 31 Geo. III., cap. 31, for authorizing the Crown to confer hereditary titles of honour, rank, or dignity, and to annex thereto a hereditary right of being summoned to the Legislative Council. These colonists were *Angliores Anglis*, and went back rather boldly to the days of Pitt and the spirit of the Canada Bill of 1791. "Why, if titles are open to all at home, should they be denied to colonists?" asked Wentworth. "Why should such an institution as the House of Lords (which is an integral part of the British constitution) be shut out from us?" Wentworth demanded the privilege for every class that had the energy to aspire to rank and honour. Sir Henry Parkes has put the other side in his letter to Earl Grey,[1] when he said that the radical misconception in the efforts to construct a second chamber in the

[1] *Fifty Years of Australian History*, vol. i. p. 320.

Colonies had been in the supposition that it was possible to create any kind of chamber like the House of Lords. This was impossible, and the idea had to be given up before a healthy conception of the work could be formed. Earl Grey was opposed himself to Wentworth's idea of a Colonial aristocracy, although he wished at the same time to thrust an intrusive wedge into the Australian constitutions by means of his nominated members in the Assemblies themselves, who would certainly have been as impracticable as a Colonial aristocracy. The position and functions of the Legislative Councils in Australia may still be said to be a burning question of Australian politics. As recently as December 11, 1897, the Premier of New South Wales denounced the Legislative Council, accusing that body of being influenced by class and personal motives in rejecting taxation bills. A nominated Council had, he said, become impossible, and the Assembly will set to work and reform the Council. Similar blocks have occurred before, and the Council has survived. Still, it is unsatisfactory that, under the bi-cameral system in Australia, no proper *modus vivendi* has yet been reached between the two chambers. In Melbourne it is now proposed to extend the suffrage for the Council to every male and female householder, in a bill described by the Premier (Dec. 13, 1897) as the most democratic measure ever proposed in Australia. The usual method has been to elect the members of the Legislative Council on the basis of a higher franchise than members of the Legislative Assembly.

The "House of Lords" bogey has long since been scared from the Colonies, together with all visions of hereditary titles, and of an hereditary chamber, but there has always been a latent fear in the Colonial mind that, like the Trojan horse with its armed warriors, the Council might enter the stronghold of the constitution and carry it away captive. The palladium of Colonial liberties is lodged more securely than to be the prize of any party in the state. Sometimes the Council has been used by the ministers of the day to further their own ends, and to carry out their own particular policy, if it is a burning one, such as protection. Sometimes the Council has stood between the Assembly and the people on a question of right and privilege, and has been of real constitutional service. It is not yet decided, so as to be an axiom of state, whether the Legislative Council stands best on an elective or a nominated basis, or whether it should be for a term of years or for life, or whether a system of retirement by rotation is best. Governor Weld, himself a New Zealand colonist, expressed an opinion once that nomination for life for councillors was the best method to be employed in choosing the Upper House. Whatever it is, whether nominated or elected, whether existing for a term of years or for the lives of those chosen, it is clear that the function of the House cannot be honourably fulfilled if they are to be simply those of a body registering the decrees of the Assembly. In Canada there is greater political stability under the circumstances of a confederated dominion, and it may happen that if the Australian Colonies confederate also, the federal government will be bi-cameral, and the provincial or states government will be uni-cameral. The legislative councils may disappear from the states or provinces, but their material, which is, after all, what is wanted, may reappear in the Senate of the Dominion or Commonwealth of the South.

In New Zealand the constitutional struggle assumed a slightly different phase owing to the continued presence there of the native question. Maori members sit now in the House of Representatives, elected by the natives themselves, but forty or fifty years ago it was a very different state of things. It was an axiom with Earl Grey that the Maori question must necessarily stand in the way of representative government in New Zealand, as it was impossible to give the colonists the full control of the native policy; and representative government, unless it led to a fully responsible government in all questions, including the natives, was only half a gift. According to the official theory there was always bound to be an *imperium in imperio*, just as it was at the Cape of Good Hope and along the Kaffrarian borders. In both colonies the military difficulty came first, as the Kaffirs and Maoris were amongst the bravest and best of all savages with whom the British have been brought into contact. Such savages have refused to die out, and have ended by being incorporated in the Empire, the South African, however, surviving better than the New Zealander. With these races the conflict was long, difficult, and sometimes very sanguinary, and on points of military strategy the advice of the Duke of Wellington was sought. "Construct military roads", was in brief his answer, whether through the Amatola Forest in Cape Colony or in the fastnesses of New Zealand; and it is certainly true that it is the civil engineer who, in the everlasting conflict between barbarism and civilization, holds the key. Whether in a march upon Coomassie, or in an expedition against the Kaffir hordes, or upon the Matabele, or in the campaigns against the New Zealanders, the question of a road or a line of communication is the first consideration. However, whether in South Africa or New Zealand, especially with the command of the coast-line, which made flanking movements possible on occasions, there could be but one end to the struggle.

In our present study the conflict is interesting, so far as it shows the incidence of responsibility and the burden of expenses. At one time the New Zealand disturbances had been made the ground for increasing the Queen's troops to 7000, to say nothing of the naval aid and contributions to local volunteers and military pensioners. The colonists were induced to pay, for five years, the acknowledgment of £5 per head on the Queen's troops employed for their service, on the condition, however, that we were to remit the capitation fund so raised up to the amount of £50,000 a year to them to be expended on native improvement. Up to 1861 the Duke of Newcastle maintained that "colonists in general should only pay for their police, and should be spared the task of defending themselves against foreigners and formidable tribes on their borders, but that no fixed rules could be laid down on the subject, as some colonies were poorer than others". Lord Grey endorsed this theory,[1] arguing that the home Government should keep both power and responsibility in their own hands, and protect the natives from extermination. As a criticism upon this policy Lord Norton has observed that to relieve the colonists of responsibility and allow them to revel in disturbance, aggravated by our aid and to be settled at our cost, was a policy which brings as much mischief as possible to all three parties concerned, viz. the home Government, the colonists, and the Maoris themselves. At the end of the New Zealand disturbances there was always an unseemly quarrel as to the exact share of expense to be allotted to the home and colonial authorities. The home government raised the cry of selfishness against the New Zealand colonists, and the colonists retorted with the cry of mismanagement and needless expenditure. At one time the war charges were, for the colonists, £120,000 a month, for England, £240,000; and it was clear that war might be a profitable game to play for contractors and for colonists in want of relief from losses sustained in war. It was in 1863 that "Native Affairs" were all handed over to the colonists by the Imperial

[1] Hansard, June 24, 1862.

Government. With the establishment of full colonial responsibilities over every state department, native or otherwise, in New Zealand the war-clouds rolled away. The colony was growing, colonists were becoming more prosperous, gold was discovered in New Zealand, and, further, on the moral side, a distinct advance was made in the views of the duties and obligations of the white colonists towards the Maoris. The old wild random days of bush warfare were over, the back of native rebellion was broken, and educational agencies were at work. Sir George Grey, a governor well known both in South Africa and New Zealand for his native policy, had set on foot a native commission, and established native villages and councils, and induced the home government to contribute a special grant for native improvement. Year after year much was done on the philanthropic side, and the New Zealander, unlike the Tasmanian, has been preserved so far to share the glories of the British Empire as a partner in a colonial constitution.

New Zealand was remarkable for the multiplicity, at one time, of its provincial legislatures. By the Imperial statute, 15 and 16 Vict., cap. 72, which conferred a constitutional form of government, a New Zealand hexarchy was established, each member of it governed by a superintendent and provincial council. But as time went on, the tendency of colonial opinion was towards centralization, and, as Lord Norton has put it, "the New Zealand hexarchy began to look out for an Egbert, not to conquer, but to cement an union of government, and for an Alfred to turn the local superintendents into chief magistrates of divisions". This tendency, taken together with the abolition of provincial areas and the substitution of counties, was practically a sign of the federating spirit, and, as far as governing expenses went, a more economical arrangement. There was too much "government" in a young colony when there were (1) municipal, (2) provincial, (3) general councils.

The native question in New Zealand, also, rendered political centralization necessary and expedient. Colonists are not always disinterested; and as the native difficulty was confined mainly to North Island, there was a strong party in the Middle or South Island ready to argue that the Maori disturbances meant little or nothing to themselves. The same kind of feeling existed in the Cape Colony formerly when the eastern and western provinces were in existence, the colonists of the west, who lived five hundred miles from the Kaffrarian border and the scene of native revolts, never realizing fully the dangers and perils of their fellow-colonists in the east.

The constitution of New Zealand is broadly based now, none more so amongst all our British colonies. The former "Belgravia" of the colonies has long ago renounced all deeply aristocratic and conservative leanings. If anything, it is a land of political and social experiments, where, for example, women possess the franchise equally with men. The terms of the franchise for men, acquired by one year's residence in the Colony, might well be copied by President Kruger of the Transvaal, whilst every adult Maori has a vote for a Maori member. How would such tolerance go in South Africa, where the paltry blanket vote is the *bête noir* of the Afrikander?

Chapter IX.

The Growth of Colonial Constitutions— South Africa.

When Great Britain took over the Cape in 1795, it was found that the Netherlands East India Company had paid very little attention to the political and social development of South Africa, and had discouraged, as a rule, European immigration, keeping their eyes fixed steadily upon the East and the markets of the East, and regarding Table Bay only as an important half-way house between East and West, where the outward- and homeward-bound merchantmen could rest and recruit. The Malay population at the Cape was imported thither by the Dutch, and became, and still are, useful servants. The Dutch mercantile policy was pursued for a hundred and fifty years—*i.e.* from 1651-1795. The governing body, a very exclusive order, were called "The Council of Policy", and consisted of eight members: (1) the Commander or governor, (2) the secunde, (3 and 4) the two military officers highest in rank, (5) the fiscal, (6) the treasurer, (7) the salesman, (8) the garrison bookkeeper. There were also certain public bodies, such as: (1) the Burgher Council, (2) the Church Council, (3) Board of Militia, (4) the Matrimonial Court, (5) the Orphan Chamber, (6) the Court of Commissioners for petty cases; but one and all subject to the Court of Policy, and in no sense popular bodies.

The term Free Burgher was a complete misnomer, the first burghership being simply a change from the position of paid to unpaid servants of the company. The burghers were trammelled and confined in all things, and the orders and proclamations were so rigid that it would have been impossible to carry out the penalties therein except with the utter ruin of the burghers. The officials at the castle at Cape Town inflicted all kinds of vexatious rules of etiquette upon the unfortunate inhabitants, and the ceremonial of their court was as hard and rigid as that of any despot, extending to the sumptuary laws, the prescribing of certain kinds of fashions of apparel, the definitions of the various grades of society. The title of senior and junior merchants was a very exclusive one in the old Dutch Government, and had a peculiar significance. Only the governor, the fiscal, or attorney-general, the secunde, and the commandant of the castle were counted as "*opper koopmanner*" or senior merchants. The grades were as strictly laid down as in John Locke's *Constitution of Carolina*, drawn up for the proprietors on feudal and old-world lines. The Church was allied closely to the State, the clergyman taking rank as a merchant, but between the officials and the burghers there lay a huge social gap. Above all towered the stately and powerful Chamber of XVII., which, from their headquarters in Holland, swayed the destinies of the Dutch East India Company. In the Cape itself despotism had taken deep root, the foundations of tyranny were firm, the term "Colonial freemen" had lost all significance of the meaning of the liberty which freemen in Europe enjoyed. The heads of the government and the original burghers knew that freedom here was the mockery of a name, that burghership was a state of subserviency to the Company; and the new-comers, whatever their European views of the rights of citizenship, were constrained to bow their heads and yield. Dependent on the government, if in all things obedient, they might prosper in their private circumstances. But to assert any political right, or to murmur against exactions, entailed confiscation of their all, separation from their families, exile to the Mauritius or to some penal station.[1]

Such was the unpromising material upon which British colonization had to build in South Africa, but until the British ships came there was not the slightest chance for freedom or franchise. The only freedom the nomadic Boer families enjoyed was the anarchical freedom of the veldt, where, far away from all kinds of central administration, they lived like the Cyclopes of old.

English military rule, which succeeded the Netherlands' mercantile rule, was, of course, bureaucratic, as we should expect, but together with the English came the idea of a freer colonial life. For two hundred years, chiefly in North America, England had been learning the lessons of a free colonial life shaping its own destinies. She had met Holland in many parts of the world, by sea and land, in the East and along the shores of the Western Continent, and had just supplanted her in Ceylon; but it was under very curious political circumstances that she first met the strange Boer amalgam in South Africa, nominally Dutch, but to a great extent, and by extraction, French. Many of these were in silent or overt rebellion against the old cumbrous Dutch Company at Cape Town, and had tried for generations to "trek away" into the desert to escape from them. The main official hold over them was exercised through the Landdrosts and Veldt Cornets, who guided a very rough and primitive system of local government.

Military rule lasted with fair success until the days of Lord Charles Somerset, when a quarrel arose between Government House and two champions of the early South African press, already alluded to, viz. Thomas Pringle, a poet journalist, a friend of Sir Walter Scott, and John Fairbairn. We are reminded of a similar

[1] Greswell's *Africa South of the Zambesi*, p. 166.

Growth of Constitutions—South Africa. 221

dispute in New South Wales between Wardell and Wentworth, champions of a free press, and Governor Darling, on matters of Colonial administration in 1830–1831. The two South African pressmen had brought with them from Great Britain notions of liberty which were inconsistent with the *régime* of a military governor, and there was no doubt that they were badly used. The dispute at the Cape ended in a concession, granted by Mr. Huskisson, who had charge of colonial affairs, and it was notified, after a long process of negotiations, that the press in South Africa would be under the protection of the law. This was certainly a point gained in the history of constitutional development, and led to the establishment of the rule that, in the British Colonies, free criticism of public acts and policy, considered as such, was allowable.

In 1835 constitutional progress was made in the Cape Colony by the formation of an Executive Council, and of a Legislative Council of twelve, six of them being official and six of them unofficial members. At the same time the colony was divided into the eastern and western provinces. Some of the difficulties attending an extension of a more fully representative government at the Cape were pointed out in a despatch (April 15, 1842) written by Lord Stanley to Sir George Napier, Governor of the Cape. First of all there was the fact of the great distances of many of the districts of the colony from the capital, which would prevent their having their due weight at Cape Town; and, secondly, the heterogeneous character of the population, divided as it was into so many races. The first difficulty, at least, common to more colonies than one, and exemplified in Australia, where the colonists of Port Phillip complained of being so far from Sydney, might be dealt with either by establishing separate legislatures or removing the Legislature to some more central point than Cape Town.

Here is the old question of the proper and most convenient place in a young country for the seat of government and for the metropolis, a question settled in old countries by a variety of circumstances, geographical and otherwise, working continuously for generations, but always a vexed question in large colonial areas. In Canada, New Zealand, and the Cape, there have been as many claimants to be "the Capital" as cities and islands of old to the birthplace of Homer. At the Cape, after much deliberation, in 1850–1851 it was concluded that the best thing was to allow Cape Town to be still the seat of government. A glance at the political map of South Africa as it existed in 1850 would seem to warrant the idea of provincial separation. There was a distance of five hundred to six hundred miles between the provinces, by a hard and, in those days, perilous land journey. Wild beasts and wandering hordes of natives were a real danger fifty to sixty years ago in South Africa. The coast journey was emphatically a dangerous and disagreeable one; there were no good landlocked harbours anywhere, and the Cape politician who came from the east to take part in the deliberations of the Council or Assembly at Cape Town had to embark in a surf-boat on an open roadstead like Port Elizabeth or East London. Again, there was a sufficient distinction between eastern and western politicians and their aims and policy to warrant almost a separate Legislature. The English immigration of 1820 to Algoa Bay had formed an epoch in Cape history, and the growth of Albany was very different from the growth of the western districts. Eastern and western industries were different, the *vigneron* of the west leading quite a separate life of his own, out of touch with the frontiersmen of the Kaffrarian border. Moreover, there was no Kaffir question in the west, and it was round this Kaffir question and its proper solution that the destiny of the country hung. To use a rough parallel, the social and political differences between the eastern and western provinces of the Cape Colony were nearly as great as those which parted the British colonists of Upper Canada from the French Canadians of Lower Canada.

South Africa is a country of which Earl Grey speaks with the greatest "reserve" in his letters to Lord John Russell, and the country has always been the *bête noir* of home politicians. But he was really indignant when he heard of the refusal of the Cape Colonists to take the Irish convicts from Bermuda, and he referred to the "extraordinary proceedings" of the inhabitants of the Colony, about which he is unwilling to use the terms which would adequately describe them. He is also evidently dissatisfied with the action of Sir Harry Smith, the Governor of the Cape at the time, who was placed between two very awkward and dangerous fires, from which he, the hero of Aliwal and of Boomplatz, found it hard to extricate himself, smart soldier as he was. There is no doubt that the anti-convict agitation strengthened the backbone of Colonial constitutionalism here as well as in Australia, and that Earl Grey really misunderstood the whole transportation theory, as it affected Colonial life. For the Cape Colonists were in deadly earnest on this subject; they had risen *en masse* and boycotted the ship in the Bay; they had formed an Anti-Convict League and set on foot a "Vigilance Committee" to watch the "pest ship" as *The Neptune* was termed; a resolution was carried in public that "it was the duty of all good and loyal subjects of Her Majesty at once to suspend all business transactions with the government". Earl Grey was convicted out of his own mouth, as he had stated it to be his opinion that no colony, which was not created in the beginning as a convict station, ought to be compelled to receive convicts; and the Cape was on a different footing from New South Wales and Tasmania. There were many persons in England who sympathized with the Cape, and in March, 1849, Sir C. Adderley moved in the House of Commons that "out of consideration for the honourable pride and moral welfare of the Cape Colony" Her Majesty would be pleased to order that the Cape should cease to be a receptable for convicts; and this motion was carried. But, to show the current of official opinion, the man who refused to "boycott" the convict ships, and supplied them with food, was knighted by the home government for his patriotism.

The Cape constitution, as elaborated by Earl Grey (1850), had one marked feature which differentiated it from the Colonial constitution which had preceded it. The official recommendation was, that the members of the Legislative Council should be elected, not nominated, and that their term of election should last ten years. Their election would be on a franchise with a high property qualification, and it was the opinion of those who framed the constitution that election would place the Council upon a more popular basis than nomination, and give the Upper Chamber more political power in reality than they possessed already. The question is, as we have seen, of great constitutional importance.

In 1872, just twenty years after Earl Grey's constitution, the first ministry under responsible government sat at Cape Town. There was no more vexed question, either at home or in South Africa itself, than the advisability of introducing the new form of government into the Cape Colony. There had been the usual friction between the Executive Council of the Government and the Cape Legislature, expressing the will of the people; in other words, to use Gibbon Wakefield's simile, the fire had been lit in the room and the chimney was closed. There was no way by which the popular will could be enforced, and when Sir Philip Wodehouse had dissolved the Assembly on a question of public retrenchment it was felt that there was a dead-lock in the machinery of government. Personally, Sir Philip Wodehouse was hostile to the introduction of responsible government, as it seemed to imply a severance of the colony from the mother-country, and, in South Africa especially, there were high reasons of State against a premature gift of responsible government.

The task of introducing responsible government was entrusted to Sir Henry Barkly, whose ideas upon the subject were known to be favourable, or at any rate more in keeping with the trend of popular and even official opinion at home. It was argued that if responsible government had turned out such a good thing for British North America and Australia it would be equally advantageous to the Cape Colony. Sir Henry Barkly, one of the most able and courteous of our Colonial governors, was equipped with the latest experience, as he had filled the post of Governor in Victoria. He came, therefore, prepared to introduce, if not to push, this great measure of constitutional reform. Curiously enough, the opposition came from the Legislative Council, that upper chamber, elected by constituents, which Earl Grey had placed in the constitution as a moderating force. Upon the first introduction of the bill for responsible government the Assembly carried it by 34 to 27 votes, no very decisive majority as the figures show. The Legislative Council, in a full house, rejected it by 12 to 9.

Some Colonial reformers might have thought that, under the circumstances, it was expedient to hold back and not to run the risk of even seeming to force such an important measure upon the colonists, about whose unanimity there were unmistakable doubts. But in 1872, at the beginning of the session, Sir Henry Barkly announced that he was authorized and instructed by

Her Majesty's Government to re-introduce the bill, and upon this occasion the second reading was passed in the Legislative Assemby by 35 to 25 votes, and in the Legislative Council by the narrow majority of 11 to 10. This last majority hinged upon the wavering allegiance of two members of the western divisions of the Cape Colony, Dr. Hiddingh and Mr. De Roubaix, who were finally induced to withdraw an opposition they had previously offered to the bill and to the principle it implied.

Careful politicians who have watched closely the history of South Africa during the last generation have frequently asked themselves the question, whether the gift of responsible government to the Cape, with all it involved, was premature or not. South Africa, it must be remembered, as a field for political experiments, was not British North America, nor was it Australia or New Zealand. The presence of the Boers and of the native population made the case different at once. The truth is, that the pushing British element was ready for the change, but the Boer peasantry living in the country were not, their political training having been absolutely neglected in past times. Yet, in reality, by the introduction of responsible government the destinies of the Cape were handed over to the Dutch electors, who were in the majority by two to one. Would it not have been cautious, if not wise, if the Colony had been kept in leading-strings a little longer, perhaps another twenty years, so as to give time for the education of the Dutch or Boer voter, and a breathing-space in the midst of the native problems? True it is that the Boer or up-country voter was inert and apathetic, and not at all ready to take advantage of his voting power in the new constitution, so much so that he was almost regarded in the old days as a *quantité négligeable*. But the power was there all the same, and it only needed the right time and favourable circumstances to hatch this apparently dormant political egg. Unlike the United States of America, and its feverish, excitable life, fostered and encouraged, if not wrought up, into more dangerous electrical exhibitions by professional politicians, the veldt existence in South Africa is somnolent and drowsy and very difficult to arouse. Not that the Boers have no political memories, or, indeed, only short ones; for they remember certain sores continually, such as the bad management of the Emancipation Act, whereby they were cheated out of their compensation money, or such an episode as that of the punishment for rebellion "at Slachters Nek" is brooded over with as much vindictive earnestness as any Covenanter thought over his historic grievances.

This political life lay quiescent till the Boer War and the days of the Afrikander Bond, that curious awakening of veldt life incident upon quicker developments and easier means of communication. Then, for the first time, Tadpoles and Tapers were seen in the homesteads and the quiet villages of South Africa, speaking often as advisers of a simple farmers' association for the improvement of agriculture, but in their inner hearts political propagandists of the cry, "Africa for the Afrikander". If we analyse more closely the meaning of the term "Afrikander", it would, we suppose, exclude the "African", or aboriginal inhabitants of South Africa, as well as the European immigrants.

In South Africa there is a system within a system, a question within a question, and a whole series of minor influences at work which, in the philanthropic and religious world especially, have been the lasting puzzle and problem of politicians at home, and have certainly hindered constitutional growth. There is no British colony which has afforded so constant a theme to Exeter Hall platforms as South Africa; there is no sphere where missionary and evangelizing enterprises have had so great a scope and so free a play; there is no country where it has been harder to disentangle pure and righteous motives from selfish and sinister political aims. The battle has raged mainly round the question of the status of the Hottentots and Kaffirs, and this was a first principle in politics. Until this was settled it was hard to proceed to adopt even the form or the outline of a political constitution. Amongst the Cape Colonists themselves there has always been a party hostile to native enfranchisement of any description, whilst there have been at the same time a section in favour of it. When the "Draft Ordinances" were discussed, Mr. Porter, a well-known colonist, adopted the line of a low franchise, together with the admission of the coloured classes into the constitution as voters. The opposite policy seemed to him a policy of suspicion, exclusion, and unworthy prejudice; and so strongly did he feel on the subject that he said he was ready to tear the draft ordinance to pieces if his suggestions were not adopted. This gives us a glimpse into the internal divisions of the Cape at the very moment when fuller representative government was being extended to it. For a long time afterwards the policy and spirit generally of Mr. Porter were reproduced by Mr. Saul Solomon, a very able and influential Cape politician, who was always strong enough to form a clique if not a party at the Cape, and was in constant sympathy and communication with the Aborigines Protection Society and Exeter Hall at home. But the native question itself requires a discriminating hand. What philanthropists might have been justified in giving to Hottentots and Malays could not be bestowed with the same advantage upon the Kaffir hordes. The great Kaffir question, indeed, overshadows all others.

On the other hand, there was the silent influence of the Boer party in South Africa, who have never admitted, even in their republican constitutions, the theory of race equality, and have always regarded Bushman, Hottentot, and the Kaffir as the Gibeonite of their society. Their deep-rooted opinions and prejudices are discernible in the "Grondwet" of the republics of the Orange Free State and the Transvaal. Connected as the Boer element is all over South Africa by family ties, by religion, and by traditions, it is not to be wondered at if its antipathies have profoundly modified the general view of a considerable section of the colonists of South Africa. Were we dealing with the British element by itself, as in New Zealand, it would have been easier to arrive at general conclusions even upon so controverted a point as the status of the native element, whether Hottentot, Malay, Kaffir, or even of Indian immigrants, in the South African constitutions. As it is, the matter is, generally speaking, *sub judice*, and we are still waiting upon events.

From the administrative point of view the home Government endeavoured to concentrate imperial authority in South Africa in the person of the Governor of the Cape Colony, and, with this object in view, has invested this official with a special commission, and extra powers as "High Commissioner of South Africa". The governorship of the Cape Colony is therefore a unique official post. In addition to the ordinary duties of a constitutional governor of a "responsible" Colony, he has enormous extra-territorial responsibilities extending over many spheres of administration. In the triangular duel so often going on between "Blacks, Boers, and British", he is often compelled to take a part, and to be an arbiter in the midst of many and jarring interests. It was, doubtless, the formidable native question in Kaffraria which, thirty or forty years ago, gave rise to the High Commissionership of South Africa. In 1860 Sir George Grey, the Governor of the Cape Colony, held also the title of Governor of British Kaffraria, then constituted a separate province, as well as that of the High Commissionership of South Africa. There were several reasons why this office should have been called into existence at the Cape, the chief amongst them being the pressing necessity that a responsible British official of high standing should keep an ever-watchful eye along the Kaffrarian borders, and be "the eyes and ears" of the great queen across the waters. He should be a strong and merciful administrator, standing, if need be, between the Boers and the natives, or colonists and natives, as the impersonation of imperial justice and honour.[1] The Commission issued to Sir Bartle Frere was of a very wide nature, as the political horizon in South Africa was widening, and there was a hope of South African confederation. "He held control over all the territories adjacent to the Cape Colony, or with which it might be expedient that Her Majesty should have relations; he was enjoined to take all measures and do all that could lawfully and discreetly be done for preventing the recurrence of any irruption into Her Majesty's possessions by hostile tribes, and for maintaining the said possessions in peace and safety; he was also required to invite and obtain the co-operation of the government of the Orange Free State, or of any foreign power, towards the preservation of peace and safety in South Africa, and the general advancement and welfare of its territories." Rarely had a British governor wider and more discretionary powers. One of the effects of the Zulu war was to deprive Sir Bartle Frere of part of his commission. In June, 1879, Lord Wolseley succeeded him as "High Commissioner of the Transvaal, Natal, and all the adjoining eastern portion of South Africa". He also superseded Lord Chelmsford in the command of the army, and Sir Henry Bulwer as Governor of Natal. In 1880 Sir George Colley succeeded

---

[1] See *Fortnightly Review*, May, 1896. Article by W. Greswell.

Growth of Constitutions—South Africa. 231

Lord Wolseley as Governor of Natal and High Commissioner of South-East Africa. The tragic death of Sir George Colley at Majuba, and the recall of Sir Bartle Frere cleared the ground for a fresh arrangement, or rather for a return to the former state of things. Lord Rosmead was called upon as governor of the Cape to fill the duties also of High Commissioner of South Africa.

This brings us to very recent history, and to a very turbulent period of recent South African history. In addition to the Pretoria Convention, the late Lord Rosmead had to take up the task of the Basuto award, of the resumption of Basutoland by the Imperial Government, of the Convention of London, and of the establishment of a protectorate in Bechuanaland. The question is, how has this combination of duties and their centralization of authority worked practically in South Africa? However able and just the High Commissioner of South Africa may be, it may fairly be pleaded that the task of supervision is now almost beyond his control. It has certainly tended to centralize all South African political life at Cape Town and in Cape Colony. Some have questioned whether this is an advantage. It might have been better if Her Majesty's High Commissioner had been a more detached official and living in a more central part of South Africa, which is now being extended northwards at a most rapid rate. The work of imperial administration in South Africa depends largely upon the character, status, and abilities of the High Commissioner.

The constitutional history of Natal is of a comparatively peaceful character, and has not been marked by any great struggles. In 1843 the district of Natal was proclaimed by the governor of the Cape Colony to be a British colony; in August, 1845, it was made by letters patent part of the Cape Colony, but only until November of the same year, when it was made a separate colony, with a Lieutenant-governor and an Executive Council, still, however, subordinate to the Cape. It was not till 1856 that Natal was made absolutely distinct. Its affairs were then managed by a Governor and by an Executive Council and a Legislative Council of a composite character, partly elected and partly nominated. A fully "responsible" government was rather slow in coming to Natal, chiefly owing to the presence of the Kaffirs and the difficulties of the native question. At the present moment there are said to be 500,000 Kaffirs living within Natal territory,[1] whilst the white population was only estimated in 1891 to be 46,788. However, in 1893-1894, not altogether without some misgivings in certain quarters, Natal gained a "responsible" government. The two houses, the Legislative Council, created by nomination, and therefore differing from the upper chamber at the Cape, together with a House of Assembly, elected by a popular suffrage amongst the European population, were inaugurated with all due formality, and a new phase in constitutional history began.

In broad outline, therefore, we can detect a very remarkable family likeness between the constitutions of Canada, of Australasia, and of South Africa, as they all resemble the prototype at home. The differences in detail between the form of government in England and her colonies are numerous, and can scarcely be recapitulated here. Generally speaking, the constituencies are more broadly based in the latter. In the Canadian Dominion Government the election of the House of Commons is by ballot on a franchise almost equal to "manhood suffrage", and it may be said that in the election of the members of the provincial Legislative Assemblies every male adult has a voice. In the Cape Colony, where, contrary to the Canadian rule, both houses are elected, voters have to satisfy a small pro-

[1] *Proceedings of Royal Colonial Institute*, 1895-1896, vol. xxvii. p. 198.

perty qualification, and be in receipt of salary and wages of not less than £50 per annum, or not less than £25 per annum with board and lodging. The conditions of this £25 qualification, like that of the 100 dollar qualification in New Brunswick, are not hard to fulfil. In the Australasian Colonies manhood suffrage with a small property or residentiary qualification of six months generally is the rule. In Tasmania the voter must have or earn £60 per annum. In New Zealand all the adult Maoris have votes for the four special Maori constituencies. Nor are the qualifications for membership of the elected assemblies hard to fulfil in Queensland, no property qualification being required for either house. Theoretically there is the most perfect equality in all our self-governing colonies, and there is nothing practically in the way of any man who wishes to exercise his vote, or to go higher and offer himself for election to the electors of the country as a parliamentary candidate.

If we look a little closely into the scale of representation in our "responsible" colonies, and examine the proportion of members to electors, we shall discover that all these colonies are extremely well represented. In the United Kingdom there are 570 members of the House of Commons, representing an estimated population in England, Scotland, Ireland, and Wales of 37,740,283 for the year 1891, that is to say, one member represents a population of about 66,000. Turning to the nine colonies of the Cape, Natal, New South Wales, Victoria, Tasmania, South Australia, Queensland, Western Australia, New Zealand, and referring to the basis of the last official census summaries of 1891, we shall find the population to be as follows, which we may compare with the representation of the Legislative Council and the Legislative Assembly. In the Cape and Natal the native population is excluded, in the Australasian Colonies it is included.

	European Population (1891).	REPRESENTATION.	
		Legislative Council.	Legislative Assembly.
I. The Cape Colony,	376,812	22	76
II. Natal,	46,788	11	37
III. New South Wales,	1,132,234	60	141
IV. Victoria,	1,140,405	48	95
V. Tasmania,	152,619	18	36
VI. South Australia,	320,431	24	52
VII. Queensland,	393,718	39	72
VIII. Western Australia,	49,782	15	30
IX. New Zealand,	626,658	40	74
Total,	4,239,447	277	613

or one member for 4817 inhabitants.

The scale of representation in Canada requires a separate statement, as there is a dual system in existence there: (1) that of the Dominion, (2) that of the Provinces. In the Dominion Government the Senate numbers 80, and the House of Commons 215 members, or collectively 295 members. Taking the 1891 population of 4,829,411, the proportion of members to population will be one member for about 16,000 inhabitants. Proceeding further to the scale of Provincial Representation it will be as follows:—

	Population, 1891.	REPRESENTATION.	
		Legislative Council.	Legislative Assembly.
I. Quebec,	1,488,586	24	65
II. Ontario,	2,112,989	—	92
III. Nova Scotia,	450,523	21	38
IV. New Brunswick,	321,294	—	41
V. Prince Edward Island,	109,088	—	30
VI. Manitoba,	154,442	—	40
VII. British Columbia,	92,767	—	33
VIII. N. W. Territories,	99,722	—	29
Total,	4,829,411	45	368

or one member for about 11,000 inhabitants.

If we went a little further into the figures of the population and of the representation of our self-governing colonies in Canada, South Africa, and Australasia, and omitted the Upper Houses, we should find that with the 215 members of the Canadian House of Commons, and the 368 members of the Legislative Assemblies of the Provinces of Canada, and the 613 members of the Legislative Assemblies in South Africa and Australasia, we could count up a goodly total of 1196 legislators. Taking the whole population of our self-governing colonies as 9,068,858, according to the census of 1891, the average of representation would be one member to about 7500 colonists, a proportion that does not err on the side of under representation, although it must be recollected that the conditions of a young and rising country with vast areas coming into administrative control are not those of an old country with historic constituencies.

In one particular the Colonial system of government differs from that of the mother-country, and it is in the fact that legislators are paid for their services in cash and in certain allowances. In the Canadian Dominion Government each member of the Senate receives £250 a session, and each member of the House of Commons £2, 10s. a day, with a maximum of £250 a session. In the Provincial Legislature, Ontario, Quebec, and British Columbia give the members of their Assemblies £1, 10s. a day with travelling expenses; New Brunswick, £75 a year; Manitoba, £100. Turning to Australasia, New South Wales gives each member of the Assembly £300 per annum; Victoria, £300 per annum; South Australia, £200 per annum; New Zealand, £150 per annum. In the Cape Colony the members of both houses are paid at the rate of £1, 10s. a day, with travelling allowances. The general rule, therefore, throughout the "responsible" Colonies of paid legislators enables the poorest man, if he so chooses, to be a representative of his town or district.

The Septennial Act does not find favour in the Colonies, and in Canada the usual term is four years, in the Australasian Colonies three years. The position of the Legislative Councils or the Upper Houses in our responsible Colonies is, from a constitutional point of view, extremely interesting. As we have seen, some colonies adopt the uni-cameral system, and dispense altogether with the Council after having tried it; in some colonies the principle of nomination obtains, in others that of election. In the Cape Colony the Council is elected, but a member must be the owner of immovable property in the colony of not less value that £2000, and must be not less than thirty years of age.

In New Zealand we are struck by the lavish way in which the suffrage is given to the Maoris. But it must be remembered that, with a comparatively small and stationary native population, this concession carries with it no possible seed of danger. Moreover, the Maori vote is limited to the Maori constituencies. This theoretical equality is really a vote-as-you-please doctrine confined to a well-marked sphere, and cannot apply to such a country as South Africa, where the native is in a numerical majority and promises to increase still more. The problem in South Africa is, how to deal with the native and how to govern him; also, how far he may be permitted to govern himself. In South Africa we have one problem inside another. There are certain tendencies which make for an oligarchical, or at any rate a less democratic, form of government in South Africa than in the rest of our responsible Colonies.

Such, in brief outline, are the main political and territorial features of our Colonial Empire. It has been built up, as we have seen, by the colonizing activity of the

British race, and rests chiefly for its continuance and success upon trade and commerce. The extensions of this Empire, covering so many portions of the world both in the tropical and temperate zones, suggest a free interchange of all products. It also includes some of the best and most prolific mineral-bearing districts in the world, and gold, silver, and copper mines attract in their wake population, thus encouraging agriculture and pastoral pursuits. Moreover, the Empire is both insular and continental. The islands of the world over which the British flag flies are not only useful as posts of observation, and as ocean "quadrilaterals", but also as centres of tropical and subtropical industries. The West Indies are the insular supplement of Canada, the Fijis of New Zealand, and Mauritius group of South Africa.

In building up our "Second Colonial Empire" there have been many perilous crises, especially in Canada, as we have seen. The best commentary on the doubts and trials of those days in Canada, sixty years ago, may be found in the words of Sir Wilfred Laurier, the French-Canadian premier, spoken at an Imperial banquet in London during the Jubilee year (June 18, 1897). During these years there had been, said Sir Wilfred, many changes, but there had been no change in the loyalty of French Canadians. Canada was free, and freedom was her nationality. There was no jealousy, because it was the proud privilege of men of this generation to see the banners of England and the banners of France entwined together and floating victoriously on the banks of the Alma, on the heights of Inkermann, and on the walls of Sevastopol. Elsewhere Sir Wilfred said that, although proud of his French descent, he was "British to the core", because there was not a man in Canada to-day of French origin who did not realize that he found under the flag of England far more freedom than he could have enjoyed under the flag of France.

Thus Sir Wilfred spoke with the voice of a federated Canada.

The growth of the idea of federalism and the general tendency of the Colonies to be united more closely with one another, and also with the mother-country, is one of the most marked political features of the latter years of the Victorian era. There is, on the one hand, "Intercolonial Federation", which applies to the political amalgamation of groups of Colonies, thrown together by the mere fact of geographical propinquity, and, on the other, "Imperial Federation", a wider term involving a more ambitious programme and a far closer amalgamation of diverse interests. Federalism, in its modern sense, should be the child of constitutional development and the crowning product of popular representative government. Thus we say, truly enough, that when Lord Durham advised the union of the two Canadas, Upper and Lower, in 1838, he was laying the foundation of the great Canadian federation. Such a federation is clearly distinct from the *kriegsverein*, or purely military federation, which leaves little room for constitutional practice and theory. Yet, somehow, we feel that the British Empire, which rests largely upon constitutional growth, and is in its essence an empire trusting to peace and commerce, needs some kind of *kriegsverein*, with the motto of "Defence, not Defiance". There are wars going on almost continually upon the borders of our ever-growing Empire, rising in importance from mere punitive expeditions to such a formidable campaign as is now going on (1897–1898) upon the frontiers of India, but these are only the *simulacra belli* compared with the unmeasured catastrophe of a war with a first-class European power. Fortunately, the sphere of warlike operations would be limited to the sea, and it would be practically impossible for "the elephant to fight the whale". Still, the issues of maritime warfare are uncertain, especially when we take into consideration the formidable character, nowadays, of weapons of offence. There is no one who can say that the exploits of such French seamen as Surcouf, the daring Malouine privateer, who preyed so successfully upon British commerce in the Eastern seas from the Isle of France at the end of last century, would not be repeated on some future occasion by a French or other European enemy. Then,—in 1790-1800,—we are told that the merchants of Calcutta stood aghast. "Commerce was at a standstill, our cruisers were outwitted, and on more than one occasion, in spite of their heavier metal, were compelled to haul down their flags to the pigmy privateers hailing from the port of St. Malo." Our maritime commerce is many times greater now than it was a hundred years ago, and in a corresponding ratio our sea-risks are greater. Fortunately, the merchants of Great Britain and of her Colonies have, in their marine insurance policies of the last generation or so, thought little of the risks from "the king's or queen's enemies". There has been no serious enemy at sea to Queen Victoria. But it would be puerile, nay criminal, to suppose that our vast maritime empire, with its business estimated at the trade-value annually of £911,000,000, exclusive of foreign trade in British bottoms, will never be exposed to serious risk. The feverish haste with which European nations are striving to strengthen their navies and to dispute Great Britain's supremacy at sea is a notorious feature of the age. Great Britain and her Colonies are free from the frightful burden of conscription which weighs like a nightmare upon the nations of Europe, and causes them to regard with undisguised envy and jealousy the untrammelled and prosperous lives of the citizens of our great Empire. But if we are exempt from the overwhelming tasks of frontier defence by land, it is all the more incumbent to utilize our opportunities for defence by sea, and to spare no expense to make this thoroughly effective. For all those who enjoy the privileges of the *Civitas Britannica* this naval defence ranks as the first and firemost of all civic duties. All discussions on federation pivot around this one great paramount duty of common defence. Last century it was the merchants of Calcutta who stood aghast at the ravages of French privateering, but in any naval war of the future, not only the merchants of Calcutta, but the whole trading and mercantile communities of such colonial centres as Melbourne, Sydney, Adelaide, Montreal, Quebec, Capetown, Port Elizabeth, Hong Kong, Singapore, Colombo, and scores of prosperous centres of colonial trade might be thrown into a fever of apprehension and alarm. So quick and sudden are the turns of modern warfare that irreparable mischief might be done along the highways of commerce before any effectual counter-blow could be struck. Great Britain might finally emerge victorious, as before, but at a terrible sacrifice, especially if her plans of naval co-operation with her Colonies were immature or still a subject of the slightest doubt or dispute.

"Si vis pacem, para bellum." There can be no motto more true than this as applied to the case of Great Britain and her world-wide Empire, scattered in so many portions of the globe. The duty of self-defence falls upon all, upon colonists as well as upon those who live in the mother-country. In our "First Colonial Empire" North American colonists were not slow in fighting the battles of Empire in North America itself, and many a hard-won victory bears witness of their prowess against the French. Our "Second Colonial Empire" has risen into wealth and prominence more peacefully during the Victorian era, but it stands in need of help from Colonial arms, of contributions from Colonial exchequers. That there is the spirit and wish to help in the task of defence is illustrated in many ways in our Colonies, notably by the aid given in the Sûdan campaign by the Australian contingent, and by the general acquiescence of the Australian delegates at the Colonial Conference of 1887 in the chief principles of imperial defence. The offer of a battle-ship from the Cape, or its equivalent in an annual contribution, is another more recent sign of an awakening sense. Still, however powerful individual example is, or however gratifying isolated and sporadic acts of patriotism are, to an overburdened mother-country, it is felt that something more definite, more reliable, and more systematic is required. If the integrity of our vast Empire, built up by such untold sacrifices in past time of men and money, really depends upon the question of imperial defence, then this question dwarfs all others immediately. If our first and only line of defence fails us, it is surely idle then to speak of the Empire of Great Britain as the embodiment of any principle of religion, politics, trade, or civilization. It will have perished, a factor no longer to be considered in the economics of the world.

The late Poet Laureate uttered a warning note when it was whispered that England's fleet had been suffered to decay, and that her coaling-places and outposts were neglected:

> "You, you, if you should fail to understand
> What England is, and what her all-in-all,
> On you will come the curse of all the land
> Should this old England fall
> Which Nelson left so great".

Appendix.

The following are in outline the main features of the Canadian Constitution :—

I. By the British North America Act the Executive Government and authority of and over Canada, as well as the command-in-chief of the land and naval militia, and of all naval and military forces of and in Canada, were declared to be vested in the Queen.

II. The Parliament consists of the Queen, the Senate, and the House of Commons. The Queen is represented by the Governor-general, who is assisted by a Privy Council, to which belong all those who are and have been advisers of the Crown; the acting portion of the Council, however, consists only of the ministry of the day.

III. The Governor-general is appointed by the Queen, and holds office for five years. He takes no part in legislation, but assents in the Queen's name to all measures which have passed both the Senate and the Commons. He may, however, refuse such assent, or may reserve bills for Her Majesty's consideration. He may also disallow Acts of the Provincial Legislatures, within one year of their having been passed in the Province.

IV. The Senate is composed of members appointed for life by the Crown under the Great Seal of Canada. A Senator is entitled to be called Honourable. He must be a British subject, born or naturalized, have passed the age of thirty years, be a resident in the Province for which he is appointed, and hold property to the value of 4000 dollars (£800) above all liabilities. His seat becomes vacant if he fails to attend two consecutive sessions of Parliament, if he becomes bankrupt or takes advantage of any insolvent law, or is attainted of treason or convicted of felony. The Speaker, who must be a Senator, is appointed by the Governor-general, and 15 members, including the Speaker, form a quorum. Each Senator receives 1000 dollars (£200) per annum. The Senate consists of 80 members, and so chosen that 24 belong to Ontario and 24 to Quebec. Bills of all kinds, *except money bills*, can be originated in the Senate.

V. The original number of the members of the House of Commons was 181, but in accordance with the provisions of the British North America Act, and in consequence of the admission of new provinces and territories, and of the power of amalgamation originally given in the Constitution, this number has been increased to 215, distributed as follows:—Ontario, 92; Quebec, 65; Nova Scotia, 21; New Brunswick, 16; Manitoba, 5; British Columbia, 6; Prince Edward Island, 6; the North-West Territories, 4. By section 51 of the British North America Act it was provided that the number of representatives for Quebec should always be 65, and that the other provinces should be represented in such proportion to the population, as ascertained at each decennial census, as the number 65 would bear to the population of Quebec. Members are paid at the rate of 10 dollars (£2) a day, if the session is less than thirty days, and 1000 dollars (£200) for the session, if over 30 days. All bills for appropriating any part of the public revenue, or for imposing any tax or impost, must originate in the House of Commons, and must first be recommended by message of the Governor-general. The House must be called together from time to time by the Governor-general in the name of the Queen, under the Great Seal of Canada, but there must be a session of Parliament once at least in every year, and twelve months must not intervene between the last sitting of one session and the first sitting of the next.

VI. The concurrence of the Governor-general, the Senate, and the House of Commons is necessary before any measure can become law. Every member of the Senate and of the House of Commons must take the oath of allegiance before taking his seat.

VII. The exclusive legislative authority of the Parliament of Canada extends to all matters connected with the following subjects:—
1. The Public Debt and Property. 2. The Regulation of Trade and Commerce. 3. The raising of money by any system of taxation. 4. The borrowing of money on the public credit for public works. 5. The Postal Service. 6. The Census and Statistics. 7. Military and Naval Defence. 8. The salaries of the government officials. 9. Beacons, buoys, lighthouses. 10. Navigation and shipping. 11. Quarantine and marine hospitals. 12. Sea-coast and inland fisheries. 13. Railways, canals, ferries, and portages. 14. Coins and currency. 15. Banks and

Appendix. 245

the issue of paper money. 16. Savings-banks. 17. Weights and measures. 18. Bills of Exchange. 19. Interest. 20. Legal tender. 21. Bankruptcy and insolvency. 22. Patents. 23. Copyright. 24. Indians and Indian reserves. 25. Naturalization and aliens. 26. Marriage and divorce. 27. Penitentiaries.

Passing on to the Provincial Constitutions, it must be remembered that the Act of 1867 provided for four, viz. those of Ontario, Quebec, Nova Scotia, and New Brunswick. With regard to Nova Scotia and New Brunswick, their constitutional history was slightly different from that of Ontario and Quebec, as they had received constitutions at an earlier date. In Nova Scotia the Assembly was elected, first of all, for no definite period, but continued during the pleasure of the Governor. The House elected in 1770 was called "the Long Parliament" of Nova Scotia, and lasted till 1785. In 1792 a Septennial Act was passed. In 1840-1 a large number of reforms took place, and the representation of the maritime Provinces was put upon a more liberal and democratic basis. Both on the part of Nova Scotia and New Brunswick there was a good deal of opposition to the Confederation Scheme, but ultimately this was removed.

For each Province the Governor-general appoints a Lieutenant-governor to hold office for five years.

1. The Legislature of Ontario consists of one chamber only—the Legislative Assembly—numbering 82 members, elected for 4 years.
2. That of Quebec of a Legislative Council of 24 members, appointed by the Crown for life; and a Legislative Assembly of 65 members, elected for 4 years.
3. That of Nova Scotia of a Legislative Council of 17 members, appointed by the Governor for life; and of a Legislative Assembly of 37 members.
4. That of New Brunswick of a Legislative Council of 17 members, appointed by the Governor for life; and a Legislative Assembly of 41 members.

At the passing of the British North America Act provision was made for the admission of other Provinces besides the first four. It was made lawful for the Queen (Articles 146 and 147), with the advice of the Privy Council, on addresses from the Houses of Parliament in Canada, and from the Legislatures of

Newfoundland, Prince Edward Island, and British Columbia, to admit them upon the conditions expressed in the addresses, subject to the provisions of the British North America Act. In case "Rupert's Land" and "the North-West Territory", which was the general name given to the vast prairies stretching beyond to the "Rockies", wished to be united, an address from the Parliament of Canada was required. The Confederation, therefore, of 1867, whilst sufficiently important in itself as a consolidating measure, carried with it the germs of greater things. In May, 1870, the Province of Manitoba, which was carved out of the Great North-West, was incorporated with the Dominion, in July, 1871, British Columbia, and in July, 1873, Prince Edward Island followed suit. Newfoundland, which is a fishing resort both for French and British, according to treaty, still remains outside the Confederation. For many generations the French Shore right, by which the French claim exclusive privileges along several hundred miles of coast, from Cape Ray to S. John, has been a standing political difficulty.

The constitutions of Manitoba, British Columbia, and Prince Edward Island resemble those of the other Provinces. There is a Lieutenant-governor in each. Manitoba has an Assembly of 40 paid members, elected for 4 years, but no Council, resembling Ontario in this respect. British Columbia is also governed on the uni-cameral system, and has an Assembly of 33 paid members. Prince Edward Island began with a Legislative Council of 13 members, but that has been abolished, and there is now an Assembly of 30 members. New Brunswick has also dispensed with her Council. The Provinces of Quebec and Nova Scotia alone retain the bi-cameral system. One reason we may possibly make for the preference evidently shown in favour of the one-chamber system of Provincial Government in Canada may be this, namely, that the two-chamber system involves too heavy a drain upon the time and services of the public men of Canada. Moreover, the necessity of an upper chamber, which is supposed to be a check upon hasty legislation, is not so pressing and imperative in a Province, forming one member of a federal dominion with specific powers assigned expressly to it, as it would be in a detached Colony.

The position of what was termed on the British North America Act of 1867, "Rupert's Land and the North-West

Appendix. 247

Territories ", requires a little clearer explanation. In the first place, the name takes us back to the original charter of 1670, when Prince Rupert obtained from Charles II. a grant of land stretching from Lake Superior to the Rocky Mountains, from Manitoba to Athabasca, an area equivalent to that of Europe, and the haunt of roving Indian tribes and fur-hunters. This was a vast territorial monopoly, and it lasted for two hundred years. Manitoba is not mentioned as a Province in the British North America Act, as its existence as such was a subsequent development, and followed chiefly upon the enterprise of the new rush of settlers. Manitoba and the Red River Valley were found to be some of the finest wheat districts in the world, although the country was only known for a long time from its association with the Wolseley expedition.

Manitoba was the first-fruits of the Great North-West. But in 1882 four provisional districts appeared upon the map, viz. Assiniboia, Saskatchewan, Alberta, Athabasca, with the city of Regina in Assiniboia as the governing centre. At first these Territories were governed by a Lieutenant-governor, subject to instructions given by order-in-council at Ottawa, or by the Secretary of State for Canada. But since 1888, when these distant Territories were mapped out into electoral areas, there was an Assembly of 22 (now 29) members. They began by requiring a subsidy from the Dominion Government, but in course of time, as colonization marches forward, they will take their position as populous and powerful limbs of the great confederacy. There were five judicial districts, two in Assiniboia, two in Alberta, and one in Saskatchewan.

The discovery of rich gold-mines on the Klondak or Klondyke River, at the extreme north-west of the district of Athabasca, must have an effect upon this part of the Dominion. As it stands at present, the machinery of government is not sufficient, and a new judicial district, if not a new Province, at the head of the Yukon River, will be probably the latest addition to the great confederacy. We have had the experience of gold rushes in California, in Australia, and, to a certain extent, as far as the individual miner is concerned, in South Africa; but the history of colonization lacks as yet the curious spectacle of "placer" mining in the regions of the Arctic.

Side by side with a list of the Canadian Provinces it is necessary to consider what are the exclusive powers of their various Legislatures. In each Province the Legislature may make laws relating to the following subjects:—

1. The amendment from time to time of the Constitution of the Province, except as regards the office of Lieutenant-governor.
2. Direct taxation within the Province for provincial expenses.
3. The borrowing of money on the sole credit of the Province.
4. The establishment and tenure of Provincial offices, and the appointment and payment of Provincial officers.
5. The management and sale of the public lands belonging to the Province, and of the timber and wood thereon.
6. The establishment, maintenance, and management of hospitals, asylums, charities, and eleemosynary institutions in and for the Province, other than marine hospitals.
7. The establishment, maintenance, and management of public and reformatory prisons in and for the Province.
8. Municipal institutions in the Province.
9. Shop, saloon, tavern, auctioneer, and other licences, in order to raise a revenue for provincial, local, or municipal purposes.
10. Local works, but not (*a*) Lines of steam or other ships, railways, canals, telegraphs, and other works and undertakings connecting the Province with any other or others of the Provinces, or extending beyond the limit of the Province. (*b*) Lines of steamships between the Province and any British or foreign country. (*c*) Such works as, although wholly situate within the Province, are before or after their execution declared by the Parliament of Canada to be for the general advantage of Canada, or for the advantage of two or more of the Provinces.
11. The incorporation of companies with provincial objects.
12. The solemnization of marriage in the Province.
13. Property and civil rights in the Province.
14. The administration of justice in the Province, including the constitution, maintenance, and organization of provincial Courts, both of civil and criminal jurisdiction, and including proceedings in civil matters in those Courts.
15. The imposition of punishment by fine, penalty, or imprisonment or enforcing any law of the Province made in relation to any matter coming within any of the classes of subjects enumerated in this section.

Index.

Adderley, Sir C. (Lord Norton), 14, 16, 27, 39, 49, 70, 131, 160, 175, 179, 200, 216, 224.
Adelaide, Queen, 13, 97.
Aden, 105.
Aldcorn, Dr., 37.
Alexandra Land, 98.
Algeria, 33, 34.
Algoa Bay, 110.
Aliwal, 19.
Angas, G. F., 82, 97.
Anti-transportation League, 199.
Arthur, Sir G., 19.
Assiento contract, 118.
Auckland, 103.
Australia, 77, 99.

Backhouse, Mr., 89.
Ballarat, 19.
Barkly, Sir H., 114, 225.
Baronets of Nova Scotia, 141.
Barrens, the, 63.
Basutoland, 13.
Bathurst, Lord, 14, 23, 64.
Batman, J., 88.
Baudin, Captain, 80.
Beaconsfield, Lord, 51.
Bechuanaland, 115.
Benthamite School, 21.
Benué, the, 123.
Berlin Conference, 123.
Bismarck, Prince, 34.
Bismarck Archipelago, 84.
Blackford, Lord, 31.
Boers, the, 113, 229.
Borneo, 104.
Boswell, 43.

Botany Bay, 80, 204.
Bougainville, 79.
Bourinot, Mr., 188.
Bourke, Governor, 86.
Bright, John, 29.
Brisbane, Sir T., 193.
Brooke, Rajah, 104, 105, 122.
Brougham, Lord, 21, 201.
Brussels, Act of, 123.
Buller, C., 39, 41, 42, 159.
Bulwer, Sir H., 230.
Burdett, Sir F., 70.
Burghash, Seyd, 126.
Burke, Edmund, 10, 132.

Camoens, 10.
Campéché Bay, 54.
Canada, 62.
Canals, Canadian, 74.
Canning, 16, 24.
Canterbury, 103.
Cape Colony, 106.
Capetown, 219, 222.
Cardwell, Lord, 13.
Cargill, Captain, 37.
Carlisle, Earl of, 28.
Carnarvon, Lord, 183.
Carpentaria, Gulf of, 81.
Castlereagh, Lord, 108.
Chamberlain, Mr. J., 52.
Chartism, 93.
Chateaubriand, 32.
Clergy Reserves, 142, 175.
Cobbett, William, 182.
Cobden School, 9.
Colbert, 37.
Colborne, Sir J., 134.

Colonial Gazette, 39.
Colonial governors, 173.
Colonial Office, 16, 31.
Colonial reformers, 17, 21, 37, 100, 153, 166.
Columbia, 70.
Company, British E. A., 126.
Company, British N. Borneo, 122.
Company, Hudson Bay, 63, 74, 122.
Company, Netherlands E. I., 117, 218.
Company, Royal Niger, 122.
Company, South African, 115, 116.
Confederation, Canadian, 40, 184.
Congo, the, 125.
Convictism, 26, 43, 46, 93, 99, 199, 223.
Cook, Captain, 64.
Coomassie, 120.
Councils, Legislative, 138.
Creoles, French, 11, 12.
Cromwell, 43, 61.
Crown lands, 95, 96.
Cuba, 118, 170.
Cumming, Gordon, 113.
Cyprus, 106.

Dalley, 187.
Damaraland, 34.
Darwin, Port, 98.
Delagoa Bay, 115.
De Mole, Count, 82.
Denison, Sir W., 207.
Derby, Lord, 18.
De Stael, Madame, 138.
De Thierry, 82.
De Tocqueville, 139, 181.
Diamond Fields, 114.
Diego Garcia, 106.
Douglas, Sir J., 66.
Dufferin, Lord, 72, 164.
Dundas, Mr., 16.
D'Urban, Sir B., 13, 111.
Durham, Lord, 14, 22, 39, 41, 62, 73, 101, 140, 146, 155.

Edinburgh Review, 39.

Egmont, Earl, 140.
Eilat Island, 106.
Ellice, Sir E., 69, 75.
Eyre, Governor, 59.

Fairbairn, John, 45, 220.
Falklands, the, 79.
Fawkner, J. P., 88.
Février-Despointes, 83.
Ferry, Jules, 33.
Fiji Islands, 103.
Foreign Office, 18, 31.
Forster, W. E., 50, 51, 119.
Fox, Mr., 139.
France, 31, 32, 34, 78.
Franklin, Sir J., 1, 64.
Freeman, Professor, 188.
Free-trade, 48, 50, 53, 58, 60, 159.
Fremantle, Captain, 91.
Frere, Sir B., 33, 114, 127, 230.
Fulton, the, 75.

German Legion, 111.
Germany, 34, 35, 114, 127.
Gimli Colony, 72.
Gipps, Sir G., 148.
Gladstone, Mr., 152, 173.
Glenelg, 13, 182, 111, 160.
Godley, Mr., 37.
Gold Coast, 118.
Gold-fields, Australian, 98, 99.
Goldsmith, Oliver, 43.
Gosford, Lord, 148.
Grahamstown, 110.
Grenville, Sir R., 86.
Grey, Earl, 13, 25, 26, 27, 94, 119, 200, 205, 223.
Grey, Sir Charles, 148.
Grey, Sir George, 216, 229.
Griqualand West, 114.
Grote, G., 21.
Guizot, M., 83.

Hamilton, Alexander, 185.
Hargreaves, 206.
Hausaland, 123.
Hayti Republic, 59.

Index.

Head, Sir Edmund, 178.
Head, Sir Francis, 19, 164.
Herbert, Sir Robert, 31.
Hiddingh, Mr., 226.
Hinckes, Sir F., 172.
Hindmarsh, Governor, 97.
Hinds, Bishop, 37.
Hobart, Lord, 15.
Hobhouse, Sir C. Cam, 70.
Holland, King of, 114.
Hong Kong, 105.
Hume, Joseph, 148.
Huskisson, Mr., 221.

Indemnification Bill, 172.
Institute, Royal Colonial, 47, 48.
Ireland, 21, 151, 152.

Jamaica, 58, 59.
Johnson, Samuel, 43.
Johnston, Sir H., 125, 128, 129.
Juan, 170.

Kaffirs, 112, 228.
Kaffraria, 7.
King George's Sound, 90.
Kipling, Rudyard, 46.
Kirk, Sir J., 127.
Klondike, 71, 74.
Kowloon, 105.
Kruger, President, 20.
Kuriah Muriah Islands, 106.

Labouchere, H., 138, 152, 153, 183
Labuan, 104.
Lagos, 118.
Lanyon, Sir Owen, 20.
Laurier, Sir W., 131, 177.
Leader, Mr., 20, 150.
Lewis, Sir G. C., 23, 24, 133.
Liberia, 119.
Livingstone, David, 1, 121.
Locke, John, 7, 139, 174.
Lowe, R., 141, 197, 210.
Lyttelton, Lord, 37.

Macarthur, John, 193.

M'Carthy, Justin, 204.
Macdonald, Sir John, 185, 186.
Machar, Agnes, 46.
Mackenzie, William Lyon, 148.
Mackinnon, Sir W., 126.
Madagascar, 33.
Maine frontier, 68.
Malacca, 104.
Manilla, 78.
Manitoba, 7, 64, 65, 72.
Maoris, The, 85, 214.
Marquesas Islands, 83.
Marshall, J., 84.
Martineau, Harriet, 41.
Massah Islands, 105.
Melbourne, Lord, 13, 160.
Melbourne City, 88, 98.
Melville Island, 98.
Mennonites, 72.
Merivale, Herman, 30-39, 55, 56, 61, 62, 140, 178.
Metcalfe, Lord, 168.
Mexico, 41, 68.
Mill, J. S., 21, 22, 23, 39, 171.
Mills, Mr., 30.
Molesworth, Sir W., 21, 49, 172.
Monroe doctrine, 55.
Moselekatze, 113.
Murray, R., 97.
Muscat, Sultan of, 106, 126.

Napoleon, Emperor, 80, 107.
Natal, 113, 232.
Nelson, 82, 101, 187.
Neptune, The, 26.
Netherlands, The, 78, 107, 108.
New Britain, 34, 84.
New Caledonia, 83.
Newfoundland, 132, 161.
New Guinea, 34, 84, 88.
New Holland, 78.
New Plymouth, 101, 102.
New South Wales, 80, 86, 207.
New Zealand, 37, 82, 83, 216.
Nigeria, 18, 118, 120.
Noble, John, 26.
Nootka Sound, 64, 67.

Norfolk Island, 85.
North, Lord, 189.

O'Brien, W. Smith, 37.
O'Connell, Daniel, 37, 144, 152.
Oman, 126.
Orange, Prince of, 107.
Orange Free State, 113.
Oregon, 10, 70, 71.

Pakington, Sir J., 16.
Palmerston, Lord, 84.
Papineau, 134, 146, 149.
Parkes, Sir H., 197, 209.
Parnell, Sir H., 16, 24.
Peel, Mr., 92.
Peel, Sir R., 144.
Perim, 106.
Perouse, 80.
Phillip, Governor, 80, 193.
Pitt, Mr., 80, 136, 137, 139.
Plimsoll, 38.
Port Elizabeth, 110.
Porter, Mr., 228.
Portuguese Colonies, 171.
Pottinger, Sir H., 19.
Pringle, 45, 220.
Pritchard, Consul, 83.
Privy Council, The, 188.

Quarterly Review, 119, 161, 162.
Quebec Act, 135.
Queensland, 86, 87.

Radicals, Philosophical, 21.
Rae, Dr., 80.
Raffles, Sir Stamford, 104.
Railway, C. P., 73.
Raleigh Travellers' Club, 46.
Récidiviste Question, 84.
Reciprocity Treaty, 177.
Reform Bill, 36.
Reid, Wemyss, 51.
Representation, Parliamentary, 233.
Rhodes, Cecil J., 115, 116.
Rhodesia, 124.

Richelieu, Cardinal, 37.
Rintoul, R. S., 44.
Rockies, The, 74.
Roebuck, A., 20, 40, 41, 182.
Roman Catholics, 176, 191, 192.
Rosebery, Lord, 186.
Rosmead, Lord, 104, 163, 231.
Roubaix, Mr., 226.
Rupert's Land, 62, 72.
Rusden, Mr., 94, 102, 103.
Russell, Lord John, 21, 27, 36, 39, 81, 100, 143, 150, 151, 152, 165, 194.

Salisbury, Lord, 8, 52.
San Francisco, 70.
San Juan, 70.
Scott, Sir W., 66, 220.
Seeley, Sir J., 9, 51, 52.
Seigniories, 62, 175.
Selkirk, 11, 65, 66.
Septennial Act, 230.
Sheep, Merino, 107.
Shire, River, 125.
Sierra Leone, 82, 118.
Singapore, 104.
Sirah Island, 106.
Slave Emancipation, 58, 60, 112, 118.
Slave-trade, 118, 126.
Smith, Goldwin, 31, 41, 48, 51.
Smith, Sir Harry, 223.
Smith, Sydney, 15, 46, 112.
Society, Royal Geo., 47, 126.
Socotra, 106.
Sokoto, 123.
Solomon, Mr. Saul, 228.
Somaliland, 106.
Somerset, Lord Charles, 45.
South Australia, 89, 97.
Spanish Colonies, 170.
Sparrman, 11.
Spectator, The, 39, 44.
Stanley, Captain Owen, 83.
Stanley, H. M., 33.
Stephen, Sir J., 38, 89.
Stirling, Captain, 89, 90, 91.

Index.

St. Malo, 79.
Suffrage, Women's, 236.
Sugar bounties, 60, 61.
Sussex, Duke of, 101.
Swan River, 89.

Talleyrand, 81.
Tasmania, 78, 80.
Tchad, Lake, 121, 128.
Telegraphs, 52, 98, 129.
Tennyson, Lord, 46, 188.
Texas, 68.
Thompson, Deas, 206.
Thompson, Powlett, 154, 164, 186.
Thouars, Captain, 83.
Thunberg, 11.
Tonquin, 33.
Tories, The, 25, 161.
Torrens, Colonel, 95, 96.
Tory, The, 100.
Transportation, 201.
Transvaal, The, 35, 113.
Trollope, Anthony, 103.

Ulloa, 170.
Ulundi, 114.
United Empire Loyalists, 145, 181.
United States, The, 84.

Vancouver, Captain, 69.
Vancouver Island, 66, 67.
Van Diemen's Land, 78.

Vane, Sir H., 43, 147.
Venezuela, 55.
Venice, 8.
Victoria, Queen, 52.
Victoria Colony, 87, 88.
Virginia, 86.
Vlaming, 89.

Waitangi, Treaty of, 83.
Wakefield, Colonel, 100.
Wakefield, E. G., 30, 37, 38, 39, 95, 99.
Walvisch Bay, 114.
Watermeyer, Judge, 109.
Weld, Governor, 213.
Wellington, Duke of, 103, 187, 214.
Wentworth, C., 94, 197, 211.
West Africa, 49, 118.
West Australia, 89, 93, 98.
West Indies, 54-61.
Whately, Archbishop, 30, 102.
Whigs, The, 36, 39, 112, 153.
William IV., King, 148.
Wodehouse, Sir P., 13, 225.
Wolfe, General, 10.
Wolseley, Lord, 230.
Wordsworth, William, 59, 169.

Yarra, River, 86.

Zambesi, R., 24.
Zanzibar, 126.
Zulus, 114.

www.ingramcontent.com/pod-product-compliance
Lightning Source LLC
Chambersburg PA
CBHW032109220426
43664CB00008B/1196